ARMS CONTROL

ARMS CONTROL
New Approaches to Theory and Policy

Edited by

NANCY W. GALLAGHER
Wesleyan University

FRANK CASS
LONDON • PORTLAND, OR

First published in 1998 in Great Britain by
FRANK CASS PUBLISHERS
Crown House, 47 Chase Side
Southgate, London N14 5BP

and in the United States of America by
FRANK CASS PUBLISHERS
c/o ISBS, 5824 N.E. Hassalo Street
Portland, Oregon 97213-3644

Copyright © 1998 Frank Cass Publishers

Reprinted 2002

Website : www.frankcass.com

British Library Cataloguing in Publication Data

Arms control : new approaches to theory and policy
1. Arms control
I. Gallagher, Nancy
327.1'74

ISBN 0-7146-4813-2 (cloth)
ISBN 0-7146-4363-7 (paper)

Library of Congress Cataloging-in-Publication Data

Arms control : new approaches to theory and policy / edited by Nancy
W. Gallagher.
   p. cm.
   Includes bibliographical references (p.) and index.
   ISBN 0-7146-4813-2 (cloth). -- ISBN 0-7146-4363-7 (pbk.)
   1. Arms control. I. Gallagher, Nancy W., 1961-
JZ5645.A76 1998   97-41623
327.1'74--dc21   CIP

This group of studies first appeared as a special issue of
Contemporary Security Policy, Vol.18, No.2, August 1997, 'Arms Control: New
Approaches to Theory and Policy'.

CONTENTS

List of Abbreviations

ACDA	Arms Control and Disarmament Agency
BWC	Biological and Toxin Weapons Convention
C³I	Command, Control, Communications and Intelligence
CD	United Nations Conference on Disarmament
CFC	Chlorofluorocarbons
CMA	Chemical Manufacturers' Association
CTBT	Comprehensive Test Ban Treaty
CTRP	Cooperative Threat Reduction Program
CWC	Chemical Weapons Convention
DoD	US Department of Defense
DoE	US Department of Energy
EPA	Environmental Protection Agency
EU	European Union
G-21	Group of twenty-one non-aligned states
GPS	Global Positionings System
HEU	Highly enriched uranium
IAEA	International Atomic Energy Authority
IDC	International Data Center
IMS	international monitoring system
INF	Intermediate Nuclear Forces
Kt	Kiloton
NAM	non-aligned movement
NGO	Non-governmental organization
NNWS	non-nuclear weapon state
NPT	Nuclear Non-Proliferation Treaty
NTB	nuclear test ban
NTM	national technical means
NWS	nuclear weapon state
OSI	on-site inspection
OSIA	On-Site Inspection Agency
P-5	Permanent five members of the UN Security Council
PNE	peaceful nuclear explosion
PTBT	Partial Test Ban Treaty
SCFR	Senate committee on Foreign Relations
START	Strategic Arms Reduction Talks
T-3	Threshold (underclared) nuclear weapon states
TRI	Toxics Release Inventory
UNSCOM	United Nations Special Commission

Bridging the Gaps on Arms Control

NANCY W. GALLAGHER

A decade has passed since the superpowers started a series of arms control initiatives that now symbolize the beginning of the end of the Cold War. The passage of time, however, has not resolved disputes about the role of arms control in moderating the US-Soviet rivalry or preserving peace in the post-Cold War world. Some analysts believe that arms control was and always will be a dangerous illusion. Others continue to treat it as a useful but peripheral process that can reduce the costs and risks of competitive security policies. Still others see both the need and the opportunity to make broad-based arms control an essential component of a fundamentally more cooperative approach to global security.

The recent history of the Chemical Weapons Convention (CWC) contains evidence to support each conflicting conception of arms control. The Conference on Disarmament (CD) tried and failed for two decades to move from the 1925 Geneva Protocol's weak prohibition on the first use of chemical weapons to a verified ban on their manufacture, storage, and use even for retaliatory purposes. Negotiations finally geared up as the Cold War wound down, the USSR reduced its resistance to intrusive verification, and American military planners realized that they would gain more from strong international measures to prevent chemical weapons proliferation than they would from the ability to retaliate in kind against a chemical attack. The agreement signed in January 1993 is the most ambitious arms control accord to date: it completely forbids an entire category of weapons, provides for intrusive inspections and an array of other transparency measures, entrusts significant decision-making authority to the international control organization, and contains automatic penalties to punish non-participants. Many observers saw the CWC as a 'security milestone' on the road to a more cooperative post-Cold War security system.[1] They predicted rapid entry-into-force given the treaty's popularity abroad and in the United States, but although the new Clinton administration gave strong rhetorical support to the accord, it prioritized domestic issues and continued to treat arms control as a peripheral concern. By the time that the accord was ready for a ratification vote in September 1996, enough opposition had crystallized that the vote was postponed until after the presidential elections. Critics claimed that the end of the Cold War made arms control less necessary and more dangerous because the sole superpower must be prepared to protect itself and others from threats posed by 'rogue' states with no respect for international norms or treaty obligations. Although this position was defeated when the CWC ratification vote finally occurred in April 1997, arms control supporters were disheartened by the difficulty of translating diffuse support for cooperative security into the rapid negotiation, ratification, and implementation of a landmark accord.

Other arms control issues provide further evidence of unprecedented achievements and continuing frustrations. Over the last decade, the superpowers have agreed to cut their nuclear arsenals by more than 70 per cent, yet the reduction process has been obstructed by Russia's refusal to ratify the 'inequitable' START II and American resistance to begin START III negotiations until its predecessor is ratified. Decisive cooperative action averted potential proliferation disasters in Iraq, North Korea, and the Ukraine. The formal nuclear non-proliferation regime, however, is in a holding pattern: the Nuclear Non-Proliferation Treaty was extended indefinitely in May 1995, but no binding obligations were accepted to improve compliance or address problems posed by 'threshold' states outside the regime. The CD finally achieved near-unanimous support for a comprehensive test ban treaty (CTBT) in the summer of 1996, but the only way to satisfy key states, such as the United Kingdom and Russia, was to accept rigid entry-into-force provisions which strengthened Indian opposition and may prevent the ban from ever being fully binding. Now the CD has a broad agenda, but no practical plan of action. No country wants the next step to disadvantage them because they lack confidence that concessions will be reciprocated on issues of greater concern.

This pattern of uneven progress leads one to ask whether arms control's contributions to security are limited by enduring features of international politics, or if more can be done to promote cooperation given the political, military, economic, and technological changes that have occurred over the last decade. This policy debate parallels arguments among academics about the prospects for cooperation in the current international system. Yet, surprisingly little communication and cross-fertilization has occurred between theorists and practitioners, even though arms control is one of the security issues where the theory/policy gap is thought to be smallest.

This essay argues that arms control innovation and achievement have been hampered by competing conceptions of arms control among security specialists, as well as a widening divide between arms control policy experts and other international relations scholars. The notion that all members of the arms control community share a few basic principles is true only at a level of generality that obscures far more than it illuminates. A more useful approach is to show how debates about the ends and means of arms control reflect fundamentally different assumptions about the nature of international politics. Ironically, though, arguments over the future of arms control have more in common with theoretical debates from the Cold War years about such issues as deterrence stability than with more recent advances in international relations scholarship. Insights from theory can make recurring debates more productive and suggest new ways of thinking about the opportunities and obstacles for arms control in the post-Cold War world.

The essays in this volume are part of a project to increase dialogue and encourage creative reconceptualization of arms control theory and policy. To this end, we have defined arms control broadly to encompass any type of cooperative measure meant to reduce the costs and risks associated with the acquisition, threat, and use of military force. This includes legally binding restrictions on particular weapons, reciprocal unilateral restraints on destabilizing capabilities or practices, and bilateral or multilateral efforts to address the root causes of insecurity. Various authors concentrate on different aspects of this problem. Starting with such an expansive definition shows what the authors have in common and why they often have such difficulty communicating.

Is Arms Control Immune from the Theory/Policy Gap?

International relations theorists and foreign policy practitioners are struggling with similar problems in the post-Cold War world. Both must determine how much the world has changed and decide which security strategy is most appropriate for current conditions. The world does not look significantly different from the ivory tower than it does from the trenches where policy battles are fought. Scholars are more apt to critique than applaud current policy, yet their criticisms reflect a range of worldviews and often amplify debates already occurring in closed-door policy meetings.

Despite these commonalities, 'thinkers' and 'doers' often operate in such divergent ways that they fail to hear each other, or even recognize that the other group has something interesting to say. The results are wasted effort, unnecessary duplication, and frustration both for practitioners who lack the time and detachment needed for long-term planning, and for scholars who wonder whether their research really matters. The problem is particularly acute for anyone who wants international politics to move in a much more cooperative direction. Entertaining alternative approaches and demonstrating their superiority, developing pragmatic policy measures, securing domestic and international approval, and implementing fundamentally new arrangements require a more concerted effort than does making incremental modifications to practices developed during the Cold War.

In *Bridging the Gap*, Alexander George maintains that the gulf between theory and practice has been wider on security issues than on international economics or law.[2] He attributes this to the clash of cultures between the academic and the policy worlds. Social scientists with incomplete data typically seek abstract generalizations about causal relationships among a small number of variables. Decision-makers tend to rely more on experience as they search for pragmatic ways to balance trade-offs between the policy's quality, its domestic popularity, and its practicality given competing demands for time and resources.

Although practitioners often recoil from the word 'theory', they must use worldviews, implicit assumptions, and other 'generic knowledge' to simplify complicated issues and select strategies despite incomplete, ambiguous, or contradictory information. Uncertainty, complexity, and changeability in the post-Cold War policy environment increase practitioners' need for intellectual tools to help them adapt existing policies and imagine innovative responses to changed conditions. Academics fear that policy-makers still utilize oversimplified maxims from Hans Morgenthau and other post-Second World War realists, while policy-makers feel that 'much of today's scholarship is either irrelevant or inaccessible'.[3] The organizational culture of academia reinforces rigid disciplinary divisions while most security problems have political, economic, technical, cultural, and ethical dimensions. Moreover, the reward structure of academia continues to favour scholarship written within a few narrow research paradigms and published by theoretical journals or high-prestige university presses. Cuts in government funds for policy-relevant research, combined with decreased foundation support for scholarly projects on traditional security issues, weaken two of the main bridging mechanisms used during the Cold War. Thus, the gulf between theory and policy is growing even though the need for policy-friendly theory is greater than ever.

George sees arms control as one of the few security issues where the perspectives of academics and policy-makers have traditionally converged. The development of nuclear weapons held such revolutionary implications that a small group of strategists and scientists with close ties to both worlds founded the field of strategic studies and arms control. The core tenets of 'classical' arms control – that the interests of both superpowers could be served through cooperative measures to reduce incentives for pre-emptive attack, decrease the level of destruction should war occur, and lower the costs of deterrence stability – were largely developed by collaborative study groups and published in a few popular volumes, such as a 1960 special issue of *Daedalus*, and Thomas Schelling and Morton Halperin's 1961 book, *Strategy and Arms Control*.[4] Contributors to what Jennifer Sims has dubbed the 'Cambridge Approach' differed in the emphasis placed on political and technical factors. Yet, they generally agreed that tacit bargaining and formal negotiation could slow the spread of nuclear weapons, shape force structures so that initiating a nuclear attack would be unmistakably irrational, and minimize non-rational reasons for deterrence failure, such as misperceptions or inadvertent escalation.[5]

Traditional arms control has withstood attacks by academics and policy-makers from both ends of the political spectrum. Critics have questioned the rationality of deterrence, challenged the morality of nuclear weapons, alleged that the Soviets (now other 'rogue states') neither accept the logic of arms control nor honour their treaty commitments, and promised greater security through unilateral steps such as the Strategic Defense Initiative and counter-proliferation. The classical approach still has many strong adherents, though, partly because nobody has developed an intellectually coherent and equally compelling alternative.[6] For example, a collection of essays published in honour of the thirtieth anniversary of the *Daedalus* special issue shows a surprising degree of consensus that the primary function of arms control is still to stabilize deterrence, even though the contributors differ about how this should be done and whether arms control can also serve more ambitious objectives in the post-Cold War world.[7]

The appearance of consensus, or continued convergence by default on the classical arms control approach, is problematic for several reasons. First, it masks important disagreements among members of the arms control community. The assumptions underlying different approaches are rarely contrasted explicitly, so confusion results and conceptual richness is lost. Second, the pseudo-consensus decreases incentives for interaction between arms control policy experts and international relations theorists because neither side sees a compelling reason to rethink arms control theory. Third, it increases tension between the types of arms control measures that specialists consider most appropriate in the post-Cold War world and the types that they can sell to members of Congress or other non-experts who still think about arms control as a minor adjunct to strategic nuclear deterrence. These gaps may not be quite the same as those that George explored, but they still have serious implications for the future of arms control.

Identifying Divisions inside the Arms Control Community

Arms control scholars, policy analysts, and practitioners care about a common set of problems and interact often enough to be considered a community. For example, most arms control experts agree that nuclear weapons have had profound effects on international politics and that cooperative measures are needed to ensure that the benefits of nuclear weapons outweigh the potential costs and risks.[8] Yet, members of the arms control community are deeply divided over basic questions, such as the values that arms control should promote and the means by which it can promote them. Conflicting assumptions about international politics are embedded in arguments over arms control even though they are rarely explicitly identified, contrasted, or tested against each other. Theory can help make these debates more productive by clarifying the 'deep structure' caused by divergent worldviews[9] and considering ways to transcend or bridge these divisions.

Many disagreements about post-Cold War arms control have their roots in the different traditions that have coexisted somewhat uncomfortably under the rubric of 'classical arms control theory'. David Baldwin has argued that the field of security studies was much broader prior to the period from 1955 to 1965 when most arms control classics were written.[10] In the years between the First and Second World Wars, many scholars and policy-makers were idealists, for they saw democracy and self-determination, education and international understanding, economic interdependence, international law and arbitration, disarmament, and collective security as the keys to cooperation.[11] During the decade after the Second World War, security specialists had a more complex and ambivalent conception of the world. They believed that states had both competing and common interests, and that security was a goal to be balanced against other objectives, such as economic growth and individual liberties. They also thought that security could be pursued through many means, including military, diplomatic, and economic statecraft, and recognized that unilateral attempts to enhance security could threaten other states into counter-measures that left both sides worse off. Finally, these specialists paid close attention to the connections between national security and domestic affairs.[12] In short, many of the issues that interest arms control experts today were the subject of study long before the 'classics' were written.

By the mid-1950s, international relations theory was dominated by realist assumptions of a world where unitary states maximize relative power and seek security as their highest goal. The focus of security studies had narrowed to a technical question: how could states manage their nuclear arsenals to enhance national security, given the potential for a catastrophic nuclear war?[13] Strategists such as Thomas Schelling, Herman Kahn, and Albert Wohlstetter drew heavily on systems analysis and game theory when thinking about techniques to balance the utility of nuclear weapons against the need to increase deterrence stability, limit destruction, and avoid dangerous arms races. Other members of the Cambridge (Massachusetts) arms control community continued to raise issues of concern to earlier traditions, such as the impact of arms control on economic well-being and individual psychology, the effects of public opinion and international organizations on arms control choices, and the possible reciprocal relationship between arms control and democratization in the USSR.[14] As the classical approach was elaborated, popularized, and translated into specific arms control initiatives during the 1960s and 1970s, though, many of these nuances were submerged beneath the emphasis on bilateral bargaining and deterrence stability. By the late 1970s, 'arms control' had taken on an even narrower definition for many critics and referred simply to the seemingly futile effort by the superpowers to negotiate legally-binding reductions in their strategic nuclear arsenals.[15]

Current arguments about the future of arms control reflect this diverse legacy. One can conceptualize recent debates in terms of a realist-idealist spectrum roughly defined by beliefs about the conditions under which arms control can enhance security and the means through which it can accomplish its objectives. Such a theoretical spectrum inevitably over-simplifies some individuals' beliefs. Still, it reveals that experts mean radically different things when they discuss cooperative steps to reduce the costs and risks associated with the acquisition, threat, and use of military force. As a result, similar disputes recur in different contexts, alternative logics lead to vexing arms control dilemmas, and popular initiatives are typically 'first step' measures that can be justified as serving contradictory long-term objectives.

Shades of Realism

Scholars and policy-makers at the realist end of the spectrum assume that states operate in a self-help system since the world lacks either a central government or enough solidarity that states can count on each other for assistance. Realists also assume that wars occur when countries with conflicting interests calculate that the benefits of aggression outweigh the costs and risks. A favourable balance of power is the most reliable deterrent, so arms control is attractive only if it serves this end.

At the far end of the realist-idealist spectrum are total sceptics, such as Colin Gray, who think that formal arms control is almost always irrelevant or unwise.[16] Since Gray believes that political conflicts force states to worry about relative military power, he maintains that arms control is inherently paradoxical because the more conflictual a relationship is, the less likely adversaries will be to negotiate and uphold strategically significant limits on military power. Policy-makers at this end of the spectrum may present one-sided proposals as part of a propaganda campaign to win favourable international opinion or mobilize domestic support for increased defense spending – as critics accused the first Reagan administration of doing. However, arms control sceptics oppose actually signing and ratifying an accord unless it locks their state into a position of permanent superiority without placing any significant constraints on its military capabilities.

More moderate realists, such as Richard Betts, do not take a purely zero-sum view of international politics, but see legally binding arms control as a way to stabilize the strategic balance that only makes sense in a static security environment where potential threats are known, alignment patterns are obvious, and technological breakthroughs in unconstrained military capabilities are unlikely.[17] Because these conditions were satisfied during most of the Cold War, Betts supported arms control measures that left the West and East with nuclear and conventional capabilities sufficient to prevent either side from gaining more than it would lose from an attack. Given the uncertainties associated with the end of the Cold War, though, Betts prefers that states now make unilateral decisions about military reductions. He fears that legally binding commitments might hinder appropriate adjustments to threatening developments or exacerbate crises if signatories abrogate an accord for ostensibly defensive reasons.

Like Gray and Betts, Marc Trachtenberg assumes that arms races are a symptom, not a cause, of political conflicts. Although Trachtenberg considers arms control to be the 'icing on the cake of political accommodation', he contends that the superpowers can use negotiations and informal conversations about desirable military arrangements to manage and institutionalize the improvements in their political relationships.[18] Yet, Trachtenberg asserts that arms control assumes primary importance only when serious political problems are addressed under the guise of arms control negotiations. For example, he sees the emerging norm of non-proliferation, with its implication that sovereign states do not have an inalienable right to acquire nuclear weapons, as crucial to legitimizing great power efforts to 'discipline and set limits to the power of weaker and less responsible states'.[19]

The Middle Ground

In the middle of the spectrum are scholars and policy-makers who believe that arms control can make modest, but useful, contributions to security even when mistrust and uncertainty are high. This group assumes that sovereign states remain the main actors in international politics, have a mixture of common and conflicting interests, and prefer to rely primarily on self-help security strategies. Although these analysts do not believe that a comprehensive cooperative security system is possible under current conditions, they favour partial arms control measures to address security problems that might lead adversaries into an arms race or war that neither side desired.

Arms control can help national decision-makers resist pressures for destabilizing weapons acquisition due to 'non-rational' factors such as technological momentum, bureaucratic interests, or private economic incentives. One study of superpower arms control found that its most positive function was to reduce uncertainty and increase predictability so that military planning need not be based on self-fulfilling worst case assumptions.[20] Many Cold War arms control accords, including the 1959 Antarctic Treaty and the 1972 Anti-Ballistic Missile Treaty, tried to avoid counter-productive insurance-seeking by prohibiting military capabilities that neither superpower currently wanted itself nor wished for the other side to obtain unilaterally. The Register of Conventional Arms established by the UN in the early 1990s is also based on the hope that exchanging information can help members predict more accurately whether particular arms transfers will enhance or erode long-term security.

Operational practices that could lead to inadvertent war are another potential cause of deterrence failure that middle-ground arms control measures can address.[21] Such Cold War accords as the 1971 Accidents Measures Agreement and the 1972 Incidents at Sea Agreement reduced risky behaviour and facilitated crisis management should an accident occurred. During the 1980s, some arms control supporters argued that large numbers of secure second-strike nuclear weapons would be more stabilizing than small arsenals, as long as military systems were designed to minimize the potential for warning failures, loss of control by national command authorities, and escalation from a regional conflict.[22] With the threat of Russian aggression extremely low, however, other analysts have argued for radical reductions in both superpowers' nuclear capabilities because many operational problems, such as safe storage for fissile material and secure central control over Russian nuclear weapons, would be more manageable if a few hundred, rather than a few thousand, warheads were involved.[23]

Some middle-ground scholars and policy-makers believe that misperceptions, not objective conflicts of interest, are the primary cause of arms races, security dilemmas, and deterrence instabilities. If so, one way for suspicious states to be safe, yet non-threatening, is to adopt force structures and operational practices that are better suited for defense than offence. For example, the 1990 Conventional Forces in Europe treaty limits five categories of predominantly offensive weapons and restricts their deployment to preclude a large-scale surprise attack.

Since it can be difficult to determine which capabilities and behaviours are 'aggressive' and which are 'defensive' or 'benign', another goal of arms control is to provide information about intentions. Confidence-building measures negotiated since the mid-1980s by the Conference on Security and Cooperation in Europe typify this objective. Rather than restricting the size of military exercises, these accords specify that the more potentially threatening the exercises might seem to neighbouring states, the more obligations exist to provide reassurances through prior notification, exchange of information, and foreign observation. While the chances that a spiral of misperceptions could lead to nuclear war in Western Europe are significantly smaller now than during the Cold War, analysts in this tradition still believe that confidence-building measures can ameliorate security dilemmas associated with rising regional rivalries.[24] They also see verification and transparency as a means for participants in the nuclear, chemical, and biological weapons control regimes to enjoy the economic benefits of dual-use technologies without undue concerns about proliferation.

Another function favoured by those at the middle of the arms control spectrum involves the process, rather than the end-product, of arms control negotiations. Here, the argument is that even though the superpowers rarely accepted arms control measures that did more than codify existing defense plans, the countless hours spent negotiating helped both sides recognize their interdependence, realize the need for mutual restraint, and gradually develop a patchwork of tacit rules and partial regimes that kept the Cold War from exploding.[25] Rational choice scholars see the bargaining process as relevant to such things as players' reputation for resolve and their ability to make credible commitments. Scholars who do not treat states as unitary actors with fixed interests view the negotiating process as important to the formulation of national preferences and perceptions about the other side.[26] The more optimistic these analysts are that the process of negotiating increasingly comprehensive arms control accords will transform foes into friends, the closer they are to the idealistic end of the security spectrum.

Versions of Idealism

More idealistic members of the arms control community do not view the current security environment through rose-colored glasses. Rather, they see a host of serious problems that require cooperation to eradicate the root causes of insecurity. Scholars and policy-makers at this end of the spectrum define security in broad terms to include not only safety from physical harm posed by external military forces, but also freedom from coercion by one's own government, shields from economic deprivation and societal discrimination, and protection from environmental degradation.[27] The goal is not just to avoid war, but also to increase justice and equality, both because they are valuable in their own right and because order is more likely to break down when groups have grievances that are not being addressed satisfactorily through peaceful political processes. For example, while realists urge the great powers to establish non-proliferation norms that suit their own interests and enforce export control regimes that deny weaker states access to weapons of mass destruction, idealists counter that discriminatory supply-side strategies will motivate less powerful states to seek military capabilities that they might not have desired otherwise.[28] Whereas realists view the world as an anarchic system of independent sovereign states, moreover, idealists argue that it is moving toward an increasingly interdependent global society in which non-state actors – international organizations, transnational corporations, subnational ethnic groups, terrorists, and private individuals – play an increasingly influential role in creating and solving problems that cross national boundaries.[29]

Different idealists draw conflicting implications for arms control from this conception of international security. Some take a very narrow view of arms control and dismiss it as part of a 'minimalist' approach to threat reduction via strategic deterrence, crisis management, and other traditional tools of military statecraft. For example, Francis Beer charges that arms control deals only with the symptoms, not the causes, of war. He calls instead for 'maximalist' strategies to create lasting security by reforming, reconstructing, and ultimately transcending the current international system.[30] Arms control could contribute directly to some of Beer's recommendations by reducing the role of force in international politics and subordinating the military sector to other aspects of domestic society. Such demilitarization could, in turn, promote other goals, such as decreasing human rights abuses and reallocating funds from military expenditures to economic development, education, health, and environmental protection. Still, Beer seems to suggest that arms controllers should, at best, be actively trying to put themselves out of business.

Other scholars and policy analysts see broad-based arms control as an integral part of cooperative security regimes. One recent study argued that the diffusion of technology, the internationalization of economic activity, and the disintegration of political authority in key regions of the world have created new threats that cannot be handled effectively through containment, deterrence, or denial of access to particular weapons capabilities.[31] Therefore, the authors propose a new approach to security – 'cooperative engagement'. They argue that states with fundamentally compatible security objectives should reassure each other that their militaries exist solely to defend home territory by voluntarily negotiating and enforcing comprehensive agreements about the appropriate size, concentration, technical configuration, and operational practices of deployed forces.[32] Such arrangements would decrease peace-loving states' incentives to have large national militaries while simultaneously reducing potential aggressors' ability to accumulate the means of attack before the rest of the world took preventative actions. The authors argue that enlightened self-interest is already motivating many states, corporations, and public interest groups to make behaviour more transparent. They urge decision-makers to approach arms control as a mutually beneficial form of regulatory management meant to minimize undesirable side-effects from legitimate activities, rather than as an adversarial process where participants are constantly worried about cheating and uneven relative gains. For these analysts, the end of the Cold War offers an opportunity to make cooperative security a more explicit part of policy, to integrate and expand the patchwork of existing arms control measures into a comprehensive regime, and to develop mutually acceptable arrangements for dealing with problems such as defense conversion and humanitarian intervention.

Synthesis or Dysfunctional Divisions?

Some scholars have tried to synthesize this spectrum of perspectives on arms control into a single picture by proposing that different ways of looking at the issue are appropriate for different time periods, issues, and regions of the world. For example, Patrick Morgan postulates three alternatives for international politics that amount to (1) a realist world where the great powers remain strongly concerned about security and relative power; (2) a middle-ground world where residual security concerns are muted and mixed with cooperative interactions on other issues, and (3) an idealist world where security concerns have virtually disappeared, states calculate self-interest within a collective-welfare framework, and cooperation is facilitated by diffuse reciprocity and a lengthy shadow of the future.[33] Morgan argues that the trend in great power relations has been from the realist toward the idealist world, but that elements of each conceptual framework can be discerned if one examines different states' approaches to diverse issues, such as aid to Russia, free trade, and American involvement in European affairs. Other analysts agree that arms control in Western Europe reflects the evolution of a 'pluralistic security community', but maintain that the incentives for cooperation are decidedly mixed in Eastern Europe, while the structure of politics remains highly Hobbesian in much of the developing world.[34] Such attempts at synthesis are an improvement over one-size-fits-all approaches toward arms control, but they do not end arguments about both the conditions which characterize a particular situation and the prospects for speeding different regions' evolution toward cooperative security.

In short, conflicting conceptions of arms control continue to cause confusion and wasted energy inside the arms control community. Since they stem from enduring disputes about the nature of international politics, it is unlikely that they will be resolved any time soon. Theoretical analysis can clarify the basic points of agreement and disagreement. For example, arguments persist about the accomplishments of superpower arms control because some analysts measure formal treaties' very minor effects on military capabilities while others attribute major changes in perceptions, preferences, and behaviour to the arms control process writ large. Likewise, contrary to the common belief that some approaches are 'technical' while others are 'political', most groups along the spectrum see arms control as having both components, but they conceptualize the relationship between the two factors in different ways.

Distinguishing among the diverse approaches that have been lumped together under the rubric of 'traditional arms control theory' can help scholars move from meaningless dichotomies and sterile debates toward conditional generalizations about the circumstances and pathways through which various arms control options can enhance security. A fuller understanding of the conceptual richness in past research can also help post-Cold War policy-makers uncover valuable insights that were superseded or overshadowed by the emphasis on arms control's ability to stabilize superpower nuclear deterrence.

A more explicit awareness of the theoretical assumptions behind arms control preferences may also help members of the arms control community build support for their proposals. Each theoretical approach is vulnerable to standard criticisms that can be anticipated, if not always avoided. Sixty years ago, E.H. Carr urged policy-makers to blend realism and idealism, because pure realism lacks a vision to motivate action and moral standards by which options can be judged, while pure idealism lacks a clear understanding of current conditions and a practical plan for moving from what is to what ought to be.[35] Carr's call for a synthesis suggests one reason why a public opinion backlash forced the early Reagan administration to reduce its confrontational rhetoric and resume negotiations with the 'evil empire'. It also suggests that widespread public approval for the abstract principles of cooperative security may not produce Congressional support for a specific arms control agreement because opponents can always find one 'hard case' where optimistic assumptions about shared interests and mutual restraint might not be met.[36]

However, proposals based on middle-ground assumptions about mixed motives, misperceptions, and security dilemmas are hard to sell to non-experts because they take a long time to explain and are often counter-intuitive. In an age of shrinking soundbites and short attention spans, the 'ends against the middle' phenomenon will intensify without new strategies to answer criticisms based on a less complex conception of international politics.

Reversing the Rift between Arms Control Policy and International Relations Theory

Mapping current arguments about arms control policy onto old disputes about international relations theory also reveals that conceptual innovation has not kept pace with changes in post-Cold War arms control. The split between realists and idealists is as old as the field itself. Many arguments made by middle-ground members of the arms control community correspond to compromise theories developed in the 1970s and 1980s, when neoliberal institutionalists such as Robert Axelrod, Robert Keohane, and Kenneth Oye put cooperation back onto the research agenda of mainstream international relations.[37] Likewise, policy debates about whether the primary purpose of arms control should be to maximize the credibility of retaliatory threats or minimize the risk of inadvertent war mirror theoretical arguments developed during the last decade of the Cold War about the 'rationality' of deterrence.[38]

Numerous observers have noted the *ad hoc* and uneven nature of attempts to adapt arms control principles and practices to post-Cold War conditions. For example, Brad Roberts' critique of US non-proliferation policy also fits other countries and arms control issues:

> In neither government nor academe does one find a sense of how the new strategic environment has redefined what responses to proliferation are both necessary and possible, or a concept of how these pieces of the puzzle fit together. The result is an emphasis on fine-tuning old approaches, a tendency to apply outdated conceptual models to new challenges, and disarray in policy.[39]

Many recent trends in international relations theory address issues of direct relevance to post-Cold War arms control, yet have received little systematic attention from policy analysts and practitioners. The gap between members of the arms control community and scholars working on other aspects of cooperation theory exists for many of the reasons that George identified. It also reflects internal divisions among the international relations subfields. Whereas questions of war and peace were once considered of primary importance for all international relations scholars, the discipline now contains several separate-but-equal subfields with their own specialized vocabulary, concepts, and technical data. Some of the most innovative work on international cooperation has roots in political economy, psychology, or sociology, rather than traditional security studies. Because arms control involves much more than bargaining between two unitary rational actors seeking to maximize the net utility of their nuclear arsenal, it is important both to present other research in a way that is policy-friendly and to encourage more policy-relevant research on other questions of concern to arms control practitioners.

The essays in this volume stem from a project sponsored by the networking organization Women in International Security to increase communication between arms control policy-makers and scholars working on related aspects of cooperation theory. The contributors represent various theoretical and professional perspectives. The papers show how new thinking about cooperation can address problems that plague numerous arms control issues, such as the complexity of national arms control decision-making and multilateral negotiations, the challenges of reaching domestic and international agreement on verification, and the need for arms control strategies that put technical limits in the context of broader political settlements. Our goal was not to replace classical arms control theory or devise a comprehensive new policy agenda, but to initiate a dialogue that might ultimately have such ambitious results. Preliminary versions of most essays were presented at a July 1996 workshop in Washington, DC, then revised on the basis of feedback from policy-makers, analysts, and other workshop participants. The essay by Gloria Duffy is an extended version of her keynote address, while the contribution by Amy Sands is an elaboration of her commentary on the need for theory to consider more fully the many messy realities of the policy-making process. Since the point of the project was to expand arms control discussions and include more diverse perspectives, we purposely avoided imposing a single analytical framework on all of the contributions. We have, however, tried to maximize accessibility by avoiding technical jargon, specialized concepts, obscure references, and 'insider' debates of interest only to a small circle of academics or policy-makers.

The Changing Arms Control Environment

Participants in our project reached a high degree of consensus on the kinds of change that have occurred in the security environment since the classics of arms control were written, but we, like our predecessors, disagreed about the implications for arms control. Emily Goldman's essay on 'Arms Control in the Information Age' provides the most detailed picture of these changes, including the decline in superpower hostility and the rise of regional rivalries with ambiguous alignment patterns; the rapid diffusion of knowledge-intensive technologies that exacerbate some assymetries yet give weak players ways to offset others' advantages; and increasingly complex relationships between political, military, and economic issues.

Ann Florini and Gloria Duffy maintain that such changes have eroded states' ability to cope with security problems on their own, and thus require innovative forms of cooperation. In 'A New Role for Transparency', Florini suggests that governments no longer monopolize control over the main threats to security because many causes of potential instability are societal (e.g. overpopulation, inequitable resource distribution, environmental degradation) and many dangerous materials and technologies also have beneficial uses that lead to widespread availability. In contrast to formal inter-governmental arms control, therefore, Florini proposes a more decentralized approach. She uses similarities between non-proliferation and environmental detoxification to argue that strengthening the norm of transparency can change incentive structures so that individual states and corporations will voluntarily adopt measures that decrease the dangerous side effects of legitimate activities.

Gloria Duffy draws on her experience as US Deputy Assistant Secretary of Defense from 1993 to 1995 to explain why a growing number of security problems cannot be addressed effectively through traditional forms of defense, deterrence, or arms control. Like Florini, Duffy assumes that states and economic actors have a common interest in cooperative measures to prevent new 'threats without threateners'. Rather than blaming information shortages as the cause of choices with sub-optimal consequences for all concerned, though, Duffy considers situations where states want to cooperate, but lack the necessary expertise, financial resources, or internal control – a problem sometimes called 'involuntary defection'. Her essay offers numerous concrete examples where close involvement by US government officials and business leaders helped foreign leaders recognize potential problems, such as unsafe storage of fissile materials and underemployment of nuclear scientists, then obtain the resources required to implement a mutually beneficial solution. For Duffy, the biggest challenge is not persuading former adversaries to cooperate, but convincing the US Congress that a small investment in 'preventive defence' can make a major contribution to American security.

Emily Goldman agrees that changes in the security environment increase the need for cooperation, but she is less optimistic that a natural harmony of interests already exists among the relevant players. Goldman maintains that narrow restrictions on technical capabilities made sense during the Cold War because the rivalry was clear, the threat was high, the cleavages were hardened. Moreover, both superpowers had secure retaliatory capabilities, and could largely control the supply of weapons to other countries. Given the uncertainty, complexity, and fluidity of the post-Cold War security environment, Goldman argues that arms control can help shape political relations, not just respond to them. As long as conflicts of interest exist, though, anyone who wants sophisticated weaponry can eventually obtain it and even crude weapons can do tremendous damage to the fragile fabric of information-based societies. Therefore, Goldman argues that attempts to limit military capabilities must be embedded in broader political and economic settlements that increase satisfaction with the status quo and create the conditions for cooperative security.

Rather than depicting what she calls 'bridging strategies' as a new approach to arms control, Goldman draws parallels to the broader conception of arms control that existed before the nuclear age. She presents the Washington Treaty System, a web of agreements covering relations among the great powers in the Pacific between the World Wars, as a successful bridging strategy for rivals with asymmetrical capabilities. She applies lessons drawn from the success and eventual collapse of this system to the Middle East today, and argues that arms control must actively seek to influence both capabilities and intentions, because one cannot assume either that compatible interests already exist or that they will emerge as an automatic by-product of the arms control 'process'.

Managing Complexity in the Arms Control Process

In one way or another, each essay examines the consequences for arms control of the increase in interested actors at both the domestic and international levels. For example, Goldman notes numerous complications that arise when arms control must address asymmetries not only among regional rivals with different weapons 'niches' and military paradigms, but also between regional states and external powers. Florini and Duffy, by contrast, stress the benefits of involving new actors in the arms control process, such as the contributions that non-governmental organizations can make to compliance monitoring and the added resources that commercial firms bring when arms control is linked to profitable projects.

Rebecca Johnson uses her first-hand knowledge of the CD's struggle over the comprehensive test ban treaty to analyse the pros and cons of conducting nuclear negotiations in a forum with more than sixty members. When Russia and the US finally agreed to resume serious CTB negotiations, some analysts urged the new Clinton administration to formulate the basic features of an accord in bilateral talks or private discussions among the five declared nuclear weapon states (NWS). US officials preferred to use the CD, in part because arms control supporters hoped that involving many non-nuclear states would intensify pressure on potential hold-outs. Since the NWS viewed the CTB more as a non-proliferation measure than a constraint on their own arsenals, they also thought that a treaty drafted by the CD would have more international legitimacy than one constructed and imposed by the great powers. Many theorists maintain that the prospects for cooperation decrease as the number of players grows because large numbers obscure common interests, raise transaction costs, and help free-riders escape detection and punishment.[40] Yet, Johnson suggests that the problem was less with the numbers than with the lack of appropriate techniques for managing multilateral negotiations so that the benefits outweighed the drawbacks.

One of the keys to successful multilateral negotiations is the formation of coalitions to compensate for power asymmetries, reduce cognitive complexity, facilitate communication and information exchanges, and simplify bargaining.[41] The CD continues to rely on three formal groupings developed during the Cold War that ignore important cleavages and obscure strong commonalities. They also make it difficult to address the special concerns of India, Pakistan, and Israel without according them undue status because of their clandestine nuclear programmes.

Johnson also details numerous other conflicts and asymmetries that complicate multilateral negotiations. Disagreement about the ultimate objective of arms control proved to be an overarching source of tension. In addition to problems caused by unequal military capabilities and intelligence resources, other important asymmetries included differences in delegations' size, degree of commitment and continuity, level of technical expertise, and freedom to take initiatives without checking back home. Furthermore, some countries were better than others at manipulating these disagreements and bargaining asymmetries to promote their preferred outcome. To improve the prospects for a ban on fissile materials or a nuclear weapons convention, Johnson then proposes several pragmatic changes that would respect power asymmetries, yet compensate for the weak bargaining position of most states that favour radical nuclear reductions.

Amy Sands, an Assistant Director of the U.S. Arms Control and Disarmament Agency (ACDA) from 1994 to 1996, offers an insiders' view of the American policy-making process. Sands details the practical problems created by changes in the arms control environment. For example, because the economic implications of arms transfers, illicit proliferation, and arms control receive far more attention now than during the Cold War, the circle of domestic players has expanded to include the Commerce, Treasury, and Justice Departments. These organizations have little arms control experience and non-traditional perspectives on security problems. Likewise, while theorists debate the system-level effects of entering the 'information age', Sands considers how uneven access to information and unequal ability to handle information overload alters the balance of power in bureaucratic politics. Sands contends that social scientists' propensity to decompose complex problems into a collection of single-factor analyses misses important synergies between components of the policy-making process. Ironically, though, her more holistic perspective reveals yet another arms control dilemma: many factors that make American leadership so crucial for arms control success also hinder bold, effective action. Unless scholars and policy-makers radically rethink how the United States is organized to negotiate and implement arms control accords, the country with the most to gain and the most to give in support of cooperation risks the fate of weak states – involuntary defection.

The Effects of Ideas and Domestic-International Interconnections

Two other themes that cut across contributions involve the impact of ideas on arms control preferences and the interconnections between domestic and international decision-making processes. Most classical arms control theory took superpower interests as given, then explored the possible arms control options and bargaining strategies that would maximize relative gains for their country or absolute gains for both states. Since the superpower rivalry no longer seems like a fixed feature of international politics, however, scholars are examining how states form and change their policy preferences. Much of this research draws heavily on psychology and sociology.[42] As Goldman writes, 'what actors do in large part reflects how *they* perceive and understand their environment'.[43] Thus, it matters how states define themselves and others, and what behaviours they associate with those identities. Some scholars maintain that policy-makers in the United States and developing countries still rely heavily on ideas developed during the Cold War, and that this antiquated 'sociology of arms control' explains the lack of progress on proliferation and regional arms control.[44] Others argue that rising interdependence is causing states to redefine sovereignty so that it no longer means freedom to act independently and secretly, but instead connotes 'membership in reasonably good standing in the regimes that make up the substance of international life' – a change with major implications for expectations about arms control compliance.[45]

If identities and expectations are constructed through social interaction, one must decide whether the relevant reference group is all members of the international system, as in Florini's research on the evolution of norms,[46] or is located at the state, organization, or individual level of analysis. For example, feminist theorists have explored how gendered assumptions define individuals' interests and constrain their choices concerning the use of military force, although scholars have yet to extend this type of analysis to arms control.[47] Research showing that political and organizational culture influence military leaders' preference for offensive or defensive doctrines has important implications for using arms control as an escape from the security dilemma.[48] A state-level explanation might focus on the effects of democratization by asking whether shared political values, greater openness, and increased economic integration will increase public support for cooperation, or if nationalism and demagogic posturing will prevent leaders from engaging in unpopular, but beneficial, accords. Contrast, for example, the optimistic prediction that 'in the final analysis ... it may be more important for nuclear arms control that countries have democratic political systems, respect human rights, and trade with the world at large, than that they have nuclear weapons or the capability to make them',[49] with the difficulty that Boris Yeltsin has had in persuading the Russian Duma to ratify START II.

Another way to analyse the impact of ideas on arms control preferences is to consider how worldviews and other types of intellectual frameworks help policy-makers operate despite incomplete, ambiguous, or indeterminate information. Some analysts argue that ideas matter mainly when material interests provide insufficient grounds for choice, perhaps because conflicting interests would be served by contradictory options or because decision-makers need a 'roadmap' of cause-and-effect relationships to reach their desired outcome.[50] This essay, by contrast, has argued that conflicting conceptions of international relations have a pervasive effect on arms control choices because different groups of theorists and policy-makers make contradictory assumptions about the values that arms control should serve, as well as the means through which it can best promote them.

The final essay in this volume synthesizes themes addressed by other contributors as it examines a problem that plagues all arms control efforts: the politics of verification. In contrast to analysts who treat verification as a technical problem of increasing transparency, Nancy Gallagher argues that deciding how to evaluate compliance involves numerous dilemmas that can only be addressed through political processes. She uses a modified two-level games approach to show how ideas about verification influence coalition-building strategies and alter the likelihood that a treaty will be signed and ratified.[51] Gallagher argues that domestic debates about verification reflect the conflicting assumptions about international relations held by realist, middle-ground, and idealist theorists, but that they also involve certain shared assumptions that differ from conceptions of verification advanced by other countries. The narrow conception of verification that has dominated US domestic debates since the Cold War has hurt the prospects for significant arms control by creating counter-cooperative spirals where moves that increase the likelihood of international agreement decrease the likelihood of domestic ratification, and vice versa. Many observers predicted that verification disagreements would disappear once the Cold War was over, but as arms control seeks more ambitious goals and the number of players grows at both the domestic and the international levels, the politics of verification becomes more complex and the opportunities for blocking coalitions increase. Gallagher uses examples at the pre-negotiation, negotiation, ratification, and implementation stages of arms control to show that misperceptions can be reduced by realizing that players who call for rigorous verification are not always interested in cooperation, while those who oppose American verification demands are not necessarily planning to cheat or hoping to get arms control on the cheap.

Yet, new thinking about verification is only a start. As with so many other arms control issues, recognizing the dilemmas and trade-offs involved does not reveal easy solutions, but it does provide a more accurate and reliable guide to the issues that must be addressed.

In short, many international relations theorists outside the strategic studies subfield are engaged in research of relevance to post-Cold War arms control. By broadening the circle of academics with whom they have contact, policy-makers can have access to a wider range of analytical tools and empirical findings. Once policy-makers realize the diversity of research done since the early days of classical arms control and the modifications of the mid-1970s and 1980s, they are less likely to assume that they 'know it all already' or that the trends in academia only involve abstract modelling, epistemological controversies, and other topics ten steps removed from real world concerns. And once scholars recognize that there is not, and never has been, a single comprehensive theory to guide arms control policy, they are less likely to assume that this issue area has been 'played out' and their intellectual fortunes lie elsewhere.

Conclusion

The time is ripe for creative new thinking about arms control theory and policy. Rather than treating arms control as a 'stepchild of the Cold War',[52] of minor importance then and even less interest now, scholars and policy-makers should take advantage of a time when public support for cooperative internationalism is high and no immediate security crisis forces policy in a particular direction. To do so, though, members of the arms control community must work together to develop a clearer picture of the diverse ways in which arms control can enhance security and the circumstances under which different approaches will be most effective.[53] They also must share intellectual resources with theorists working on other aspects of cooperation theory so that they can find persuasive answers to old criticisms of arms control, as well as effective strategies for managing the new challenges of post-Cold War arms control. While the contributions that arms control can make to security will always be constrained by conflicts of interest and incentives to retain freedom of action rather than make cooperative commitments, the political, military, economic, and technological changes that have occurred over the last decade have loosened these constraints. Depending on how arms control is handled now, we may miss unprecedented opportunities for cooperation, struggle to adapt but remain in a reactive mode, or find the vision and the practical tools needed to make the security environment increasingly conducive to cooperation.

NOTES

The author would like to thank Stuart Croft, Anthony Daley, Ann Florini, Emily Goldman, Terry Terriff, and Carola Weil for helpful comments and suggestions. She would also like to acknowledge generous financial support for this project from Women in International Security and valuable editorial assistance from Nina Srinivasan.

1. Charles C. Floweree, 'The Chemical Weapons Convention: A Milestone in International Security', *Arms Control Today*, Vol.22, No.8 (Oct. 1992), pp.3–7.
2. Alexander George, *Bridging the Gap: Theory and Practice in Foreign Policy* (Washington, DC: United States Institute of Peace Press, 1993).
3. David Newsom, 'Foreign Policy and Academia', *Foreign Policy*, No.101 (Winter 1995–96), p.64.
4. The *Daedalus* special issue formed the basis for Donald Brennan (ed.), *Arms Control, Disarmament, and National Security* (New York: George Braziller, 1961). This book, along with Schelling and Halperin's *Strategy and Arms Control* (New York: Twentieth Century Fund, 1961) stemmed from projects organized by the American Academy of Arts and Sciences to explore the 'state of the art' in arms control theory. Another influential book, Hedley Bull, *The Control of the Arms Race* (New York: Praeger, 1961), had similar origins. These works were purposely written in an accessible manner and the Brennan anthology was even distributed by the Book-of-the-Month Club.
5. Jennifer E. Sims, *Icarus Restrained: An Intellectual History of Nuclear Arms Control, 1945–1960* (Boulder, CO: Westview, 1990).
6. Thomas Schelling, 'What Went Wrong with Arms Control?', *Foreign Affairs*, Vol.64, No.2 (Winter 1985/86), pp.219–33.
7. Emanuel Adler (ed.), *The International Practice of Arms Control* (Baltimore: Johns Hopkins University Press, 1992).
8. For a critique of arguments that nuclear weapons are inherently good, bad, or irrelevant to international politics, see Michael Brown, 'The "End" of Nuclear Arms Control', in Ivo Daalder and Terry Terriff (eds.), *Rethinking the Unthinkable: New Directions for Nuclear Arms Control* (London and Portland: Frank Cass, 1993), pp.40–4.
9. Lynn Eden and Steven Miller (eds.), *Nuclear Arguments* (Ithaca: Cornell University Press, 1989).
10. David A. Baldwin, 'Security Studies and the End of the Cold War', *World Politics*, Vol.48, No.1 (Oct. 1995), pp.117–41.
11. E. H. Carr, *The Twenty Years' Crisis, 1919–1939* (New York: Harper and Row, 1964).
12. Baldwin, 'Security Studies', p.122. For an excellent attempt in this tradition to design an agenda for post-Cold War security studies, see Barry Buzan, *People, States, and Fear*, 2nd ed. (Boulder, CO: Lynne Rienner, 1991).
13. Stephen M. Walt, 'The Renaissance of Security Studies', *International Studies Quarterly*, Vol.35 (June 1991), p.214 and Edward Kolodziej, 'What is Security and Security Studies? Lessons from the Cold War', *Arms Control*, Vol.13, No.1 (April 1992), p.24.
14. See the essays in Brennan (ed.), *Arms Control*, by Kenneth Boulding, Erich Fromm, Ithiel De Sola Pool, Lewis Sohn, Richard Leghorn, and Arthur Larson.
15. Michael Intrilogator and Dagobert Brito, 'On Arms Control', in Edward Kolodziej and Patrick Morgan (eds.), *Security and Arms Control*, Vol.1 (Westport, CT: Greenwood Press, 1989), pp.214–15.
16. Colin Gray, *House of Cards: Why Arms Control Must Fail* (Ithaca: Cornell University Press, 1992).
17. Richard Betts, 'Systems for Peace or Causes of War?', *International Security*, Vol.17, No.1 (Summer 1992), pp.5–43.
18. Marc Trachtenberg, 'The Past and Future of Arms Control', in Adler (ed.), *The International Practice of Arms Control*, p.224.
19. Trachtenberg, 'The Past and Future', pp.228–9.
20. Albert Carnesale and Richard N. Haass (eds.), *Superpower Arms Control* (Cambridge, MA: Ballinger, 1987).

21. See, for example, Scott Sagan, *The Limits of Safety: Organizations, Accidents, and Nuclear Weapons* (Princeton: Princeton University Press, 1993).
22. Intrilogator and Brito, 'On Arms Control', pp.224–7.
23. Ivo Daalder, 'Stepping Down the Thermonuclear Ladder', in Daalder and Terriff (eds.), *Rethinking the Unthinkable*, pp.69–102.
24. Robert Jervis, 'Arms Control, Stability, and Causes of War', in Adler (ed.), *The International Practice of Arms Control*, pp.187–90.
25. Alexander George, Philip Farley, and Alexander Dallin, *U.S.-Soviet Security Cooperation* (New York: Oxford University Press, 1988).
26. Joseph Nye, Jr., 'Arms Control and International Politics', in Adler (ed.), *The International Practice of Arms Control*, pp.153–73.
27. For a sampling of perspectives in this debate, see the responses to Kolodziej, 'What is Security?' that are published in *Arms Control*, Vol.13, No.3 (Dec. 1992); and the review essay by Keith Krause and Michael Williams, 'Broadening the Agenda of Security Studies: Politics and Methods', *Mershon International Studies Review*, Vol.40, No.2 (Oct. 1996), pp.229–54.
28. For the argument that US non-proliferation policy is self-defeating, see Michael Klare, *Rogue States and Nuclear Outlaws* (New York: Hill and Wang, 1995).
29. Jessica Matthews, 'Power Shift', *Foreign Affairs*, Vol.76, No.1 (Jan./Feb. 1997), pp.50–66.
30. Frances Beer, 'On Creating Security Systems', in Kolodziej and Morgan (eds.), *Security and Arms Control*, pp.279–96.
31. Janne Nolan (ed.), *Global Engagement: Cooperation and Security in the 21st Century* (Washington, DC: Brookings, 1994).
32. Janne Nolan, 'The Concept of Cooperative Security', in Nolan (ed.), *Global Engagement*, pp.4–5.
33. Patrick Morgan, 'Safeguarding Security Studies', *Arms Control*, Vol.13, No.3 (Dec. 1992), pp.475–8.
34. The term 'pluralistic security community' refers to a group of states among whom war is unthinkable and comes from Karl Deutsch *et al.*, *Political Community and the North Atlantic Area* (Princeton: Princeton University Press, 1957). See Robert Jervis, 'The Future of World Politics: Will it Resemble the Past?' *International Security*, Vol.16, No.3 (Winter 1991/92), pp.39–73.
35. Carr, *Twenty Years' Crisis*.
36. Post-Cold War opinion surveys have shown that large majorities of Americans favour cooperative internationalism. For example, 88 per cent of respondents to a 1993 poll agreed that 'because the world is so interconnected today it is important for the United States to participate, together with other countries, in efforts to maintain peace and protect human rights'. See Steven Kull, 'What the Public Knows that Washington Doesn't', *Foreign Policy*, Vol.101 (Winter 1995–6), pp.102–15. A recent study conducted by Kull and I.M. Destler also found that policy-makers misperceive public opinion to be much more isolationist than it really is. See 'Misreading the American Public On International Engagement', Center for International and Security Studies at the University of Maryland, 18 Oct. 1996.
37. These scholars argue that stable cooperation is possible in an anarchic world of self-interested states if a small group of countries can realize that policy coordination would provide absolute benefits for everyone over time, recognize who is co-operative and who is not, and reciprocate both good and bad behaviour. For examples of this approach, see Kenneth Oye (ed.), *Cooperation Under Anarchy* (Princeton: Princeton University Press, 1986). Joseph Grieco argues that this is not a synthesis position, but simply the latest incarnation of idealism, in 'Anarchy and the Limits of Cooperation: A Realist Critique of the Newest Liberal Institutionalism', *International Organization*, Vol.42, No.3 (Summer 1988), pp.485–507.
38. For a sample of positions in the rational deterrence debate, see the special issue of *World Politics*, Vol.41, No.2 (Jan. 1989).
39. Brad Roberts, 'From Nonproliferation to Antiproliferation', *International Security*, Vol.18, No.1 (Summer 1993), p.139.
40. For example, see an analysis of the free-rider problem using the economic theory of public

goods by Jessica Eve Stern, 'Strategic Decision Making, Alliances, and the Chemical Weapons Convention', *Security Studies*, Vol.3, No.4 (Summer 1994), pp.754–80.

41. Fen Osler Hampson with Michael Hart, *Multilateral Negotiations* (Baltimore: Johns Hopkins, 1995), pp.40–2.

42. For an excellent collection of essays representing this area of research, see Peter Katzenstein (ed.), *The Culture of National Security* (New York: Columbia University Press, 1996). The most direct application to arms control is Richard Price and Nina Tannenwald, 'Norms and Deterrence: The Nuclear and Chemical Weapons Taboo', pp.114–52 in that volume.

43. Emily Goldman, 'Arms Control in the Information Age', p.39 in this volume.

44. Brad Roberts, 'Arms Control and the End of the Cold War', *The Washington Quarterly*, Vol.15, No.4 (Autumn 1992), pp.39–56.

45. Abram Chayes and Antonia Handler Chayes, *The New Sovereignty* (Cambridge, MA: Harvard University Press, 1995), p.27.

46. Ann Florini, 'The Evolution of International Norms', *International Studies Quarterly*, Vol.40, No.3 (Sept. 1996), pp.363–89.

47. See Michael Stevenson and Ruth Howes, *Women and the Use of Military Force* (Boulder: Lynne Reinner, 1993). While a feminist perspective might not offer much on some arms control questions, it could provide valuable insights into problems such as disarming and demilitarizing rival factions after a civil war. In a paper on 'Gender and Arms Control' presented at the WIIS 'Bridging the Gaps' Workshop, Rebecca Grant offered some preliminary thoughts about dilemmas that feminists encounter when thinking about issues such as peacekeeping and humanitarian intervention.

48. Elizabeth Kier, 'Culture and French Military Doctrine Before World War II', in Katzenstein (ed.), *The Culture of National Security*, pp.186–215.

49. 'Preface', in Adler (ed.), *The International Practice of Arms Control*, p.xiv.

50. Judith Goldstein and Robert Keohane (eds.), *Ideas and Foreign Policy* (Ithaca: Cornell University Press, 1993).

51. On the two-level games approach to conceptualizing how the structure and strategies used in domestic politics affect the prospects for international agreement, and vice versa, see Peter Evans, Harold Jacobson, and Robert Putnam (eds.), *Double-Edged Diplomacy* (Berkeley: University of California Press, 1993).

52. Roberts, 'Arms Control', p.39.

53. An excellent step in this direction is Stuart Croft, *Strategies of Arms Control: A History and Typology* (Manchester: Manchester University Press, 1996).

Arms Control in the Information Age

EMILY O. GOLDMAN

The end of the Cold War has accelerated changes in the security context for arms control that have been underway since the mid-1980s. New threats are emerging; alignment patterns are in flux; military diversity is increasing; weapons capabilities defy conventional means of measurement and are diffusing rapidly to more and different types of actor. In particular, knowledge-intensive goods that can be converted for military use are pouring into the marketplace faster than they can be tracked, giving minor powers and non-state actors increasing access to the means with which to threaten or challenge the designs of more capable superiors. Structural and technological changes have produced a set of interrelated problems for arms control. Some problems, such as technology diffusion, have grown and taken on slightly new twists in the post-Cold War period. Others, like asymmetries in military capabilities and the rise of peer-niche competition, have always existed and been a challenge for arms control, but during the Cold War were overshadowed as efforts focused on managing a rivalry between peer competitors. The case is made here for pursuing 'bridging' strategies – namely flexible packages of asymmetrical measures that both regulate capabilities and influence rivals' motivations – to adapt arms control to the post-Cold War world and the information age. Key to these bridging strategies is the linking of structural and behavioural arms control measures to broader political and economic settlements. Bridging strategies of this type were pursued with a good deal of success in the interwar period and offer instructive insights for the present.

The Case for Adapting Arms Control

Some of the most important security developments today are those associated with the information revolution and its rapid diffusion of knowledge-intensive technologies across national borders, fed by the globalization of finance and trade.[1] New forms of social organization and dramatic shifts in technological capabilities historically have transformed modes of conflict and war,[2] necessitating new thinking about the means to prevent and reduce the risk of war. The nuclear revolution led to new thinking on arms control which diverged significantly from its pre-nuclear manifestation, disarmament.[3] The information revolution,[4] likewise, demands new thinking because the capabilities associated with it involve not only weapons, but weaponry linked with knowledge, and knowledge itself.

The information revolution has undermined many of arms control's traditional operating assumptions: that a few strong nations could monopolize new weapons; that nations seeking such arms would have to produce their own and small nations lacked the resources to do so; that the technologies upon which new weapons depended could be identified, watched, and controlled; and that states were the only proliferators.[5] The security impact of the information revolution will depend upon the new capabilities it delivers, the types of target and range of rivals that can be threatened, and the way those capabilities are exploited by national militaries and non-state actors. Knowledge-intensive technologies may become weapons of choice because of their non-lethal character. Corporate information warfare could be employed for purposes of industrial espionage at a time when industrial secrets often wield the strategic leverage of military secrets.[6] Global information warfare could target entire industries, countries, or global economic forces.[7] Moreover, non-state actors as well as lesser state powers can potentially exploit these technologies to disrupt vulnerable governmental and commercial infrastructures.

Even if one is sceptical about the impact of the information revolution on military competition, and on regional and global power balances, changes in the structure of the international system and in the interaction dynamics among its rivals have led some analysts to conclude that arms control can no longer effectively manage international rivalry.[8] First, traditional assumptions about the identity of relevant actors and adversaries who would engage in arms control have fallen by the wayside. Familiar and clearly defined threats have disappeared. Traditional great powers are experiencing limited retrenchment. New powers are emerging, but their intentions are unknown. Unfamiliar threats, such as weak states armed with weapons of mass destruction, have risen in prominence, along with unconventional challenges posed by non-state actors such as narco-terrorists, religious fundamentalist groups, and ethnic and nationalist movements.

Second, the devolution of power toward regional centres of influence represents a dramatic change in system structure. Regional arms control efforts have always been complicated, but they were overshadowed by the global bipolar rivalry of the Cold War which pitted two groups of competitors against each other. The increasing prominence of multipolar rivalry that characterizes most regional sub-systems highlights the difficulty of implementing arms control arrangements which simultaneously bridge asymmetries between powerful outsiders and regional powers, and between regional powers and their smaller neighbours.[9] In South Asia, for example, arms control arrangements between India and Pakistan must consider, on the one hand, the role and influence of more capable extra-regional players like China, and on the other hand, how limitations which stabilize the India-China dyad will leave India too capable in relation to other regional neighbours. Bipolar rivalries continue to exist, but they are embedded in complex multipolar relationships.

Third, the notion of stability upon which much of the logic of Cold War arms control rested is more complex and multidimensional in the regional settings of today, particularly since the overarching bipolar structure of conflict has disappeared. The absence of historic, political, territorial, and economic ties between the superpowers that could exacerbate their rivalry[10] made it easier to focus on stabilizing their military rivalry as a way to manage the overall relationship.[11] Most of today's regional military rivals are tied closely together geographically, historically, and economically. Their military disputes are entangled with long-standing territorial, ideological, religious, ethnic, and economic differences, in large part because the rivals in question exist within a regional systemic context. These highly complex interrelated non-military relationships and disputes make it much more difficult to isolate the military dimension of rivalry for regulation.

Arms control is also complicated by the absence of formal structures which help to define regions and adversaries. The CFE negotiations benefited from their formal-alliance-to-formal-alliance context. But if one considers the Middle East as an example, alignment patterns are ill defined. Israel defines the Arab coalition broadly, while most Arab states cannot agree among themselves on a stable coalition against Israel.[12] The Arab states face regional Arab as well as non-Arab rivals, internal threats to regime stability, and extra-regional rivals like the United States.[13] These increasingly complex threat structures (internal and external) affect motives for acquiring military capabilities and complicate the arms control enterprise.

Finally, Cold War arms control developed in response to a rivalry where the threat was clear and high, and where cleavages were hardened. Because the intensity of the rivalry was so high, managing and stabilizing the rivalry, as distinct from resolving it, became the proximate goal of arms control efforts. To many, arms control seems unnecessary when levels of hostility are low or declining.

In sum, arms control sceptics focusing on the uncertainty about potential rivals, declining hostility among the Cold War powers, and the complexity of regional rivalries argue that much of arms control addresses problems whose time has come and gone. This view reflects an overly narrow and context-specific conception of arms control – one that is geared toward negotiating formal limits on opponent capabilities to reduce the risks of competition and stabilize rivalry between hostile peer competitors. Changes in the structure of the international system, in the identity and capabilities of relevant actors, and in the interaction dynamics among key players do not devalue arms control so much as they demand that arms control advocates develop more innovative approaches.

For example, the case of high hostility is but a subset of the potential ways to characterize threat environments. More attention should be paid to the role arms control can play when rivalry is low, escalating, and diminishing. These three scenarios share a common characteristic: because hostility is not so high as to preclude some resolution, even if only a partial one, of the underlying disputes that feed incentives to arm, it is not necessary to confine the goals of arms control to the minimalist one of managing rivalry. At other levels of intensity, arms control can focus also on modifying intentions to prevent potential rivalries from developing into rigid cleavages, and to ensure that a diminishing rivalry continues along its downward trajectory. The level of hostility in the United States-Russian relationship has lessened significantly, but arms control still has a role to play to ensure that the military rivalry continues to subside or at least does not reverse course. The level of hostility also introduces the notion of timing. The absence of distinct alignments means that windows of opportunity may exist to pursue arms control proactively, rather than reactively in a Cold War managerial mode. Finally, while the dynamics of regional rivalries may indeed be complex, more non-military dimensions of the relationship exist for potential exploitation in the arms control process. Above all, arms control needs to adapt to the information revolution, which is stimulating different patterns of competition among different types of competitors, with drastically different capabilities, who are likely to engage in different types of warfare.

Traditionally, arms control has either regulated and constrained capabilities through structural arms control – the supply side of the equation – or modified the intentions and ambitions of rivals through behavioural arms control – the demand side of the equation. Structural arms control aims at regulating the quantitative and qualitative characteristics of weapons (numerical ceilings, reductions, and constraints on, or elimination of, specific types of weapon); controlling the spread of capabilities (supplier controls, export cartels, and non-proliferation regimes); and limiting the disposition of weapons (basing and deployment agreements, weapons-free zones, and buffer zones). Behavioural arms control aims at building confidence and trust, assessing intent, and increasing transparency regardless of capabilities (information exchanges, intelligence sharing, military observers, on-site inspections, and notification of exercises); and resolving political conflict. The two sets of goals can overlap. Regulating the deployment of capabilities through basing agreements can reduce tensions and influence the ambitions of adversaries. Increasing transparency can build mutual trust and lead to concrete limits on capabilities.

Cooperative security is one approach to arms control that has gained currency in the post-Cold War era. It concedes the importance of both structural and behavioural arms control measures. It attempts to link, or bridge, supply-side and demand-side arms control measures – like confidence- and security-building measures, deployment agreements, limits on force size, weapon types, and operational practices – that are already part of the arms control repertoire. The goal is to alter the motivations and ambitions of national military establishments by creating a situation of defensive sufficiency. Mutual commitments to regulate the size, concentration, technical configuration, investment patterns, and operational practices of military forces[14] will prevent the accumulation of the means for war, and make surprise and pre-emptive attacks, and organized aggression, virtually impossible.

Defensive sufficiency presumes that conflict at the political level is not an issue. As Janne Nolan summarizes, 'it presupposes fundamentally compatible security objectives and seeks to establish collaborative rather than confrontational relationships among national military establishments. The basis for such collaboration is mutual acceptance of and support for the defense of home territory as the exclusive national military objective and the subordination of power projection to the constraints of international consensus.'[15] By presupposing the compatibility of security objectives, however, the cooperative security approach to arms control may not be possible to implement in the context of many contemporary rivalries.[16] Yet when security objectives are not fundamentally compatible, arms control need not revert to the minimalist mode that was so prominent during the Cold War. Arms control can influence motivations at the national political level if linked to broader political and economic settlements that exploit the potential for asymmetric reciprocity across issue areas.[17] This approach holds the most promise for adapting arms control to the problem of technology diffusion stimulated by the information revolution, and to changes in system structure and international rivalry resulting from the end of the Cold War. These challenges will now be explored, followed by a discussion of why bridging strategies of this sort are necessary for managing technology diffusion and promoting asymmetric reciprocity, particularly when rivalries lack the more abstract nature of East–West military competition with its relative symmetry in capabilities and few sources of objective conflict.[18]

Technology Diffusion

Technology diffusion is not a new problem in the post-Cold War world, but it has taken on different dimensions, particularly when one considers the spread of information-related technologies. The diffusion of capabilities associated with the information revolution promises to change the identities and broaden the capabilities of actors able to threaten national, regional, and global security. It can empower traditionally weak states in unprecedented ways because revolutionary dual-use technologies, like computer and software capabilities, are not capital intensive and do not require a huge industrial capacity to exploit. They can be developed or acquired relatively easily and quickly,[19] enabling smaller powers with older, less capable platforms to deliver high-tech smart firepower. India, Israel, South Korea, and Taiwan already possess significant computer software capabilities.

With new information technologies, non-state actors can also increase their leverage against states, shifting the balance of power between state and non-state actors. Geoffrey Herrera argues that sub-state actors benefit from new technologies more than states because they gain 'access to forms of communication previously monopolized by states, and because some of the new technologies are best used by smaller, less-centralized organizations'.[20] The Zapatistas in Chiapas Mexico and the Chechens in Russia manipulated the global media and used communication networks to sustain their uprisings and challenge state authority. New information capabilities make protest against the state easier, cheaper, and more effective.

In addition to expanding the identities of relevant units and their capabilities, the spread of information warfare capabilities poses new types of threat for the most technologically advanced military forces and societies. According to Richard Harknett, what distinguishes the information age is the network, and the strength of the network rests on its degree of 'connectivity', be it on the battlefield or in society at large.[21] Connectivity creates opportunities for great advances, but it also breeds potentially serious vulnerabilities. Attacks on societal connectivity – 'netwar' – target the very linkages upon which modern societies rely to function: communication, financial transaction, transportation, and energy resource networks. For societal connectivity to be a useful target, 'a society must be dependent enough on these networks to make their loss important',[22] so the loss of connectivity is not likely to be as prohibitive for a low-tech society as it is for a state like the United States. Nor is it necessary to be a high-tech networked society to have access to information warfare capabilities.[23] Terrorist organizations and organized crime groups can launch netwar attacks. As new capabilities empower new types of actors, particularly non-state actors whose organizational forms are not hierarchical and bureaucratic, the utility of arms control efforts that focus on state-to-state relations as a means to reduce the risks of conflict and war declines.

What is true for the networked society is also true for the networked military. Connectivity can dramatically enhance the lethality of military forces, but it also increases their vulnerability to 'cyberwar' attacks.[24] These include the techniques of electronic warfare (jamming, deception, disinformation, destruction) that deny and disrupt information flows, the use of software viruses to destroy, degrade, exploit, or compromise information systems, and the destruction of sensing equipment. Like their societal counterparts, information-intensive military organizations are more vulnerable to information warfare simply because they are more information-dependent, while an adversary need not be information-dependent to disrupt the information lifeline of high-tech forces.[25]

Nolan, in her study of ballistic missile proliferation, described the changing international technology market and how over time it has undermined the assumption of 'technological stratification', which supported a type of stability. Industrialized states assumed they could 'retain sufficient technological superiority to stay ahead of and to counter threats posed by the growing military capabilities of developing nations'.[26] But in efforts to capture markets, generate foreign revenue, and share the costs of development and production, advanced countries began exporting more sophisticated equipment and entering into technology-sharing arrangements. To promote modernization, develop their national technological infrastructure, and enhance their international status, developing states began pursuing independent defense industries and exporting their wares for revenue. These motivations continue to drive diffusion today.

Nolan also explained how the ability to control proliferation has diminished as technology, rather than finished weapon systems, diffuses. Distinguishing between civilian and military exports has also become more difficult since commercial technologies increasingly have military applications.[27] Information technologies exacerbate these dynamics because they are driven as much by the civilian commercial economy as by government-sponsored military research and development. They are critical for success and competitive advantage in the global economy, so the ability to monitor and control their dissemination, let alone develop a normative consensus on the desirability of control, is highly questionable. The nations of the South, in particular, view with suspicion efforts of the industrialized North to limit technology transfers because of the discriminatory implications that extend well beyond the military realm to affect modernization and the eradication of sources of social unrest in civil society.[28]

Since the end of the Cold War, the academic and policy communities have concentrated on understanding and containing the spread of mass destruction weapons. As a result, we have greater knowledge about this type of proliferation problem. But the dynamics associated with the spread of mass destruction weapons are not the same as those associated with what Henry Sokolski calls 'non-apocalyptic' proliferation, the spread of weapons and technologies which are not mass destructive but that still pose threats against which the most militarily superior states have little or no defence.[29] Arguments for developing a strategy to control the spread of capabilities like computing and software are not nearly as compelling as in the case of weapons of mass destruction, because of an underlying tension inherent in the technology. As John Arquilla points out in his analysis of high performance computing capabilities, 'Efforts to safeguard national power advantages over others, associated with exclusion [i.e. a preclusive strategy], engender commercial costs in terms of market share. Similarly, openness fosters economic competitiveness, while tending to erode advantages in relative power over actual and potential rival states.'[30] A non-proliferation paradigm based on the notion that 'none is best' is not easily transferable when dealing with the competing priorities introduced by many dual-use technologies.

The internationalization of the high technology market is not new; nor are the problems associated with the spread of dual-use technologies or knowledge itself. But what is different is that the diffusion of information technologies feeds, and is in turn fed by, the pursuit of asymmetric or offsetting strategies, as opposed to emulation strategies, of capability acquisition. So while Nolan's analysis of ballistic missile proliferation in the developing world emphasizes the disappearance of an international hierarchy as the military forces of developing countries improve, those forces need not compete on the same terms as advanced countries. They need not strive to acquire peer capabilities, but simply to degrade superior capabilities cheaply and effectively.

Some analysts contend that many advanced technologies are too complex for less sophisticated users to exploit,[31] so we should not be concerned with the amount of information technologies available but with the sophistication of the users. Undoubtedly, however, developing nations will try to exploit new capabilities, particularly given demonstration of the superiority of advanced technologies in the Persian Gulf War. Moreover, states with military institutions that are less reified and have fewer entrenched interests than those of the United States may in fact be able to adapt more easily to the organizational and doctrinal requirements of waging 'cyberwar'.[32] Finally, regional rivalries are likely to be an important motivation for developing states to adopt and exploit new capabilities rapidly.

Peer-Niche Rivalry and Asymmetrical Capabilities

One of the most striking facets of the contemporary security context is the absence of competition among core industrialized powers. The dominant axis of military rivalry is no longer between peer competitors. Even US military planners are more concerned about rogue nuclear states than they are about an emerging peer competitor. Changes in system structure and evolving unit-level capabilities that are being fed by technology diffusion have produced a shift from peer rivalry to peer-niche rivalry. The 'peer-niche' characterization draws attention to different strategies for acquiring capabilities, namely whether rivals opt to emulate or offset the capabilities of their adversaries.[33] This creates significant problems for structural arms control in particular because peer-niche rivals by definition have highly asymmetrical military arsenals.

Peer competitors possess roughly similar capabilities across the board. Niche competitors strive to inhibit or defeat peer actions through asymmetric responses designed to offset or degrade superior peer capabilities. Niche competitors can acquire weapons of mass destruction to deter, deny, and punish a state with superior capabilities. Cruise missiles, mines, diesel-electric submarines, and unmanned aerial vehicles can offset superior conventional forces, particularly when coupled with improved civilian C^3I capabilities and navigational enhancements like GPS-based guidance systems and commercial space assets.[34] By increasing the accuracy of long-range stand-off munitions like cruise missiles and unmanned aerial vehicles, Differential Global Positioning System products can be exploited by weaker states to enhance their ability to project power more accurately and to deter outside intervention by technologically superior states.[35] Pre-emptive information warfare attacks, like the covert sabotage of computer systems,[36] can also be employed against high-technology forces that rely on information dominance. Similarly, information-dependent societies are more vulnerable to the infiltration of computer networks, databases, and the media for the purposes of deception, subversion, and promotion of dissident and opposition movements.[37] Finally, technologically advanced militaries historically have coped poorly with non-high-tech capabilities, particularly those employed by 'People's War' strategies in wars of national liberation. Niche competitors can employ low intensity conflict threats such as guerrilla warfare, terrorism, or special operations against down-link stations. In sum, a niche competitor need not acquire the capabilities to defeat a peer, but just those to deter the peer from intervening or deny the peer the ability to exploit its superior capability.[38]

Inferior powers have always sought ways to degrade the capabilities of their superiors. But today, the relative cheapness and accessibility of new technologies, many of which do not require the infrastructure needed for developing and operating more complicated systems,[39] mean that more technologically advanced societies do not command the advantage they once might have.[40] Moreover, technological change has been broadening and accelerating in recent times, giving competitors a rich menu of military innovation to choose from. From the seventeenth to the mid-twentieth centuries, military innovations tended to increase the power differential between great and lesser powers, but this is no longer the case. Weapons of mass destruction, even if used only for terror purposes, can function as equalizers. Advanced conventional capabilities exist side by side with weapons of mass destruction and with the panoply of low-tech capabilities like guerrilla warfare and terrorism. Advanced information-based societies and high-tech national military establishments are increasingly capable, but also increasingly vulnerable. Eliot Cohen compares the emerging military order to a medieval one, characterized by 'strategic obscurity'.[41] Warfare is not a sphere exclusive to states, and armed forces defy comparison because military technology varies widely among combatants and strength varies greatly depending on who is fighting whom.

Contrast this situation with the Cold War, in which the chief rivals were peer competitors with roughly symmetrical capabilities in key strategic weapon systems. The very notion of the 'arms race' implies peer competition. Quantitative races are attempts to out-build an adversary in a particular weapon system. Qualitative technological innovations lead to races to acquire the superior weapon. In this sense, a qualitative race can be conceived as a series of quantitative races. So the arms race metaphor, which underlays the arms control problematic, pitted two rivals striving to emulate the weapon systems of the other.[42] Emulation produced a degree of symmetry in capabilities that greatly facilitated structural arms control and made it a mainstay of the US-Soviet arms control agenda.

Asymmetries in capability always exist among rivals. Clearly the American and Soviet nuclear arsenals were not identical in quantitative or qualitative terms. The United States relied more heavily on SLBMs and the Soviet Union on ICBMs. Still, the superpower arsenals were roughly equivalent in certain key measures of military effectiveness. It should come as no surprise that the strategic nuclear rivalry was the one most successfully regulated during the Cold War. Today, however, even the notion of a key strategic weapon is questionable given the diversity in capabilities across potential rivals and the absence of any particular weapon that might operate as strategic nuclear weapons did in the US-Soviet context. Nor does the notion of tiers of military capabilities[43] help much, because it presumes a hierarchy of power when the current situation has become quite anarchic. Arms control does not require the presence of a clear key weapon to succeed, but consensus on what the strategic system of the day is does create a common currency for negotiation. The arsenals of most rivals lack a symmetry in key capabilities and there is no cause to expect this to change in the near future. Despite the claims made by proliferation optimists,[44] newly emerging nuclear powers do not possess secure second-strike capabilities to produce the condition of mutual vulnerability so crucial to the notion of strategic stability upon which structural arms control between the superpowers rested.

At the conventional level, as Barry Posen notes, military forces are inherently dissimilar and these asymmetries increase when accompanied by differences in the 'military format' of rivals – the totality of components of combat power, which includes doctrine, technology, recruitment, training, armament, and organization.[45] In the Middle East, for example, the Arab states rely on a mass mobilization format while Israel has integrated science and technology into every aspect of its armed forces to produce a high-tech format. The choice of format derives from many factors – differences in strategic depth, casualty sensitivity, and access to the military industrial base of the advanced industrialized nations. The results, however, are significant force asymmetries – Israel possesses a nuclear monopoly and air power superiority while the Arab states have more numerous mass armies and chemical weapons capabilities[46] – that complicate structural arms control efforts.

The superpowers also faced no serious sub-national conflicts or internal demands for force that significantly complicated efforts to stabilize their military rivalry. Internal security demands and sub-national conflicts, which are endemic in developing states today and have in fact been encouraged by the break-up of the Soviet Union and the international community's support for national self-determination, mean that national governments need to acquire military capabilities to deal with rising internal threats to security, in addition to long-standing external rivalries.[47] This complicates arms control efforts, particularly when rivals are geographically contiguous and military forces can readily be shifted from internal to external duties.

For all these reasons, structural arms control measures are likely to fail if pursued on their own.[48] An informative example comes from the pre-nuclear era when political and military leaders strove to develop a 'yardstick' or a formula to assess military value across different military units.[49] They found the notion infeasible, and they were simply trying to compare naval assets, even within a single class – cruisers. Moreover, the rivals in question shared a common view of the basic principles of warfare. Approaches concentrating on the relationship between instabilities in military balances and the outbreak of war were a mainstay of US-Soviet arms control, but they presupposed some agreement on the meaning of rough parity, and on how different weapons affected stability. The basis for such symmetry in capabilities was unique to the Cold War superpower rivals. It proved illusive before the Cold War and it does so after as well.

New interaction dynamics, the result of structural and technological changes, pit rivals with incomparable force structures and weapons inventories, and raise the profile of newly emerging threats from below. Asymmetries in strategic objectives, resources, and willingness to assume risks and accept costs will shape how competitors approach and attempt to exploit opportunities presented by new military technologies. Yet those capabilities are as likely to reflect an asymmetric response to a rival's capabilities as a symmetric response, because matching a superior power military capability for military capability is an immensely costly way to degrade superior power in the face of far cheaper alternatives.

Peers have always had to attend to the asymmetrical strategies designed to avoid their strengths and exploit their vulnerabilities. A classic example comes again from the interwar period when the junior naval power, France, developed a large submarine force to offset Great Britain's battleship supremacy. For the first time, a continental enemy could imperil Britain's maritime lifelines without building a superior navy. While the British wanted to abolish the submarine through arms control, the French refused to be forced into competing with the British in building battleships, which were of marginal utility for a junior naval power.[50] This was not an insignificant dispute in the arms control process, because the failure to impose limits on submarines precluded significant restrictions on anti-submarine craft, contributing to a renewed arms competition in the cruiser category. The problems for arms control are compounded today as the accessibility and affordability of new offsetting capabilities level the playing field even more. Historically, the arms control process has failed to solve the problem of adapting when rivals pursue strategies to offset rather than emulate each others' capabilities.

The problems of asymmetric capabilities and acquisition strategies rise even further when different paradigms of war, which produce different military formats, coexist. If recent wars employ new techniques that demonstrate or portend a dramatic increase in the lethality of combat, such as occurred with the Gulf War, familiar paradigms of conflict and war may be upset. Some believe the information revolution has the potential to render traditional approaches to warfare obsolete by overcoming one of the most difficult problems in warfare: finding the opponent. The assumption is that once the opponent's location is known, he can be targeted, most likely hit, and destroyed. Both sides are presumably aware of this, so that future hostilities can be visualized as a struggle for information dominance.[51] As Martin Libicki explains, 'if visibility equals death, then the nature of conventional warfare (as apart from strategic nuclear warfare or irregular conflict) shifts from force-on-force to hide-and-go-seek'.[52] Warfare will continue to be about bending the opponent's will, but no longer by destroying the enemy's physical capacity 'attrition-style' or inflicting pain 'punishment-style'; rather, it will aim to control the opponent's ability to conduct war 'paralysis-style'.[53]

The new form of war introduced by the information revolution is not likely to displace previous war forms entirely, just as the contributions of past military revolutions have co-existed.[54] But it does promise to increase the range of military *diversity* and certainly calls into question much of the supporting intellectual capital for arms control. 'Stability', for example, was a concept which was studied and practised with the aim of managing the military relationship between two competitors and their respective alliance systems. Stability assumed comparable measures of military effectiveness. It also presumed a shared understanding of the role of nuclear weapons in war. Nuclear weapons were distinct from all other weapons because warfare at the nuclear level could no longer be seen as a means to a political end.[55] Their utility lay in deterring war rather than winning it. Arms control sought to stabilize this deterrent relationship by bolstering the condition of mutual assured destruction.

As the dynamics of warfare shift and competing strategic paradigms coexist, the tools for managing rivalry and reducing the risk of war must also adapt. An informative example comes again from the interwar period. The rivals in question did not possess different paradigms of war, but they did have competing conceptions about the role of naval power, naval warfare, and naval arms control. Even at this level, the problems proved daunting. The British and French shared mutual security interests in Europe; neither viewed the other as an enemy; no one seriously believed they would go to war. Politically, there were few obstacles to arms limitation between them, providing a highly favourable set of political conditions to negotiate arms control. Yet they were unable to agree on how to reconcile different doctrinal and force structure preferences because they had different paradigms of naval warfare, one maritime and Mahanian, the other continental. As a maritime power with long trade routes to defend against commerce raiding, the British wanted to limit naval vessels by category to strike a balance among fleets alone as fighting units. As a continental power, the French wanted naval arms control to proceed in tandem with the control of land-based forces. Short of that, the French would agree only to ceilings on total naval tonnage to permit maximum flexibility for transfer between categories of ships.

The interesting new twist today centres on some distinctive qualities associated with information warfare capabilities. Previous military revolutions, like those associated with the rise of industrial warfare in the mid-nineteenth century and mobile warfare in the early twentieth century, required a significant industrial infrastructure to develop, produce, and maintain. By contrast, information warfare capabilities do not require huge financial resources to acquire and exploit. Moreover, these technologies need not be employed in the way the United States has used them to be effective.[56] They can be used to offset superior capabilities by striking at vulnerable lines of connectivity.

Bridging Strategies to Manage Technology Diffusion

The diffusion of information technologies suggests the necessity of recasting arms control to deal with the uncertainties introduced by the ongoing information revolution and the loss of control by national governments over new means of organized violence. At one level, we must address intentions, for ultimately they matter most. At the same time, we must not ignore the capabilities question, but recognize that it is not only traditional platforms or weapons of mass destruction that are at issue but a whole range of developing conventional capabilities and information technologies. Moreover, we can never hope to control information flows completely because of the rapid and myriad paths of diffusion that are inherent in dual-use technologies. For democratic, social, and economic reasons, we probably do not want to.

Innovative supply-side regimes that monitor and control the diffusion of dual-use technologies without totally denying their transfer have been proposed in an effort to balance the need to halt proliferation with the need to promote economic growth and social stability. Denial gives way to disclosure.[57] On the supply side, the idea is to create incentives on the part of suppliers as far down as the level of the firm and on the part of financial intermediaries to provide information for the creation of databases that regulators can use to allow the uninhibited flow of dual-use technologies while ensuring they will be used in civilian applications. On the demand side, the idea is to create incentives for recipient governments to reduce excessive military expenditure and to provide matching import data to supplement the export data required by the supply side of the regime. One sort of demand-side incentive would tie development aid to regime compliance by designing conditionality constraints for bilateral and multilateral aid transfers.

Various obstacles would need to be surmounted: accommodating different national institutional structures; establishing common regulatory and enforcement standards to circumvent competitive deregulation; establishing common conditionality priorities for aid; and strengthening national bureaucratic and legislative capacities for self-reporting, which are likely to be deficient in states in a process of transition to democracy, but can even be burdensome for the United States.[58] Still, proponents argue that such a regime, geared towards managing capabilities, would receive wide support. Regulators recognize the inability of national governments to cope with the proliferation problem. Corporations will accept some regulation in exchange for continued liberalization of world trade, finance, and technology transfer. Societies will welcome the opportunity to divert resources from defense into more productive avenues, promote economic development, and enhance national security in the process.[59]

Such an analytical approach to the arms control process starts from the premise that national security is a public good. Proliferation is then cast as a problem of economic regulation, in Wolfgang Reinicke's words, 'an economic activity that, although permitted in general, must be transparent so that public authorities can monitor it and avoid the occurrence of market failure, providing a public good, in this case, a nation's security'.[60] The regulative orientation builds on work in the field of economics and presumes a notion of rationality where actors are instrumentally motivated to pursue their self-interests and make choices according to a utilitarian cost-benefit logic.[61] This operating premise may make sense in the confines of the realm within which it was developed, namely the economist's focus on the behaviour of firms in competitive markets. We might be reasonably confident that such a regulatory regime would eventually come to enjoy the support of private corporations. We should be far more sceptical, however, about the compliance of social actors, particularly those nations or non-state actors that fill out the demand side of the equation and who may now or at some future time desire to exploit the military applications of dual-use technologies.[62]

The regulatory approach to arms control assumes the interests of societal actors just as it assumes the interests of corporate actors. Yet most area specialists who study security cooperation in areas like the Middle East and South Asia concur that the motives operating defy a singular characterization, if only for the reason that in many cases the military controls the state or a group depends on the military to control the state. A more useful set of starting premises comes from the cognitive orientation of anthropologists and sociologists.[63] From this perspective, 'Interests are not assumed to be natural or outside the scope of investigation: They are not treated as exogenous. Rather, they are recognized as varying by institutional context and as requiring explanation.'[64] What actors do in large part reflects how *they* perceive and understand their environment.

A regulative orientation views the external world as objective. Social actors act independently of social context, based on a set of self-interests in response to incentives and constraints operating in the environment. A cognitive orientation, by contrast, views the external world as the product of social processes, shaped by the social relations and beliefs of actors operating within it. Social actors act based on self-conceptions and cultural beliefs. Nolan's analysis of the context of defense investment in the developing world illustrates the pertinence of the cognitive orientation. She argues that efforts in developing states to achieve independence in defense production are not based on rational calculations of economic development needs or military requirements. While developing countries should recognize the diseconomies involved in diverting scarce resources away from modernization and social welfare initiatives, as well as from more efficient military investment programs that exploit comparative advantages, the 'desire to achieve an independent capacity to develop weapons ... is not restrained by any traditional logic of economic or military efficiency'. Rather, 'the principal rationale for producing weapons is to demonstrate sovereignty'.[65] The cognitive orientation suggests the complexity of the demand side of the proliferation equation, which will vary across national and regional contexts, and over time.

Given the nature of technology diffusion today, supplier regimes are important, but they are not enough. A comprehensive regime to manage the proliferation of information and other dual-use technologies requires demand-side participation to complement supply-side compliance. It must come to terms with the factors – domestic, regional, and global – compelling states to exploit dual-use technologies for military purposes, rather than assuming the motivations away. Michael Moodie summarizes this sentiment when he writes that the impact of technology on society and security affairs is the product of human choice: 'Technology may shape the context within which choices are made, create new paths open to the chooser, or change the calculations of costs and benefits associated with certain courses of action. The result, however, is determined by individuals. It is not the technology itself that is beneficial or harmful, but how it is used.' So the basic task of those who seek to manage technology, which includes the arms control community, 'should not be focused on the technology itself, but on channeling the choices of those to whom technology is available'.[66] Particularly because of the widespread availability of emerging technologies and the dramatically reduced costs of acquiring them, the issue is no longer the ability to acquire and produce capabilities but the will and political choice to do so.

One goal of arms control, therefore, should be to channel those choices with incentives and disincentives, recognizing that the structure of incentives will vary among states, between state and non-state actors, across regional contexts, and over time. Some recent examples from the nuclear proliferation area include the steps taken to convince Ukraine to relinquish its strategic nuclear weapons and the North Koreans to freeze and dismantle their nuclear facilities. Ukrainian leaders forfeited their nation's strategic nuclear arsenal, but only after receiving security assurances from Russia and the United States, guarantees of economic compensation from Russia, and $177 million in aid from the United States to deactivate their missiles. Ukrainian leaders stressed a desire to relinquish their strategic nuclear arsenal, but only if they received in return compensation for the loss of power, prestige, and respect conferred on them by being the world's third largest nuclear power.[67] Force reductions were tied to security guarantees and economic compensation, addressing the factors motivating the Ukrainians to cling to their nuclear arsenal.[68]

Assessment of the success of the North Korean Agreed Framework will have to wait several years in order to gauge North Korean compliance.[69] The North Koreans agreed to freeze and eventually dismantle their nuclear facilities in return for compensation in a host of other areas: economic and technological assistance to build light water reactors, compensation for alternative sources of energy in the meantime, assurances that nuclear weapons will not be used against them, a United States commitment to take steps to establish full economic and diplomatic relations, and delay of IAEA inspections of undeclared nuclear sites for several years.[70]

The ability of arms control measures, like those described above, to influence the motivations of prospective proliferators is admittedly a daunting task. Any determined state can acquire both nuclear and emerging non-nuclear capabilities given sufficient financial resources. The point of divergence between advocates and sceptics of such bridging strategies is on whether the cost-benefit calculations of would-be proliferants can really be altered. That assessment can only be made on a case-by-case basis, and calculations will shift over time. The challenge becomes one of identifying windows of opportunity for such initiatives. Those windows tend to open when rivalries are diminishing or just beginning to escalate.

Bridging Strategies to Promote Asymmetric Reciprocity

Asymmetries in the capabilities of regional rivals also require a different emphasis in arms control, one that can be pursued in tandem with more familiar behavioural arms control practices like CSBMs, but which recognizes the continued importance of structural arms control and seeks to adapt it with bridging strategies. Such a bridging strategy was employed quite successfully between the world wars to regulate multilateral political, economic, and military rivalry in the Far East and Pacific.[71] In 1922, Great Britain, the United States, and Japan entered into a web of agreements over military, political, and economic issues in order to reinforce their mutual security in China, a highly unstable region of the world in which each was heavily invested. They negotiated treaties to reduce their naval forces; limit the major offensive weapon system of the day, the battleship; freeze the status quo of base fortifications; demilitarize the western Pacific and establish spheres of influence there. Stabilizing military balances by granting each Pacific power defensive superiority in its respective sphere and by reducing the ability to bring war to one's adversary was a critical dimension of the arms control process. But the treaty powers also recognized the potentially explosive political and economic competition among them brewing in the Far East which was threatening to erupt into an all-out arms race. Limits on naval armaments, they knew, would not promote confidence unless linked to specific understandings regarding China. Moreover, they recognized that one power, Japan, had significantly greater interest in the region by virtue of historic and economic ties, and geographic proximity. The treaty powers addressed these underlying problems and asymmetries with a series of related political and economic agreements. They negotiated general principles to coordinate their diplomatic efforts, regulate economic commerce, and establish norms for intervention in China.

The Washington treaty system helped transform the Anglo-American relationship from one of burgeoning competition to one of political consensus. It terminated the Anglo-Japanese alliance, the cornerstone of British and Japanese policy in the Far East since 1902 and a major source of friction in Anglo-American relations. It also successfully managed competition in a region of tremendous instability for almost a decade. It is instructive for the present era for two key reasons. First, the Pacific powers acknowledged that the security issues in question were interrelated so closely that a solution to one issue could not be worked out in the absence of a simultaneous, coordinated solution to the other issues. Second, the treaty powers built this notion into the arms control process.

By the late-1920s, the security system began to unravel. The causes of collapse are complex; there is no scholarly consensus on why cooperation failed, or on whether the experience should be viewed as a partial success or a total failure.[72] Three factors seem instrumental in its unravelling. Two were beyond the ability of the treaty powers to control: worldwide economic depression and the nationalist unification of China. One was reasonably within the treaty powers' control – how arms control and related political disputes were managed – but by the late 1920s the treaty powers elected to separate the arms control and political tracks, moving forward on the former at the very time that the premises of political cooperation were crumbling. In an effort to protect and extend force limitations at the London Conference of 1930, they neglected the more profound political threats to security emerging in the Far East and failed to renegotiate the political compromises upon which cooperation was initially erected.

What are of particular interest for the present are the unintended consequences that resulted from seeking to reduce the potential for conflict in narrow military terms while failing to relate those understandings to broader considerations of general stability. Facing escalating threats from Nationalist forces to their special interests in China – interests which had been recognized by the West in 1922 – the Japanese revised their local security requirements upwards. In 1930, force ratios codified Japan's local naval superiority, but negotiations only considered the military balance. The arms control treaties, as a result, were perceived by a majority in Japan – and not just the military – as a challenge to national status and prestige both regionally and globally. By not acknowledging the dramatically changing events in the Far East and their much greater impact on Japanese interests, the British and Americans inadvertently undermined the domestic foundations of Japan's cooperative diplomacy with the West. Failing to relate the political and military dimensions of security contributed to the fall from power of those leaders in Japan committed to arms limitation and cooperation with the West.

The Washington treaty process of 1922 represents one way to adapt arms control to rivalries that lack the relatively abstract nature of the East-West military competition. In the context of many regional rivalries today which have deep historical and political roots, working to stabilize the military relationship without addressing underlying sources of political turmoil may prove counter-productive in important ways. Actors may not be able domestically, nor may it be possible conceptually, to separate out the military dimension of the relationship as was possible in the US–Soviet context. The military and political tracks need to proceed in tandem and ideally be inter-linked in the negotiation process. Particularly instructive is the comparison between the arms control processes employed in the Far East in the 1920s and in the 1930s. In the earlier decade, arms control was designed to promote asymmetric reciprocity across issue areas. In the later decade, reciprocity was confined entirely to the military sphere.

The Middle East today is a region fraught with asymmetries – geographic, demographic, economic, cultural, ideological, and civil–military.[73] Overlapping and cross-cutting threats and shifting alignments exist, as well as significant internal threats to security. This has resulted in the absence of a single central balance, and the presence of massive asymmetries in the quality and quantity of weaponry. Notions of parity and symmetry make no sense in this context. For these reasons, Geoffrey Kemp concludes that the relevant players need to 'subscribe to the principle of asymmetric reciprocity. The key adversaries must accept, a priori, the fact that strategic asymmetries cannot be removed and that there can be no neat symmetric formula for reducing military forces and limiting military deployments and technical capabilities.'[74]

The question becomes how to operationalize asymmetric reciprocity.[75] Clearly it must be extended beyond the realm of military practices because of the tremendous asymmetries in capabilities and differences in military format among rivals. The naval limitation negotiations of the 1920s provide a model of asymmetric reciprocity that bridges military and non-military issue areas. Concessions over military capabilities were made palatable because they were accompanied by trade-offs in other issue areas. The Middle East peace process provides a vehicle for pursuing this type of arms control. It encompasses bilateral negotiations among the immediate players in the Arab–Israeli conflict over territorial withdrawal, border demarcation, security arrangements, and political rights of the Palestinians. It also includes multilateral negotiations that engage a wider set of participants and issues. Five separate working groups cover arms control and regional security, regional economic development, refugees, water resources, and the environment, issues deemed vital to the future security of the region.

The inclusiveness of the process suggests at first glance an understanding that arms control and political relationships must evolve in tandem given the structural context. Arms control must be part of the larger conflict resolution process. That said, however, the process has suffered from lack of coordination among the five separate working groups, and from lack of integration between the multilateral and bilateral talks.[76] While there is a recognition of the interrelationship between the two sets of processes, there has been, according to Joel Peters, 'a poverty in the analysis of [the multilateral track's] role and contribution to the peace process'.[77] He notes that the multilateral process was always perceived as subordinate to and dependent upon the bilateral process, useful for discussing technical issues but 'separable from the primary issues at stake'.[78]

Arms control can be a proactive process, going beyond efforts to stabilize the military situation, contributing to the resolution of political conflict. But this requires that negotiations bridge issue areas, balancing sacrifices in one area with gains in others. At a minimum, the physical separation among the multilaterals, and between the multilateral and bilateral tracks, needs to be overcome. If the conceptual separation were also reduced, it might help convince the relevant parties and their domestic audiences that military-related concessions need not undermine national security.

Conclusions

Arms control as a tool for managing rivalry and reducing the risk of war must adapt to the structural changes associated with the end of the Cold War and to the technological dynamics associated with the information age. The rising importance of regional rivalries that are no longer influenced by the overarching bipolar superpower conflict, coupled with the rapid diffusion of knowledge-intensive dual-use technologies, means that arms control must adopt a new set of operating assumptions. New actors with new capabilities have emerged on the scene. Rivals possess asymmetrical capabilities, military formats, and paradigms of war. No single key strategic weapon system exists to serve as a basis for agreement on the indices of power. A clear-cut bipolar rivalry has given way to more complex multipolar rivalries, in which military competition is tightly enmeshed with a whole host of non-military disputes. The logic of the bridging strategies presented above is to expand the horizon of arms control well beyond the arena of military capabilities and practices, because the nature of military rivalry and military capabilities today diverges in important ways from the Cold War nuclear age model. The goal is to reduce the non-military as well as the military incentives to resort to force or to intimidation by the threat of force in addition to the military incentives to resort to force. By linking non-military with military concessions, the arms control process can marry negotiations over territorial conflicts, environmental and resource disputes, refugees, economic development, new security structures, and norms and procedures for intervention in areas of conflict with more familiar arms control tools of limitations and reductions, bans on use and deployments, and confidence- and security-building measures. The ultimate objective should be not just to limit the means of destruction, but to reduce the perceived utility associated with military assets by viewing arms control as one strategy for transforming underlying identities and interests. This requires attending to regional and domestic contexts, and to the ways rivals understand their threat and opportunity environments.

Arms control is no panacea. It cannot do it all. It faces significant challenges in developing ways to promote asymmetric reciprocity and manage technology diffusion. But it adapted to the bipolar superpower rivalry in the nuclear age; it has the potential to adapt more effectively to multipolar regional rivalries in the information age.

NOTES

The author would like to thank Andrew Ross, Amy Sands, and Nancy Gallagher for their comments and suggestions.

1. Alvin and Heidi Toffler, *War and Anti-War* (New York: Warner Books, 1993), pp.236–7.
2. The Tofflers, for example, argue that the way we make war reflects the way we make wealth. War reflects society's mode of production. Less sweeping arguments have been made by military historians, who point, for example, to the advent of nationalism that transformed

warfare after the French Revolution. The nuclear revolution is the clearest example of a purely technological change that led to new modes of warfare. The information revolution is the product of changes in both technology and social organization.

3. In 1961, seven books were published which reflected the new thinking on arms control: Bernard B. Bechhoeffer, *Postwar Negotiations for Arms Control* (Washington, DC: The Brookings Institution, 1961); Donald G. Brennan (ed.), *Arms Control, Disarmament, and National Security* (New York: George Braziller, 1961); Hedley Bull, *The Control of the Arms Race* (New York: Praeger, 1961); David H. Frisch (ed.), *Arms Reduction: Program and Issues* (New York: The Twentieth Century Fund, 1961); Arthur T. Hadley, *The Nation's Safety and Arms Control* (New York: Viking, 1961); Louis Henkin (ed.), *Arms Control: Issues for the Public* (New York: Prentice-Hall, 1961); and Thomas C. Schelling and Morton H. Halperin, *Strategy and Arms Control* (New York: The Twentieth Century Fund, 1961).

4. There is no consensus among historians, political scientists, or policy-makers about how to define a military revolution or a revolution in military affairs, whether these are conceptually the same, and whether we are currently passing through either one. Technological innovation often plays an important role in realizing the large gains in military effectiveness associated with such revolutions, but it is often not sufficient. Doctrinal and organizational adaptations are usually necessary. Nevertheless, at a minimum, advocates of the information revolution contend that advanced technologies associated with the information age, such as micro-electronics, computers and software, and precision guided munitions promise to shift the technological basis of military power and affect the means of military competition and advantage. For the historian's debate, see Clifford J. Rogers (ed.), *The Military Revolution Debate* (Boulder: Westview Press, 1995). Proponents of the information revolution include Andrew F. Krepinevich, 'Cavalry to Computer: The Pattern of Military Revolutions', *The National Interest*, Vol.37 (Fall 1994), pp.30–42; Alvin and Heidi Toffler, *War and Anti-War* (New York: Warner Books, 1993); Eliot Cohen, 'A Revolution in Warfare', *Foreign Affairs*, Vol.75, No.2 (March/April 1996), pp.37–54; Joseph Nye and William Owens, 'America's Information Edge', *Foreign Affairs*, Vol.75, No.2 (March/April 1996), pp.21–36. Sceptics include A.J. Bacevich, 'Preserving the Well-Bred Horse', *The National Interest*, Vol.37 (Fall 1994).

5. Toffler and Toffler, pp.236–7.

6. Winn Schwartau, *Information Warfare: Chaos on the Electronic Superhighway* (New York: Thunder's Mouth Press, 1994), pp.271–90.

7. Ibid., pp.291–311. Schwartau (p.292) argues that 'From both a competitive and combative perspective, it would be stupid for a well-financed and motivated group *not* to attack the technical infrastructure of an adversary. The vulnerabilities are clear, the risk so low, and the rewards so great. In fact, if someone wants to take on a technologically sophisticated society, the real question we should ask is not, "why would they attack the computers?" but "why wouldn't they?"'

8. Betts, for example, writes that 'Arms control could make sense in the Cold War because the relevant alignments by which stable force ratios might be estimated seemed clear and durable. By the same token, limitations on individual nations' forces could be pernicious after the Cold War because there is no logical basis by which to determine the allowed ratios before new cleavages emerge and harden.' Richard K. Betts, 'Systems for Peace or Causes of War? Collective Security, Arms Control, and the New Europe', *International Security*, Vol.17, No.1 (Summer 1992), p.36.

9. Kanti Bajpai and Stephen P. Cohen, 'Cooperative Security and South Asian Security', in Janne E. Nolan (ed.), *Global Engagement: Cooperative Security in the 21st Century* (Washington, DC: Brookings, 1994), pp.460–1.

10. See Miroslav Nincic, *Anatomy of Hostility: The US–Soviet Rivalry in Perspective* (New York: Harcourt Brace Jovanovich, 1989), pp.38–81 for a persuasive case that the U.S.–Soviet rivalry lacked authentic conflicts of interest.

11. The whole notion of the security dilemma presumes that rivalry is driven more by the interaction dynamic itself than by authentic conflicts of interest.

12. Barry R. Posen, 'Military Lessons of the Gulf War – Implications for Middle East Arms Control', in Shai Feldman and Ariel Levite (eds.), *Arms Control and the New Middle East*

Security Environment (Boulder: Westview Press, 1994), pp.70–1.

13. Ephraim Kim, 'The Threat Perception of the Arab States', in Feldman and Levite (eds.), *Arms Control and the New Middle East*, pp.81–94.
14. Ashton B. Carter, William J. Perry, and John D. Steinbruner, *A New Concept of Cooperative Security*, Brookings Occasional Papers (Washington, DC: Brookings, 1992), p.6; Nolan (ed.), *Global Engagement*, pp.4–8.
15. Nolan (ed.), *Global Engagement*, pp.4–5.
16. See chapters on South Asia by Bajpai and Cohen, and on the Middle East by Kemp, in ibid.
17. This is a difficult and ambitious task, so one's expectations must be more modest. Neoconservative critics of arms control deny that arms control could ever influence political motivations, arguing that the enterprise succeeds only when it is unnecessary. See Colin S. Gray, *House of Cards: Why Arms Control Must Fail* (Ithaca: Cornell University Press, 1992) and Robert Gordon Kaufman, *Arms Control During the Pre-Nuclear Era: The United States and Naval Limitation Between the Two World Wars* (New York: Columbia University Press, 1990).
18. Nincic distinguishes objective from derivative sources of conflict. Objective conflicts of interest involve incompatible pursuits that, in and of themselves, suffice to pit two sides against each other, and where one rival would be objectively better off only as a consequence of making the other objectively worse off. A dispute over borderlands is an example. Conflicts that are derivative assume an objective conflict exists, which may or may not be the case, and involve a contest over means required to pursue the conflict, namely over the sources of power. Nincic, *Anatomy of Hostility*, p.38.
19. Maj. Norman C. Davis, USMC, 'An Information-Based Revolution in Military Affairs', *Strategic Review*, Vol.24, No.1 (Winter 1996), p.47.
20. Geoffrey L. Herrera, 'New Information Technologies and the Future of State Security', Paper prepared for the JCISS/Security Studies Conference on the Revolution in Military Affairs, Monterey, CA, Aug. 26–29, 1996, p.15.
21. Richard J. Harknett, 'The Information Technology Network and the Ability to Deter: The Impact of Organizational Change on 21st Century Conflict', Paper prepared for the JCISS/Security Studies Conference on the Revolution in Military Affairs, Monterey, CA, Aug. 26–29, 1996, p.23. See also John Arquilla and David Ronfeldt, 'Cyberwar is Coming!' *Comparative Strategy*, Vol.12, No.2 (April–June 1993), pp.141–65.
22. Harknett, 'The Information Technology Network', pp.24–5.
23. Harknett notes that while 'the United States may have required an advanced technological infrastructure to produce the global positioning satellite system ... now all one has to do is go down to Radio Shack to purchase a GPS monitor to access the system.' Harknett, ibid., p.37.
24. Ibid., pp.32–4.
25. Donald E. Ryan, Jr., 'Implications of Information-Based Warfare', *Joint Forces Quarterly* (Autumn/Winter 1994–95), p.115.
26. Janne E. Nolan, *Trappings of Power: Ballistic Missiles in the Third World* (Washington, DC: The Brookings Institution, 1991), pp.3–8.
27. Ibid., p.5.
28. Nolan notes that 'Technologies that are at the cutting edge of Western military modernization, including advanced information processing, composite materials, directed energy systems, and biotechnologies, are to varying degrees equally vital to civilian modernization.' Nolan, *Trappings of Power*, p.6. See also Michael Moodie, 'Beyond Proliferation: The Challenge of Technology Diffusion', *The Washington Quarterly*, Vol.18, No.2 (Spring 1995), pp.190–5.
29. See Henry D. Sokolski, 'Nonapocalyptic Proliferation: A New Strategic Threat?' *The Washington Quarterly*, Vol.17, No.2 (Spring 1994), pp.115–27.
30. John Arquilla, 'Between a Rock and A Hard-Drive: Export Controls on Supercomputers', *The Nonproliferation Review* (Winter 1996), p.59. See also Wolfgang H. Reinicke, 'Cooperative Security and the Political Economy of Nonproliferation', in Nolan (ed.), *Global Engagement*, pp.178–82 for a more thorough discussion of how comprehensive export control efforts can obstruct the flow of international trade, hamper economic expansion and world growth, and stymie integration of the former east bloc and less-developed countries into the world economy.

31. Stephen Biddle, 'Recent Trends in Armor, Infantry, and Artillery Technology: Development and Implications', in W. Thomas Wander, Eric H. Arnett, and Paul Bracken (eds.), *The Diffusion of Advanced Weaponry: Trends, Regional Implications, and Responses* (Washington, DC: American Association for the Advancement of Science, 1994). See also Stephen Biddle, 'Victory Misunderstood: Skill, Technology and What the Gulf War Tells Us About the Future of Conflict', *International Security*, Vol.21, No.2 (Fall 1996), pp.139–79.

32. See 'Is There A Revolution in Military Affairs?', *Strategic Survey 1995–1996* (London: The International Institute for Strategic Studies, 1996), pp.32–3, for discussion of the 'platform-oriented traditionalists', the dominant faction which is firmly entrenched in Congress, the defense industry, and the senior ranks of the US military. Looking out five to ten years into the future, they support an incremental investment strategy, building on the huge sums already invested in existing weapons platforms.

33. 'The Revolution in Military Affairs', *Strategic Forum* 11 (Washington, DC: Institute for National Strategic Studies, Nov. 1994), p.2.

34. Thomas G. Mahnken, 'Why Third World Space Systems Matter', *Orbis*, Vol.35, No.3 (Fall 1991), pp.563–79.

35. Gregorian argues that Third World countries have a strong incentive to introduce new innovative systems, like GPS, that will significantly enhance their military capabilities. Moreover, GPS eliminates two major obstacles Third World countries have faced: incompatibility with existing systems and dependence on suppliers. GPS is easy to integrate into current systems and can be bought commercially, eliminating any major obstacle to technology acquisition. Finally, targeting for GPS-guided munitions though satellite reconnaissance is an avenue now open to many developing states. Raffi Gregorian, 'Global Positioning Systems: A Military Revolution for the Third World?' *SAIS Review*, Vol.13, No.1 (Winter–Spring 1993), pp.133–48, particularly pp.142–7.

36. Cohen, 'A Revolution in Warfare', *Foreign Affairs*, pp.45–6; see also Schwartau, *Information Warfare*.

37. Arquilla and Ronfeldt, 'Cyberwar is Coming!', pp.144–6.

38. This describes the strategic influence exerted by inferior naval powers that employed a fleet-in-being strategy to maximize the influence of their inferior assets, and by the French Navy's Jeune Ecole school, which relied on the torpedo boat and subsequently the submarine as a way to offset the capabilities of superior maritime powers. Julian S. Corbett, *Some Principles of Maritime Strategy*, 2nd ed. (London: Longmans, 1918), pp.191–9; Emily O. Goldman, *Sunken Treaties: Naval Arms Control Between the Wars* (University Park, PA: Penn State Press, 1994), pp.91–3.

39. For example, not only are missiles less expensive than manned aircraft; they are also less complicated. They require less infrastructure to develop, and less training to operate and maintain.

40. Biddle notes, however, that the relative significance of technology is affected by skill and error. His analysis of the Gulf War concludes that it was neither superior coalition technology, nor Iraqi incompetence that explains the one-sidedness of the outcome, but rather the synergistic interaction of technology and skill that allowed the Coalition's advanced technology to exploit Iraqi mistakes. Emphasizing the role played by skill differentials, he hypothesizes that technology is magnifying the effects of skill differentials on the battlefield, making skill imbalance much more important today than in the past. Biddle, 'Victory Misunderstood'.

41. Cohen, 'A Revolution in Warfare', pp.52–3.

42. Samuel P. Huntington, 'Arms Races: Prerequisites and Results', in Robert J. Art and Kenneth N. Waltz (eds.), *The Use of Force: International Politics and Foreign Policy*, 2nd ed. (Lantham: University Press of America, 1983), pp.439–72.

43. Leonard S. Spector and Jonathan Dean, 'Cooperative Security: Assessing the Tools of the Trade', in Nolan (ed.), *Global Engagement*, p.134.

44. See Waltz in Scott D. Sagan and Kenneth N. Waltz, *The Spread of Nuclear Weapons: A Debate* (New York: Norton, 1995).

45. Posen, 'Military Lessons of the Gulf War', pp.62–71.

46. Geoffrey Kemp, 'Cooperative Security in the Middle East', in Nolan (ed.), *Global Engagement*, pp.406–10.

47. Keith R. Krause, 'The Evolution of Arms Control in the Middle East', in Gabriel Ben-Dor and David B. Dewitt (eds.), *Confidence Building Measures in the Middle East* (Boulder: Westview Press, 1994), pp.274–5.
48. The Non-Proliferation Treaty has codified asymmetries but it is based on the notion that the spread of mass destruction weapons is a threat to global security and does not attempt to regulate specific rivalries.
49. Raymond G. O'Connor, 'The "Yardstick" and Naval Disarmament in the 1920s', *The Mississippi Valley Historical Review*, Vol.45, No.3 (Dec. 1958), pp.441–63.
50. See Goldman, *Sunken Treaties*, pp.94–6, 137–42.
51. See John Arquilla, 'The Strategic Implications of Information Dominance', *Strategic Review*, Vol.22, No.3 (Summer 1994), pp.24–30 for a discussion of information dominance. See also Ryan, 'Implications of Information-Based Warfare', pp.114–16 for a discussion of information manoeuvre.
52. Martin C. Libicki, 'Information and Nuclear RMAs Compared', *Strategic Forum*, 82, Institute for National Strategic Studies (July 1996), p.2.
53. This characterization was suggested by Jan S. Breemer.
54. The acquisition of nuclear weapons did not lead militaries to abandon the mobile armour tactics that Germany pioneered between the world wars.
55. See Robert Jervis, *The Meaning of the Nuclear Revolution* (Ithaca: Cornell University Press, 1989), and Robert Jervis, *The Illogic of American Nuclear Strategy* (Ithaca: Cornell University Press, 1984).
56. This point is critical for countering the claim that inferior skills will prevent developing states from effectively exploiting new technologies. The technologies can be exploited in a variety of ways and need not be integrated into military arsenals in the way the United States has. As Krepinevich correctly notes, 'as long as there are multiple competitors exploiting the potential of the emerging military revolution, the revolution itself will be likely to take several paths, if only because of the competitors' varying strategic goals, access to relevant resources, and strategic culture'. Krepinevich, 'Cavalry to Computer', p.41.
57. Reinicke extensively discusses a series of regulatory approaches to reduce information asymmetries in the market for arms and dual-use technologies and to allow authorities to regulate proliferation. Reinicke, 'Cooperative Security and the Political Economy of Nonproliferation', pp.175–234. Ann M. Florini, 'A New Role for Transparency', in this issue, makes a similar argument.
58. Antonia Handler Chayes and Abram Chayes, 'Regime Architecture: Elements and Principles', in Nolan (ed.), *Global Engagement*, pp.85, 95.
59. Reinicke, 'Cooperative Security', p.215.
60. Ibid., p.179.
61. See W. Richard Scott, *Institutions and Organizations* (Thousand Oaks, CA: Sage, 1995), pp.35–7 for a discussion of the regulative pillar of institutional analysis.
62. For a discussion of the problems with the extended economic analogy and an exclusively regulatory approach to institutional analysis, particularly the failure to consider the formation of preferences and identities, and the effects on how actors define interests and behave, see Peter J. Katzenstein, *Cultural Norms and National Security: Police and Military in Postwar Japan* (Ithaca: Cornell University Press, 1996), pp.12, 27.
63. See Scott, *Institutions and Organizations*, pp.41–5 for a discussion of the cognitive pillar of institutional analysis.
64. Ibid., p.43.
65. Nolan, *Trappings of Power*, pp.14–16. For explication of this argument see Dana P. Eyre and Mark C. Suchman, 'Status, Norms, and the Proliferation of Conventional Weapons: An Institutional Theory Approach', in Peter J. Katzenstein (ed.), *The Culture of National Security: Norms and Identity in World Politics* (New York: Columbia University Press, 1996), pp.79–113.
66. Moodie, 'Beyond Proliferation', pp.185–6.
67. 'Ukraine Finds Atom Arms Bring Measure of Respect', *New York Times*, 7 Oct. 1991, p.A6.
68. 'Aiding Peace', *Defense News* (Nov. 28–Dec. 4, 1994), p.22; 'U.S. Funds Ukraine Plan to Convert Munitions', *Defense News* (Nov. 28–Dec. 4, 1994), pp.4, 36.

69. 'North Korean–U.S. Nuclear Weapons Deal Ignites Debate', *Defense News* (Dec. 5–11, 1994), p.30; David E. Sanger, 'Who Won in the Korea Deal?' *New York Times*, 23 Oct. 1994, p.E3; Peter Grier, 'N. Korea Pact Points Up Limits of Containment', *Christian Science Monitor* 21 Oct. 1994, p.3.
70. Jeffrey Smith, 'Clinton Approves Pact with North Korea', *Washington Post*, 19 Oct. 1994), p.A1.
71. See Goldman, *Sunken Treaties*.
72. Gray and Kaufman argue that interwar arms control was a failure, while Kruzel argues that the Washington negotiations produced one of the few arms control agreements that led to significant disarmament. Joseph Kruzel, 'From Rush-Bagot to START: The Lessons of Arms Control', *Orbis*, Vol.30, No.1 (Spring 1986), pp.193–216.
73. Kemp, 'Cooperative Security in the Middle East', Nolan (ed.), *Global Engagement*, pp.406–8.
74. Ibid., p.409.
75. Kruzel posits that asymmetries can be dealt with in three ways: an agreement can contain asymmetric limitations; asymmetries may be balanced off within an accord; or compensation outside the accord may be offered for asymmetries contained within it. The first solution, he argues, is rare and unstable; the second is very difficult to engineer; the third is feasible, but he confines compensation to weapon systems that lie outside the scope of the accord, rather than considering compensation in non-military terms. Asymmetric reciprocity need not, and should not, be confined to the single arena of military capabilities and practices. Kruzel, 'From Rush-Bagot to START', pp.210–12.
76. For a good overview of the structure of the talks, see Joel Peters, *Building Bridges: The Arab–Israeli Multilateral Talks* (London: The Royal Institute of International Affairs, 1994).
77. Ibid., p.31.
78. Ibid., p.34.

A New Role for Transparency

ANN M. FLORINI

Arms control has traditionally dealt with limiting the means of destruction. When the greatest threat to security came from the potential for organized violence inflicted by an external enemy against a state, arms control logically sought to limit that danger. But as the threats to security have become more diffuse, policy-makers will need to draw on a wider repertoire of tools to reduce the potential destructiveness of less organized threats, and even emerging unintended dangers.

Over the past few decades, arms control has contributed a tool to international diplomacy that may address some of these growing threats. That tool is transparency. Transparency refers here to the provision of information by an actor about its own activities and capabilities to other actors. More and more, transparency is a norm – that is, a standard of behaviour to which actors are held, one that has become increasingly entrenched in international security relations, politics, business practices, and policies of environmental protection.[1] It has roots in many areas, from the spread of democracy to the demands of globalized business to the requirements under arms control for states to provide other states with vast quantities of information about their military capabilities and organizations.

This new norm contributed significantly to the end of the Cold War through the verification provisions and confidence-building measures associated with arms control in the 1980s, but its future role will be even more important.[2] In a world characterized by multipolarity, the diffusion of some forms of power from state actors to other types of actor, the proliferation of both weapons of mass destruction and precision guidance technologies, the widespread breakdown of political authority, and the distribution of environmentally toxic materials on a unprecedented scale, protecting humanity and the planet will demand even higher levels of transparency in regard to who has access to which materials and technologies and who is doing what with them.

It has been proposed that transparency could serve as the cornerstone of non-proliferation and broader cooperative security efforts.[3] But this raises many questions about what information should be made available, to whom, and for what purposes. One way to work through these questions is by making comparisons with another issue area where transparency already has started to play a crucial role (at least within the United States): the prevention of environmental toxification. Proliferation and environmental toxification share characteristics beyond the grave risks they pose to human well-being, risks that are not being adequately addressed by current policies.[4] Both involve the need to regulate substances that are widely, legitimately, and necessarily used in economic transactions (sometimes even the same substances). In both cases, moreover, centralized control systems which exclusively involve states will not suffice.

Thinking about how to use transparency measures to address proliferation and toxification requires a long-term perspective, because the solutions to proliferation and toxification require a substantial incubation period. Achieving the necessary degree of transparency will require a norm change. New norms do not emerge spontaneously: particularly at the international level they are often the product of concerted effort sustained over long periods.[5]

This essay looks at the problems of proliferation and toxification over the long term, describes why these problems will require a transparency-based approach, and analyses what that approach should entail. The next section examines the trends likely to alter and intensify the nature of the proliferation threat, as well as to increase demand for environmentally hazardous products and production processes that could result in toxification. The paper then discusses specific characteristics of the problems of proliferation and toxification and argues that the traditional strategies used to address these dangers – denial of access to dangerous materials and after-the-fact countermeasures – will prove inadequate in the new context. Next, it shows that alternative policies that rely on the public revelation of information about economic transactions and processes can alter behaviour more effectively than can more familiar types of regulation. The paper concludes with a discussion of the prospects for applying the transparency-based approach to proliferation and toxification at the international level.

The Trends[6]

If no policy changes are made, in the next two to three decades the world could become a much more hazardous place, with new dangers emerging from a diffuse set of actors and sources. In particular, over the next few decades, the dangers posed by the proliferation of weaponry and by environmental toxification may increase significantly. Although these are usually thought of as two quite different problems, they share many root causes. In the short term it may be possible to ignore them, or to manage them using current policies, but in the long term, to the year 2025 or so, several trends will combine to make current policies unworkable.

The information revolution is leading to widespread and rapid dissemination of knowledge about weapons of mass destruction and other weaponry. Much of the technology required for precision targeting is embedded in widely diffusing civilian information technology. Although the Clinton administration may be right that no rogue state will have the technological capability to launch a missile attack on the United States in the next fifteen years, the next thirty years could tell a very different story. By 2025, capabilities for weapons of mass destruction and for precision guidance of delivery systems are likely to be widely diffused.

Over the same period, given population pressures and rising income levels, demands for industrial products (with their associated environmental costs) will increase dramatically. By 2025, the planet will be far more crowded than it is today, with at least two billion additional people, and perhaps as many as four billion more.[7] By comparison, the current world population is about 5.8 billion people.[8]

These developments will take place in a world threatened by political instability. Most of the swollen population will be poor, with about 95 per cent of population growth occurring in poor countries and largely in the poorer segments of those societies. Most will live in cities, often in megalopolises which will have grown too fast to keep up with the demand for basic infrastructure such as sewage, roads, decent housing, and water.[9]

Disparities between rich and poor will be accentuated. Although most people's incomes will rise, income disparities between rich and poor will grow even more rapidly, because the rich are starting off at a much higher base. If China grows at a per capita rate of 7 per cent a year from now until 2025 (a rate better than the best sustained per capita growth rate ever seen, South Korea's 6.5 per cent), and the United States continues to grow at the per capita rate of 1.5 per cent, the difference in per capita income would widen from $24,500 to $35,271. Under this scenario, which exaggerates China's likely growth relative to the U.S., incomes would continue to diverge until 2041.

This is likely to be a politically fragmented world, divided by much more than national boundaries. There are hundreds if not thousands of identifiable ethnic and other groups with a reasonable claim to at least a degree of self-determination.[10] Growing numbers of such groups are clamouring for at least some of the attributes of statehood, although relatively few have the wherewithal to survive as independent polities.[11] Whatever the political organization of the future turns out to be, it will lack the relative clarity of the nation-state system as we have traditionally understood it.

These developments are more than likely. The fragmentation of political identity is already well under way.[12] The population surge will occur because the parents of that population are already born. Income disparities will grow unless the economies of the rich countries collapse. Nonetheless, because most people in that rapidly expanding population are becoming absolutely (even if not relatively) richer, demands for the products of industrial economies – cars, houses, clothes, televisions – will soar, introducing vast quantities of ill-regulated pollutants.

In short, nearly a billion people will be added to the world's population each decade, most relatively poor but all needing food to eat, a place to live, resources to consume, and a job. Their political loyalties will be fickle and are unlikely to be based on a strong sense of national identity. They may not be much moved by pleas to constrain their own still relatively low standards of living for the sake of protecting the environment. Most will live in cities, readily accessible to demagogues, for whom external enemies have historically provided an inviting target. And the information revolution will ensure both that most of the poor will be aware of the disparities in standards of living and that information on all kinds of weapons, including weapons of mass destruction, will be widely available.

One solution would be sustainable economic development adequate to improve standards of living and to create stable middle classes in most societies. Yet even under the best of circumstances, there are good reasons to believe that humanity is unlikely to grow its way out of its troubles quickly, and almost surely not quickly enough to avoid the problems described in this piece. Environmentally sustainable means of development may be possible but are not yet well developed. Furthermore, too many parts of the world lack the political and institutional infrastructure needed to develop or adopt environmentally benign new technologies at a sufficient rate and to channel capital appropriately.[13]

Thus, these trends set the conditions for greater supply of and demand for both the means of violence and environmentally hazardous materials. Diffuse, sub-state violence may emerge from frustrations and resentments inherent in inequitable development, and that violence could take the form of precisely targeted attacks on rich-country targets. It would hardly be unprecedented for demagogues to rise to power by blaming the problems of their followers on external targets. With targeting information provided by global positioning satellites and other readily available information, the currently remote targets of the rich countries may not be so inaccessible, even to sub-state actors. And not all rich-world targets will be far away. As the economy becomes increasingly globalized, firms based in one country could be badly hurt by attacks on their foreign direct investments.[14] And most if not all parts of the world will be living through the results of an uncontrolled chemistry experiment on the consequences of introducing tens of thousands of untested chemicals into planetary cycles.

Characteristics of the Problems

The apparently disparate problems of proliferation and toxification share several characteristics that make them amenable to similar solutions. Both involve the use of materials that are embedded in legitimate economic activities that cannot be readily halted, a kind of 'dual-use' problem that goes far beyond the difficulties familiar from the use of fissile materials for nuclear power. Nuclear proliferation concerns involve a relatively small number of actors and a still relatively small quantity of dangerous materials. But when proliferation is expanded to include chemical and biological weapons and delivery systems, the quantity and diversity of materials and technologies that must be viewed as part of the threat increase by orders of magnitude. Both proliferation and toxification involve increasing quantities of potentially dangerous materials or technologies because of increasing demand for those legitimate products. Both involve large numbers of actors, private and governmental, who are buying and selling these potentially dangerous materials and/or technologies on a daily basis. Success in addressing these dangers may require instituting some system of control over vast numbers of economic transactions, without stifling the economic vitality on which global well-being ultimately depends.

There are, of course, differences between control of proliferation and environmental regulation. Most important is that externalities in the environment are truly consequences that are unintended and unwanted by everyone. Companies would be quite happy to eliminate all hazardous substances from their production processes were it technologically feasible and economically profitable to do so. In the case of proliferation, however, someone wants that 'externality', meaning that there is a market for it. In the environmental case, the problem is solely one of preventing firms from free-riding, using less expensive but more hazardous technologies and substances than their competitors. In the proliferation case, it will be necessary to avoid both free-riding and deliberate circumvention of whatever control regime exists.

Yet the similarities outweigh the differences. Both will require controlling the damaging externalities of perfectly legitimate, indeed essential, economic transactions. There is likely to be very limited resources or political support for traditional regulation. Somehow, it will be necessary to permit commerce in potentially hazardous substances and technologies among many decentralized actors.

Proliferation

The dangers posed by proliferation of arms, particularly weapons of mass destruction, are well understood. Such weapons, if used, would cause massive devastation, and the more actors possessing them, the greater the risk of use. The mere possession of such weapons, even if they are not used, may greatly exacerbate regional tensions, destabilizing already volatile situations and enhancing the power of pariah states or terrorist groups. Even a single use of a nuclear weapon would break a taboo that has held for more than fifty years, in itself a powerful restraint on actors considering the use of nuclear weapons.

The proliferation threat is escalating with the diffusion and evolution of technology. The very capability to attack targets which enabled the United States to win the Gulf War so handily grew out of commercially developed technologies. It is true that no other country will come close in the foreseeable future to matching the US capability for what William Perry has described as the 'reconnaissance strike force', which includes command, control, communications, and intelligence, precision-guided munitions, and defense suppression.[15] But even lacking this full spectrum of capabilities, many countries and sub-state actors could strike out with lethal effectiveness at civilian targets, using widely available technology to locate targets, possibly combined with primitive but effective weapons of mass destruction. In short, given the realities of global economic integration, many more actors, both state and others, have or will obtain access to the technologies underlying weapons of mass destruction or the means of guiding weapons across great distances and landing them precisely on target.

Toxification

The degree of danger from environmental toxification, by contrast, is only just now being recognized. Toxic substances of all kinds are flooding the planet, the inevitable concomitant of existing industrialization practices. Toxification refers to the accumulation of toxic substances in individual biological organisms or in the biosphere generally from anthropogenic materials flows. This accumulation can have a variety of unpleasant effects, ranging from neurological harm to a single organism (as in lead poisoning) to the disruption of entire ecosystems.

The extent of the threat is unknown, and at this point unknowable, but the signs are ominous. The environmental and health effects of the more than 50,000 chemicals produced annually for use in industrial processes remain largely unexplored. Even information about who is producing potentially hazardous chemicals, where and in what ways they are being used, or how the products are being disposed of, is at best difficult to find. No one has a comprehensive overview that would make it possible to track products containing hazards or to monitor the processes that produce them.

The levels of toxic material flows being introduced by human activity go well beyond anything seen in nature, often by orders of magnitude.[16] Moreover, it is not only the levels but the total accumulation that matters. Many of the substances persist for decades if not centuries. Heavy metals such as lead, mercury, and other potent toxins, for example, were widely used for decades before their hazards became known, and these elements do not decompose into less dangerous substances. Even once the hazard is known, the economic utility of many hazardous substances can make it difficult to restrict the pollution. Much of the world still burns leaded gasoline. The best-known example of toxification may be the destruction of stratospheric ozone by man-made chlorofluorocarbons (CFCs), chemicals which until recently were widely used as refrigerants, aerosol propellants, and industrial cleansers. It was largely accidental that the harmful effects of CFC use were discovered in time for a global ban to prevent real catastrophe. It is thought possible that toxification has played a part in the decline of German forests, the demise of coral reefs around the world, and the sudden decimation of many species of frog.

The Limits of Traditional Solutions

The phenomena of proliferation and toxification will be among the most serious threats to human well-being for at least the next several decades. Yet neither traditional strategies aimed at denying access to certain goods and technologies nor other conceivable alternatives hold much promise for abating these threats.

Neither American nor broader global interests are well served by the current policy debates on proliferation and toxification. The debate assumes that the options for proliferation policy are limited to incremental changes to existing policy (a combination of diplomatic efforts aimed at dissuading potential proliferators and export controls to deny key technologies and materials to hold-out states) and/or the development of military countermeasures to deal with proliferation once it occurs. But existing policy could only be effective if the sole proliferators of concern were states, if states had full knowledge of and control over their imports and exports, and if controlling exports of a limited set of goods and technologies could prevent the proliferation of all the weapons systems and technologies of concern.

The debate over toxification policy is much less developed, having begun in earnest only with the United Nations Conference on Environment and Development in 1992. Follow-up efforts related to environmental toxification are still at a very preliminary stage. Within the United States, clean-up efforts have been harshly criticized on all sides, as epitomized by the notoriously controversial Superfund programme which was too expensive, often ineffective, and overwhelmed by the difficulty of determining whom to hold accountable for the contamination of specific sites.

A strategy that emphasizes broad-based denial of access to potentially dangerous products cannot adequately deal with either proliferation or toxification. It is useless to address toxification, because no state or reasonably small group of states controls the supply of hazardous substances used in industrial production. Even in those cases where supply could be controlled, denial of access would mean undercutting essential economic activities involving feedstock chemicals. With regard to proliferation, the denial approach has already accomplished most of what it can achieve in restraining proliferation. Much of the success of the nuclear non-proliferation regime, for example, has depended on two factors: cooperation among a small number of supplier states who restricted their nuclear exports to other countries, and the existence of technological bottlenecks stemming from the difficulty of acquiring either highly enriched uranium or plutonium to make a bomb. Neither condition still holds, even in the nuclear area. The problem of proliferation no longer consists merely of a small number of supplier states exporting nuclear goods and technologies to recipient countries. The world is awash in weapons-usable plutonium, much of it not under effective international control, and the number of existing or potential near-term suppliers of nuclear materials and technology has sharply increased. This renders inadequate the centralized, generally coercive application of regulations aimed at denying access to certain goods and technologies. Other kinds of weapons proliferation, including chemical, biological, and technologies related to delivery systems, have even fewer choke points at which controls could be applied.

The denial strategy cannot be made effective by simple extension. The sheer number of goods and substances whose exports would have to be restricted dwarfs any previous efforts at denial-based controls. No relatively short list of forbidden exports could suffice. With regard to proliferation, the threats increasingly lie in the area of computer technologies, chemicals, and biotechnology; goods and technologies with both civilian and military uses and no ready distinction between them. To give just one example, the Chemical Weapons Convention, which came into force in spring 1997, covers more than three dozen chemicals, with provision made for adding to the list.[17] Moreover, scores of states and thousands of firms are now numbered among the suppliers of all the goods and technologies of concern. With regard to toxification, there are over 50,000 chemicals used in production processes, of which only a few hundred have been adequately tested for their environmental and health effects. In this area, we do not even yet know what needs controlling. Clearly, simply banning all trade in dual-use technologies and all products containing hazardous or potentially hazardous substances is not the answer.

A *post hoc* approach has problems as well. The US Department of Defense has established a Counterproliferation Initiative that aims to equip United States forces to face adversaries who possess nuclear, biological, or chemical weapons. The initiative incorporates development of new technologies and new military strategies aimed at current or likely proliferators. Unfortunately, rather than deterring proliferation, this approach could effectively reinstate an arms race, this time against unknown opponents who may see the policy as an incentive to proliferate so as to be able to confront – or deter – the United States. And, of course, a counter-proliferation strategy is only useful after proliferation has occurred. A *post hoc* response to toxification is even more unattractive. Many pollutants of concern, such as heavy metals, cannot be effectively cleaned up once they have been dispersed into the environment, and the effects of many others are simply unknown.

A Growing Role for Transparency

In time, transparency measures may be able to do what denial strategies and countermeasures alone cannot. By allowing legitimate uses (and emissions) of the goods and substances of concern to be easily traced, transparency would make the task of would-be proliferators harder, and it would make assessing responsibility for the unwanted side-effects of toxic substances much easier. Perhaps most important, it can enlist the potent force of public opinion, while imposing much less of a regulatory burden than would exist under alternative policies.

Transparency can serve three quite different purposes. Most familiar in arms control is its *deterrent* effect: signatories to treaties refrain from violating the accords because the verification provisions make the likelihood of being caught and punished unacceptably high. Also increasingly familiar is the role of transparency in providing *reassurance*: a means by which actors can prove that they are not misusing goods and technologies. Much less known in arms control, but beginning to emerge in the environmental field, is the *revelatory* effect of transparency. As will be described below, the institution of transparency requirements can provide actors with information about the consequences of their own activities, information they would never have obtained without the requirement to do so but which, once gathered, can spur dramatic changes in the actors' behaviour. The Russian government might not have been aware of the degree to which its fissile material was unsafely stored without Washington's prodding and assistance, but once made aware, both governments found improving the situation to be in their mutual interest.

The growing acceptance of transparency could act as the basis for creating transparency systems which could serve all three goals, tracking the goods and substances of concern throughout their life cycles. They would rely primarily on self-reporting, requiring producers to provide information about the ultimate consequences of their production. In the case of dual-use technologies, firms wishing to export such items would have to provide information about the end-user. With regard to toxification, producers would be required to report not only on their emissions of hazardous substances as wastes, but on the presence of hazardous constituents (above a threshold) in the goods they produce. Such tracking would make it possible to follow a hazard throughout its life cycle.

Similarly, it may be possible to label a wide range of products and substances in such a way that they can be tracked throughout their life cycles. Los Alamos National Laboratory has developed tags that cannot be duplicated or tampered with which could be attached to a product or container. (The tags were intended to help verify compliance with the Conventional Armed Forces in Europe Treaty, so that permitted numbers of tanks and other systems could be labelled and readily distinguished from those not so labelled. The treaty's verification provisions in the end did not require the use of the tags, and they are still sitting on the shelf at Los Alamos.) Along the same lines, chemical co-tracers could be added during the manufacturing process to chemical substances which would make it possible to identify the point of origin of the chemicals.

This system could not rely solely on state-to-state negotiation. Ideally, the system would enlist the cooperation of suppliers and consumers alike to make transfers of goods and technologies far more transparent. As has been increasingly the case with arms control negotiations, at the least the relevant producers would have to be willing participants. And because such a vast range of goods and substances are now relevant to proliferation and toxification, a very significant proportion of the world's economic actors should be included.

While only a few very large firms have the resources to maintain control of their hazardous or dual-use products throughout their life cycles, information-revolution technology is making it feasible for a wide range of producers to monitor where those products go. With currently available or easily developed technologies, for example, miniature computerized tracking devices could be attached to virtually any product. This regulation by transparency would permit most economic activities to take place unhindered, but would require that they be conducted in a way that is readily monitored. Producers would be responsible for recording what hazardous constituents or dual-use technologies are contained in their products and where they go. Such transparency would make it possible to detect early efforts to acquire weapons capabilities or to dump large quantities of hazardous substances without interfering with legitimate trade. It would also greatly facilitate pollution prevention.

It requires a change of mindset to recognize that producers have an obligation to provide information concerning the contents of their products, the uses to which their products are put and the ways in which their products are disposed of. It is this normative change that will be necessary for a transparency-based approach to work. Encouraging precedents provide hope that such a norm change is not unfeasible. Nuclear power producers have long recognized a special responsibility to account for their highly dangerous materials. Chemical producers have taken some steps down this road as well, as evidenced by the Chemical Manufacturers' Association's strong support for the highly intrusive verification provisions of the Chemical Weapons Convention. As in these cases, producers can recognize that effective and reasonable regulation of the hazardous materials they use can stave off public demands for harsher regulation later on. Producers in countries that are particularly likely to impose national regulations may support international regulation as a means of levelling the economic playing field for themselves.

Indeed, the CWC provides a most compelling example of the possibilities of transparency. Any regime of reasonably effective constraints on chemical weapons capabilities requires an unprecedented degree of transparency simply because the substances at issue are ubiquitous. The same chemicals that have revolutionized agriculture and medicine in this century can be used to make chemical weapons. Because these substances are so widespread and so thoroughly integrated into the fabric of the international economy, with a few exceptions they cannot simply be banned. Instead, the verification net must be cast both wide and deep, covering an enormous range of chemicals and imposing stringent verification requirements.

The CWC divides chemicals into three categories known as 'schedules'. Each category is subject to different verification provisions. Schedule 1 chemicals are either directly usable as weapons or easily transformed into weapons, and have few if any other uses. Each party is allowed to maintain one small-scale production facility to conduct medical, pharmaceutical, and protective research with Schedule 1 chemicals, stockpiling a total of no more than one ton of these substances.[18] Such facilities will be subject to monitoring and on-site inspection as deemed appropriate by the Organization for the Prohibition of Chemical Weapons, the body established by the Convention to implement its terms.[19] Schedule 2 chemicals are generally precursors to Schedule 1 substances or are otherwise toxic, but have some recognized limited commercial uses. Facilities producing Schedule 2 chemicals will be subject to inspection if their production levels exceed certain thresholds.[20] Schedule 3 substances are those that can directly be used as chemical weapons or are precursors to Schedule 1 or Schedule 2 chemicals, but are produced in large commercial quantities. Again, facilities that produce these substances in sufficiently large amounts will be subject to regular inspection.[21] In addition, under certain conditions there can be very short notice challenge inspections 'of any facility or location in the territory of or in any other place under the jurisdiction or control of any ... state Party'.[22] These will take place according to a system of 'managed access' intended to allow states to protect sensitive national security or commercial proprietary data, while enabling the inspectors to determine whether the convention has been violated.[23] Despite the intrusiveness of these inspection requirements, the US manufacturers of the chemicals covered by the treaty, who were deeply involved in the negotiations, have been among its strongest supporters.

Centralized Control?

Clearly, states must play a key role in establishing a transparency-based system. Indeed, one way to proceed would be to create a centralized international system. The information from monitoring systems would be recorded in an international registry that would note the producer, the consumer, and the end use of a wide range of goods and substances. On the proliferation side, such a registry could then be used to determine whether an importer was attempting to acquire a surreptitious weapons capability a piece at a time, as Iraq so successfully did prior to the Gulf War. With regard to toxification, the registry would enable governments to track concentrations of hazardous products and emissions, information that could prove invaluable as more becomes known about the effects of currently untested chemicals and their interactions. Information in the registry would be subject to verification by national inspections, or the information provided by self-reporting could be gathered and to some degree verified by an international institution.

This transparency would bolster the effectiveness of a denial strategy, making any export-licensing system far more effective and efficient. Export licenses for dual-used goods and technologies could be denied if a suspicious pattern were detected long before a full weapons capability could be developed.[24] The centralized system would provide a valuable database and could allow states to coordinate their exports *de facto*.

But, as described above, a denial strategy can at best play only a small part in controlling proliferation and toxification. The centralized use of the information gathered through required transparency may improve the effectiveness of the denial strategy, but not enough to overcome its fundamental flaws. Furthermore, a proposal to establish another bureaucratic layer regulating international trade or national economic activity is unlikely to meet with a warm response anywhere.

Moreover, efforts to establish and maintain the registry could be fatally undermined by the free-rider problem, as the example of the current effort to expand the scope of multilateral nuclear safeguards illustrates.[25] Following the revelations about the extent of the clandestine Iraqi nuclear programme that ensued in the wake of the Gulf War and the concerns over the North Korean programme, the International Atomic Energy Agency (IAEA) adopted voluntary transparency measures to increase information about its members' nuclear programmes. A more radical proposal to increase the effectiveness and efficiency of its safeguards system, however, is running into a problem all too familiar to international institutions: no one wants to pay for it. In brief, as the IAEA Board of Governors has debated how to go about implementing improvements in the safeguards system that would cost the IAEA itself money, almost all members have argued in favour of the improvements. However, the members all seem to want someone else to bear the cost. While all states, other than those that hope to gain a surreptitious nuclear weapons capacity, would benefit from the existence of a more reliable centralized system of gathering information about the nuclear programmes of most of the world's countries, each state recognizes that others have that interest and therefore hopes that the others will pay the costs: the classic free-rider problem.

A Decentralized Approach

Transparency could be used quite differently, however, in ways that would avoid the free-rider problem and would help to compensate for the difficulties of the denial strategy. This alternative would rely on the revelatory power of transparency. Most firms do not seek to contribute to proliferation or toxification. They often do so out of ignorance or competitive pressures. Many companies have little idea where the various hazardous constituents of their waste streams originate and have even found that they can significantly cut costs of production and waste treatment by monitoring their own materials flows more closely. Even more important may be the role of public pressure, a highly effective means of inducing behavioural change among firms.

There are striking examples beginning to emerge in the environmental arena of transparency-based approaches to environmental protection. Until quite recently, American environmental regulation has concentrated more on process than result. It was very difficult and expensive to go out into the field and measure who was emitting what, and even harder to understand exactly what the environmental consequences of various emissions were. Instead, regulators focused on forcing companies to change their industrial processes, to replace equipment known to produce a lot of pollution with equipment known to cause less pollution. When the Environmental Protection Agency (EPA) goes out into the field, it does not measure pollution around a facility. Instead, it checks to see whether the facility has the permitted equipment and industrial processes in place.

No one has ever thought this was an ideal approach. It is bureaucratic and inflexible. Two alternatives are emerging, both of which rely heavily on the power of information to spur public – not governmental – action. In the first, the government simply requires firms to provide information on emissions or products containing hazards. In the second, non-state actors take it on themselves to use emerging technologies to monitor toxic emissions.

The Right to Know

A decade ago, the United States Congress passed a law, The Emergency Planning and Community Right to Know Act of 1986, requiring manufacturers to report annually to the United States Environmental Protection Agency on the quantities (over a baseline amount) of certain chemicals they have released into the environment or transferred to another facility.[26] That information is compiled in a database called the Toxics Release Inventory (TRI). In addition, a report must be made every time any quantity of hazardous waste greater than a set amount is released. Hazardous waste is waste containing any substance on a list maintained by the Environmental Protection Agency.

The TRI is far from perfect. It reportedly suffers from serious under-reporting and other inaccuracies. It covers only chemicals already known to be toxic, and a fierce political battle is currently raging over EPA's efforts to expand the number of chemicals listed. Yet it has had a dramatic and largely unexpected impact, reducing the emissions of the reported chemicals at the facilities covered by TRI by 44 per cent since 1988, while production of those chemicals rose 18 per cent.[27] In some cases, companies acted to revise their production processes and cut down on emissions because their reports made them aware of the money they were losing through unnecessarily wasteful production processes. In others, the motivation came from the desire to avoid suffering adverse publicity and angering local communities, who were not pleased to learn what was being dumped on them. This has occurred purely through the revelatory effect of the transparency requirement. The law imposed no new limits on the quantities of chemicals that could be released. It merely required companies to announce publicly how much they were in fact releasing.

As is so often the case, while the federal government was acting at the national level, the state of California was going further. In 1986, the same year that the TRI legislation was passed, California voters overwhelmingly approved an initiative called the Safe Drinking Water and Toxic Enforcement Act, better known as Proposition 65.[28] Under this law, the state publishes a list (updated annually) of chemicals known to the state to cause cancer, birth defects or other reproductive harm. Over 550 such chemicals were listed as of 1996. Once a chemical is listed, any business that knowingly exposes anyone to a listed chemical must provide a 'clear and reasonable' warning, through such means as labelling products, posting signs at the workplace, or publishing notices in a newspaper.

The consequences of Proposition 65 have been as dramatic as those associated with the TRI. Businesses have gone to great lengths to avoid having to give warnings that they are exposing their customers or employees to toxic substances. With no new bureaucracy or enforcement mechanisms, air emissions of some listed chemicals have fallen significantly. Businesses have reformulated production processes and products so that listed chemicals are no longer used: trichloroethylene is no longer used in most correction fluids, toluene has been removed from many nail care products, and foil caps on wine bottles no longer contain lead.

Clearly, the right-to-know approach would not by itself resolve the problem of proliferation. Some sellers and buyers would still have an incentive to conceal what they are doing. Yet the approach would represent a major step in the right direction by making transparent the vast sea of legitimate transactions within which proliferation efforts can currently hide.

Private Action

Surprisingly little is actually known about the quantities of toxic emissions coming from specific facilities. Other than the TRI reports, there are no reporting requirements, and even the TRI reports are not verified through independent measurements. Until recently, the only way to determine how much of a given substance was being emitted by a given facility at a given time was to take air samples back to a laboratory for testing. This left little scope for non-governmental actors, including local community groups, to monitor potential polluters in their midst. Now, the necessary monitoring technologies are becoming available and sufficiently inexpensive that they can be used by non-governmental organizations. For example, optical remote sensing systems that can monitor the emissions of specific pollutants from individual facilities are coming on the market.

Some of these systems are being used by community groups to keep a wary eye on facilities in their neighborhoods. For example, in California a major chemical disaster took place at the Unocal refinery in Rodeo in

August–September 1994. Over the course of sixteen days, 125 tons of caustic catalyst, including heavy metals and organics, sickened 1500 people in the community, some of whom suffer lingering health effects. In response, Communities for a Better Environment, a California non-profit organization, and local citizens obtained an infra-red optical remote sensing system (an R&D model provided by a vendor at a nominal cost), to take on the road to Bay area communities downwind of Unocal and other refineries.

Applying Transparency

These environmental cases in the United States may provide the basis for new thinking about the appropriate roles of governments and other actors in addressing the increasingly diffuse threats of proliferation and toxification. As they suggest, relying solely on the revelatory power of transparency can significantly affect the behaviour of businesses at relatively low cost to the governments, while permitting businesses a great deal of flexibility in finding the most efficient means to reduce or eliminate social harm.

There are several advantages to requiring the public provision of information as a means of controlling the undesirable consequences of legitimate economic activity. Firms that are unwittingly contributing to problems would have the information necessary to stop. Firms would become far more subject to public pressure. And perhaps most important, the transparency-based system would isolate the true problem cases: the firms, states, and groups that are up to no good would find it much harder to take cover in the legitimate economy.

It is not utopian to think that such information would motivate substantial changes of behaviour on the part of business even in the absence of public pressure. Examples abound of companies instituting significant changes on environmental grounds even in the absence of current or impending legal requirements to do so. The collaboration between McDonald's and the Environmental Defense Fund to reduce the use of harmful packaging such as Styrofoam is merely one of the better known cases. In one extreme example, Ray Anderson, the CEO of a carpet-tile manufacturer called Interface, was galvanized into action upon realizing that his own company's business was environmentally unsustainable. The company is now investing heavily in radical energy efficiency, using renewable energy sources, and attempting to produce zero waste. In the most challenging effort, the company is now proposing to lease rather than sell its carpet tiles. When the tiles wear out, the company will take them back and recycle them – a substantial change in usual business practice.[29] Firms might welcome requirements for transparency if by complying with such requirements they could shield themselves from legal liability for unwittingly selling materials to proliferators.

Nonetheless, it is likely that the more profound effect of requiring the release of information comes from the force of public opinion, and here the decentralized approach may have significant benefits. As Emily Goldman argues elsewhere in this volume, compliance on the demand side of a centralized transparency-based regime may prove very difficult, because potential proliferators may perceive their interests in ways that make proliferating more attractive than analyses of economic development needs or military requirements would lead outsiders to assume. If indeed, as she says, the goal of proliferators is to demonstrate sovereignty, the monitoring and enforcement needs of a centralized transparency-based system may be even more daunting than they initially appear. If so, the decentralized approach proposed here becomes even more attractive by comparison. Not only could it greatly increase the numbers of eyes and ears engaged in monitoring, but it could also add a much-enhanced element of social disapproval to the available punishments for buyers and (more likely) sellers of misdirected dual-use technology. Companies can be fined by governments. They can be shamed by their fellow citizens.

As has generally been the case with the information provided by the TRI, non-state actors, particularly non-governmental organizations, will have a crucial role in this decentralized use of transparency. They have the capacity to monitor and advocate action based on information about the behaviour of firms, and indeed this is often their *raison d'être*. Non-governmental organizations dedicated to specific issues often have resources to apply to monitoring that overstretched governments do not, as the frequent lawsuits brought by US NGOs against corporate polluters demonstrate. Information and analysis would not necessarily flow only in one direction, of course. Firms would obviously have an incentive to monitor whether their competitors' products are being used in socially undesirable ways. But the disinterested analysis of NGOs motivated by the promotion of socially desirable behaviour rather than the bottom line would have far greater credibility with the general public.

Problems

The idea of using public transparency as a (partial) means of coping with the growing dangers represented by proliferation and toxification raises some knotty problems. First is the issue of what goods and substances should be covered by the requirement to provide information, and what information should be provided. Businesses are likely to be averse to requirements that are as broad as the numbers of potential dangers would indicate. Both the Toxics Release Inventory and Proposition 65 are restricted to 'listed' chemicals. And despite the Chemical Manufacturers' Association's (CMA) claims of support for the TRI, when the Environmental Protection Agency tried to double the number of chemicals listed, CMA sued to stop it. (CMA lost the suit, but the case is now on appeal.)

Another problem is the issue of the capacity of some societies to take advantage of the information provided, or even to provide the information. Transparency, to be effective, requires a fair degree of technical and managerial competence widely distributed among the personnel of the state, business managers, and non-governmental organizations. It only works if the necessary information really gets out and if the civil society is able to organize and act in response to the information. This capacity is currently lacking in many parts of the world. Thus, the use of transparency as a means of addressing proliferation and toxification would require assistance in building such capacity.

At the international level, one environmental agreement provides an example of the difficulty of relying on transparency in lieu of regulation. The Basel Convention on Transboundary Hazardous Waste requires shippers of hazardous waste to receive the prior informed consent of any state to which it wishes to export such substances. Some ninety developing countries have signed a protocol noting that they do not wish to receive any hazardous wastes. But this approach is seriously flawed. Few developing countries are in a position to enforce the ban. There are no monitoring or enforcement provisions. In any case, the convention only deals with hazardous materials during one portion of their life cycle, and ignores them when they are serving as (no less hazardous) inputs or products.

A third problem has to do with the difficulty of implementing the transparency approach in a coherent fashion across the board, given the bureaucratic division of decision-making. In the United States, monitoring and control of toxic substances, for example, tends to be divided up bureaucratically according to the medium – air, water, or soil – in which the hazard is found, with the result that incentives are created for cross-media shifting of pollutants rather than their actual control. Similarly, non-proliferation efforts are divided into several different issue areas (biological weapons, chemical, nuclear, and delivery systems such as missiles) with little coordination among the regimes. This division is mirrored in the domestic bureaucratic structure of the United States, rendering it unlikely that anyone in the government will take the lead in creating a monitoring system that provides a comprehensive overview of the problems.[30]

Fourth, as mentioned earlier, some actors will not want to cease their proliferation behaviour, and transparency imposes no active constraints against them. Depending on the adequacy of the transparency regime, a voluntary transparency system could create false confidence and undermine the goal of non-proliferation. Moreover, if the price for international agreement on transparency were to be increased access to dual use materials and technologies that would otherwise have been at least somewhat constrained by denial measures, the transparency approach might actually make the situation worse.[31]

Conclusion

Once it is widely recognized that proliferation and toxification represent significant and growing dangers, governments will find themselves under increasing pressure to do something about them. Neither the denial strategy nor after-the-fact countermeasures will suffice. This is not to say that the transparency-based approach advocated here is a panacea. A decentralized system that relies on the revelatory power of transparency certainly will not resolve all the dangers of proliferation or toxification. On the proliferation side, the increased requirements for transparency on the part of firms should complement, not replace, the array of measures in place.[32] For the problem of toxification, on the other hand, where there are very few existing agreements, international negotiations may be needed in addition to the transparency measures advocated here. A permissive but transparent system is likely to be far more cost-effective for governments as well as far more appealing to the private sector than would be the expansion of the more heavy-handed approaches to which governments are accustomed.

The transparency system would require willing compliance with demands for information that has long been viewed as legitimately secret. Acceptance of a norm of transparency has already occurred to a degree unpredictable – indeed, unthinkable – a decade ago, both in arms control between sovereign states and, within the United States, regarding the environmental impact of certain economic activities. But many questions remain concerning how a transparency-based regime could balance legitimate rights of privacy and secrecy against societal needs to monitor potentially dangerous goods and technologies and how the necessary broad consensus could be formulated.

The transparency system calls for a substantial change in norms about the responsibilities of producers of legitimate civilian goods. The new norm would require that ignorance no longer be bliss – namely, that producers could not claim lack of knowledge about the harm their products or production processes could do, because they would be legally required to have and share that knowledge. Such a norm change may require altering a mindset that sees transparency as a public good – that is, as a social benefit that everyone wants to receive but to which no one perceives an individual incentive to contribute. Transparency has private benefits to an actor that provides information about itself. Transparency can allow an actor to reassure others about its intentions and performance, thus staving off more coercive regulation or the possibility of a spiral into a security dilemma. Requirements for transparency can enable firms to discover useful information about themselves without undergoing expenses to which competitor firms are not subject. US leadership will be essential to the creation of this system, and US businesses, who are already subject to some degree of transparency-based regulation, may strongly support the extension of the approach as a means of ensuring a level playing field.

The centralized registry may prove to be the ultimate goal, if all the hurdles can be overcome. But even if they cannot, the provision of information to the general public is in and of itself a useful tool. The TRI and Proposition 65 are good models, far from perfect but also clearly better than the alternatives. Transparency has advantages beyond the confidence-building role familiar from arms control, advantages that will apply both to proliferation and to toxification, or indeed to any issue area where ignorance, intentionally or not, can cause harm.

A fully effective set of policies to stem proliferation and toxification will have to include regulatory measures in addition to transparency, to deal with actors who are not susceptible to the shaming effects of publicity. But transparency alone has dramatic effects and should be pursued even if an effective and coordinated set of policies is not yet feasible. Indeed, transparency, by isolating the bad apples, may contribute to making that wider strategy more acceptable and easier to implement.

NOTES

The author is deeply grateful to John Steinbruner for suggesting that transparency could provide a means of addressing both proliferation and toxification. Nancy Gallagher's perceptive comments contributed greatly to shaping the article. Karen Florini provided both information and insight on the growing role of transparency in environmental protection. The views in this article are those of the author and do not necessarily reflect the views of the Rockefeller Brothers Fund.

1. There is a rapidly expanding literature on the role of norms in international security. See, for example, Peter Katzenstein (ed.), *The Culture of National Security: Norms and Identity in World Politics* (New York: Columbia University Press, 1996).

2. For a detailed discussion of the norm of transparency in international security, see Ann M. Florini, 'Transparency: A New Norm of International Relations' (Ph.D. diss., University of California, Los Angeles, 1995).

3. Janne E. Nolan (ed.), *Global Engagement: Cooperation and Security in the 21st Century* (Washington, DC: The Brookings Institution, 1994). See particularly the chapter by Antonia Handler Chayes and Abram Chayes, 'Regime Architecture: Elements and Principles', pp.65–130.

4. I am not contending that environmental toxification is necessarily a 'security' issue along the lines of proliferation, only that it poses a demonstrable danger to human well-being on a large scale. For good overviews of the voluminous literature and continuing debate on environment and security, see the annual Reports of the Environmental Change and Security Project, Woodrow Wilson International Center for Scholars.

5. For a discussion of how and why norms change over time, see Ann Florini, 'The Evolution

of International Norms', *International Studies Quarterly*, Vol.40 (1996), pp.363–89. For specific examples of the evolution of norms other than transparency, see: Ethan Nadelmann, 'Global Prohibitions Regimes: The Evolution of Norms in International Society', *International Organization*, Vol.44 (1990), pp.479–526; and Richard Price and Nina Tannenwald, 'Norms and Deterrence: The Nuclear and Chemical Weapons Taboos', in Peter J. Katzenstein (ed.), *The Culture of National Security: Norms and Identity in World Politics*, pp.114–52.

6. I am indebted to the participants in The 2050 Project, particularly John Steinbruner and Allen Hammond, for the general approach and some of the specific information contained in this section.

7. United Nations Population Fund, *The State of World Population 1995* (New York: UNFPA, 1995), pp.16–17.

8. United Nations Population Fund, *The State of World Population 1996* (New York: UNFPA, 1996), p.1.

9. United Nations Population Fund, *The State of World Population 1996* (New York: UNFPA, 1996).

10. Ted Robert Gurr, Barbara Harff, Monty G. Marshall, and James R. Scarritt, *Minorities at Risk: A Global View of Ethnopolitical Conflicts* (Washington, DC: U.S. Institute of Peace Press, 1993).

11. Martha Finnemore, 'Norms, Culture, and World Politics: Insights from Sociology's Institutionalism', *International Organization*, Vol.50, No.2 (Spring 1996), pp.325–47.

12. Jessica Mathews, 'Power Shift', *Foreign Affairs*, Vol.76, No.1 (Jan./Feb. 1997), pp.50–66.

13. Paul Kennedy, *Preparing for the Twenty-First Century* (New York: Random House, 1993); Thomas Homer-Dixon, 'The Ingenuity Gap: Can Poor Countries Adapt to Resource Scarcity?' *Population and Development Review*, Vol.21, No.3, (Sept. 1995), pp.587–612.

14. The rich countries could also face internal threats to their security, a problem of particular salience for the United States. At least some of the conditions prevailing in the poor countries of 2025 may be mirrored in America. If income disparities continue to grow, if urban centres continue to decay into crime-ridden islands of ignorance and despair, if America becomes divided into a society of haves and have-nots, then we may see a return to the riots and assassinations of the 1960s – this time with assault weapons, truck bombs, and possibly even chemical and biological weapons.

15. William J. Perry, 'Desert Storm and Deterrence', *Foreign Affairs*, Vol.70, No.4 (Fall 1991), pp.66–82.

16. Cheryl Simon Silver and Dale S. Rothman, *Toxics and Health: The Potential Long-Term Effects of Industrial Activity* (Washington, DC: World Resources Institute for the 2050 Project, 1995), p.6.

17. Amy E. Smithson (ed.), *The Chemical Weapons Convention Handbook* (Washington, DC: The Henry L. Stimson Center, Sept. 1993).

18. *Convention on the Prohibition of the Development, Production, Stockpiling and Use of Chemical Weapons and on Their Destruction* (Washington, DC: United States Arms Control and Disarmament Agency, Oct. 1993), Verification Annex, p.125 (hereafter Chemical Weapons Convention).

19. Ibid., p.129.

20. Ibid., p.134.

21. Ibid., p.141.

22. Chemical Weapons Convention, Article IX (8), p.33.

23. Chemical Weapons Convention, Verification Annex Part X, 'Challenge Inspections Pursuant to Article IX', pp.150–61.

24. In 1991, Germany established a national system intended to accomplish this purpose, called Kontroll bei der Ausfuhr (KOBRA). It was an on-line data collection system available to all customs offices in Germany. See Wolfgang H. Reinicke, 'Cooperative Security and the Political Economy of Nonproliferation', in Nolan (ed.), *Global Engagement*, p.183.

25. The following is taken from Stephanie Phillips, 'IAEA Safeguards: A Classic Public Goods Problem' (unpublished manuscript, Jan. 1997).

26. *Emergency Planning and Community Right-to-Know Act of 1986*, 42 U.S.C. sec. 11001–11050.

27. 61 Fed Reg. 51322 (Oct. 1, 1996). Reporting actually began under TRI in 1987, but because of problems in the reporting the first year, EPA uses 1988 as the baseline year for comparisons. The Chemical Manufacturers' Association uses the 1987 data as the baseline, and reports a 49 per cent decrease in emissions since then. 'Responsible Care Communication' Chemical Manufacturers Association, March 10, 1995, URL: http://es.inel.gov/techinfo/facts/cma/cmacommo/html.
28. The following information is taken largely from 'Proposition 65 in Plain English!' URL: http://www.calepa.cahwnet.gov/oehha/docs/p65plain.htm.
29. Donella Meadows, 'A CEO Responds to a Spear through the Heart', *Valley News*, Lebanon, New Hampshire, 28 Nov. 1996.
30. Nolan, 'Cooperative Security in the United States', pp.507–42, esp.pp.531–5.
31. I am indebted to Nancy Gallagher for this point.
32. These include, on the proliferation side, the International Atomic Energy Agency, the Non-Proliferation Treaty, the Chemical Weapons Convention, the Missile Technology Control Regime, and the United Nations Register of Conventional Arms, all of which serve important roles and should be maintained.

Beyond Defence, Deterrence, and Arms Control

GLORIA DUFFY

In the summer of 1996, US Secretary of Commerce Ron Brown and a group of United States business executives died tragically when their aircraft crashed in Bosnia. This incident and the mission which took Brown and his delegation to Bosnia dramatize the new security challenges facing the United States in the post-Cold War world, as well as the creative strategies and policies the United States must adopt to improve its own security and international security in the current environment. Today, few security threats can be addressed by traditional means. Secretary Brown's mission to Bosnia was an important metaphor for the ways in which the United States must reach out and directly apply its financial and technical resources to address the security problems in other regions of the world which can threaten its interests and global stability.

During the Cold War, it was very clear to the United States what its vital interests were, who its enemies were, what the threats were, and how it could address them. Its interests were global, because of its rivalry with another nuclear superpower, the Soviet Union. The perceived threat was Communist expansion and the major enemies were the Soviet Union and its allies. The main way of addressing these threats was through military force or the readiness to use military force through nuclear deterrence.

Beginning in the 1970s, when the nuclear arms race in itself began to be regarded as too costly for society, these traditional methods were joined by the adjunct of arms control, to reduce formally the threat where the United States and other countries could reach agreement on measures to be taken. The United States approach to security rested on these pillars of defence, deterrence, and arms control for over thirty-five years.

Following the Cold War, the United States is in a period of tremendous flux as it redefines its interests as a country, and the nature of threats to security and international stability. It is redefining its interests in an environment where the threats are shifting radically and where the methods available to address them are also changing profoundly. We face a much more complex and confusing picture today than we did during the Cold War.

Some of the threats remain quite traditional. They are still, in some cases, embodied in countries. For instance, were the communists or nationalists to come to power in Russia again, as has been a concern in recent elections, even though it is diminished in economic and military power, Russia might once again present the type of threat to its neighbours that the Soviet Union did during the Cold War. Some of China's policies in the Pacific, for example towards Taiwan, may also represent a traditional geopolitical threat to its neighbours and international stability. Iraq's invasion of Kuwait, precipitating the Gulf War, and the aftermath of repeated military skirmishes with Iraq represent another traditional nation-state threat. And in a different sense, the thirty-five civil wars under way in various areas of the globe today represent classic threats to peace and security which can be met through military force, deterrence, or the related measures of peacekeeping or other types of outside military intervention.

But many of the dangers the United States and the international community face today are more related to economic and technological factors than to geography or to direct military threats to the United States or its allies. These threats are less identified with countries than they are with forces that cross borders and boundaries. For example, terrorism, which is taking some disturbing new directions both domestically and internationally, involves primarily the force of ideas or emotions, joined together with very modest actual military power or weapons to create extensive damage, both physical and psychological, for the nations or groups that are its victims.

Terrorism aside, many of these new threats are what Rand analyst Gregory Treverton has called 'threats without threateners'. They stem from social and economic trends and technology, where there is no intent to harm someone, but the unintended by-products of these forces are threatening. Threats without threateners lie behind the instabilities caused by population growth, immigration, the vulnerability of computer systems which control so much of our society's operation, and the international drug trade. The drug trade is one of the best examples of a threat without a threatener. Those who import drugs or buy drugs in the United States or export drugs from other countries are engaging in economic transactions, and thinking only of their personal interests. They do not intend to harm United States security or international stability. Yet by-products of these individual or group activities – gang warfare, political corruption, difficulties states face in controlling their borders – threaten security and stability.

The United States has moved through two phases over the past forty-five years, first emphasizing weapons and deterrence, then adding negotiations and arms control to our strategy for dealing with threats. Both are still valid in some situations. Appropriately, our defence effort continues today to build weapons and maintain the readiness of forces to protect our security against traditional threats. And arms control continues to address problems such as nuclear testing, the further drawdown of strategic nuclear forces, restricting chemical weapons, and maintaining and expanding the Non-Proliferation Treaty. Neither approach helps very much in addressing the new types of threat described above. Many of these threats simply cannot be very effectively dealt with through military force, deterrence or traditional arms control and diplomacy. What can military force do against a problem like cyber-terrorists intent on hacking into government computer systems? Often the problems are too imminent and urgent to be the subject of long, drawn-out negotiations. Arms negotiations have often been based on symmetry – countries have agreed to reduce or eliminate weapons of similar type and number. Many security problems today are asymmetrical; for example, dismantling weapons of mass destruction poses problems for the former Soviet Union that are not particularly difficult challenges for other industrialized societies. Negotiating an effective, equitable, and universally acceptable agreement on landmines is qualitatively different from negotiating reductions in strategic weapons with the Soviet Union. Some threats, such as those posed by population growth, are too subtle to have an identifiable party with whom to negotiate or coerce with military threats. Business as usual, relying on military force, deterrence and arms control to guard our security, would not protect us from these new types of threat.

Because of the dramatically different character of such threats, a new phase has been reached which requires direct United States engagement in preventing the emergence of security threats. Increasingly, security strategy needs to move in the direction of attempting to reduce or prevent threats before they require military response – types of prophylactic or preventive measure. This represents a new approach, a third pillar in security strategy. Sometimes this approach supports arms control, sometimes it is an alternative, and sometimes it is a step beyond arms control. Slowly, sometimes all too slowly, a process is under way to adapt defence policy and strategy to integrate this new approach.

Although they have not always been identified as such, this preventive approach to security has been used successfully in several recent cases. The combination of incentives and international pressure that is being brought to bear to halt the North Korean nuclear weapons programme is an example of the preventive approach at work. Another instance is the expanding military cooperation and consultation between the United States, Japan, and other Pacific countries to deal with potential threats from China or other regional aggressors. The extensive military-to-military contacts, building bridges between the United States, NATO countries and the militaries of the new countries of the former Soviet Union are yet another example. The Clinton administration, and particularly former United States Secretary of Defense

William Perry, pioneered this preventive approach and has utilized it effectively in several areas of the world.

The most striking example of the preventive approach used successfully has been the Nunn-Lugar programme, or 'cooperative threat reduction', as it is also called. This has consisted of United States technical and financial assistance to the former Soviet countries to prevent the proliferation of nuclear, chemical, and biological weapons on the territories of Russia, Ukraine, Belarus, and Kazakhstan. It is an effort to prevent the emergence of a threat to the United States and international security and stability from that region, rather than simply to wait for the threat to emerge and then react to it later, by trying either to reduce it through negotiations, to deter it, or to take a military response against it. The process of cooperative threat reduction with Russia, Ukraine, Belarus, and Kazakhstan has bolstered arms control by helping to bring about START I ratification by these countries and supporting the implementation of START I. But it has also moved considerably beyond what arms control was able to do.

After the Soviet Union disintegrated in early 1992, 30,000 nuclear weapons were left on the territory of the former Soviet Union; 3,200 of them outside Russia in Belarus, Ukraine, and Kazakhstan. Large amounts of fissile material – highly enriched uranium and plutonium that could be used to make nuclear weapons – also remained on the territories of several new states. Ballistic missiles, strategic bombers, and all of the types of weaponry that had been accumulated during the Cold War were left in the aftermath of the dissolution of the Soviet Union. These weapons, materials, and delivery systems remain in new states where political control was uncertain, and in an international environment where countries including Iran, Iraq, North Korea have an interest in obtaining weaponry and materials related to weapons of mass destruction.

The breakup of the USSR created an urgent need for safe and secure transport, storage, and dismantlement of these weapons. Yet, the Newly Independent States of the former Soviet Union (NIS) were suffering extreme economic privation, with barely the resources to provide food and housing for their people, much less to spend the funds necessary to deal adequately with a deteriorating military complex and weapons of mass destruction.

This danger, like the drug trade and immigration, is a threat without a threatener. The force of national self-determination which propelled the various republics of the Soviet Union to become independent created the threat of diffusion of nuclear weapons among several states rather than just one. The forces of economic deterioration meant that these countries could not adequately protect the weapons and materials on their territories. And the growth of organized crime within the former Soviet republics combined with the search for nuclear weapons by rogue states outside the NIS to create dangers of diversion or misappropriation of weapons and materials. The former Soviet states did not particularly seek to threaten anyone, but the forces causing the 'loose nukes' problem nonetheless created dangers to international security.

In the fall of 1991, as the Soviet Union began to fall apart, Senators Nunn and Lugar sponsored legislation to enable the United States to use funds from its defense budget to assist these countries. The Nunn-Lugar, or cooperative threat reduction, programme was initially funded with $400 million from the defense budget. Partly because of the difficult nature of the challenge and partly from lack of experience with a concept as unconventional as the Nunn-Lugar approach, these funds were not effectively utilized until 1993, when the Aspin-Perry team arrived at the Defense Department. At that time, a sense of crisis was growing about the control of nuclear weapons and materials in the former Soviet countries. Having learned quickly that traditional diplomacy was not producing any results in dealing with this problem, the Clinton administration was determined to utilize the Nunn-Lugar programme effectively to deal with the threat of proliferation in and from the former Soviet Union. This effort had two main objectives: to encourage Ukraine, Belarus, and Kazakhstan to become nuclear-free; and to help the Russians to better protect, guard and dismantle the weapons and material on their territory.

United States offers of financial and technical assistance opened the doors for talks with the four countries about their nuclear weapons and policies. Eventually Washington concluded over fifty agreements for cooperative threat reduction projects with these countries, and obtained the commitment of Ukraine, Belarus and Kazakhstan to denuclearize and not become new nuclear weapon states. Kazakhstan became nuclear-free in the spring of 1995; Ukraine followed on 1 June 1996; and Belarus did so in November 1996. Many cooperative projects were also started with Russia. The United States, with more modest contributions by European countries and Japan, provided the four countries with material assistance to implement their decisions to denuclearize and dismantle nuclear weapons, including cranes to lift missiles out of silos and shears to remove the wings from bombers. In Russia, the assistance was used to help build a secure storage facility for plutonium from dismantled warheads. The United States is assisting the Russian Ministry of Defense to better guard and protect nuclear weapons during transport and storage. Through funding the grant-making International Science and Technologies Centers, the United States, the European Community, and Japan are helping to re-employ thousands of weapon scientists in the former Soviet Union on civilian projects. In one of the most dramatic operations under this programme, the United States removed 600 kilograms of highly enriched uranium (enough for about twenty nuclear weapons) from Kazakhstan to Oak Ridge in November of 1994.

Not only has the effort to prevent proliferation in the former Soviet Union been conducted by the United States government through diplomacy and negotiations, but there has also been a concerted societal action involving United States industry. For instance, through the Nunn-Lugar programme the Bechtel Corporation is a contractor for the Russian government and assists in planning the disposal of chemical weapons. The United States has also started sixteen defence conversion projects, pairing United States companies with defence enterprises in the former Soviet Union, helping them in the transition to produce civilian goods. These conversion projects are generating a variety of civilian goods, from low-end computers to laser pointers, through joint ventures between United States companies and former Soviet defence enterprises.

This cooperative threat reduction approach has been very successful in preventing proliferation within and from the former Soviet Union. The case of Ukraine was the most difficult problem. The United States offered assistance and was closed involved in Ukrainian decision-making, as well as providing economic support for Ukraine and security assurances. This strongly influenced the Ukrainian government's decision to become non-nuclear rather than the world's third-largest nuclear power. The last of the nuclear weapons left Ukraine on 1 June 1996, a major watershed for non-proliferation worldwide.

In addition to being effective, this preventive approach to the problem of proliferation in the NIS has proven to be both rapid and inexpensive. Moving from the concept of cooperative threat reduction, to negotiations, to agreement, to procurement, to shipping, to the use of the aid provided, to realizing the major objectives of the effort, took only about two years. The cost of the effort to the United States has been about $2.5 billion over seven years, less than one-fifth of one per cent of the annual United States defence budget.

Not all of the problems related to proliferation in the former Soviet Union have been completely solved. Cooperative threat reduction work is continuing to address the inadequate protection for fissile material in Russia, and other issues. But, most importantly, in looking at the security threats facing the United States and the means to address them, there simply was no other way to accomplish the goals of denuclearization and dismantlement of nuclear weapons in the former Soviet Union. Traditional diplomacy was tried and failed. Neither military force nor traditional arms control would have been effective. The only approach that was effective was direct engagement in the decision-making of the NIS countries about their weapons of mass destruction, backed up and supported by the technical and financial assistance of the United States and other countries.

The approach of preventive defence, of which the efforts with the former Soviet countries are the shining example, is by no means limited in its potential to cooperative threat reduction dealing with the nuclear problem in the NIS. If developed more fully, it can become the third pillar on which United States national security policy rests. Another recent case – the North Korea nuclear reactor deal – was mentioned above. In this instance, the United States, South Korea, and Japan concluded a deal with North Korea to replace with light water reactors the reactors which were producing materials usable for nuclear weapons.

Similar strategies could be used to promote other arms control objectives. The United States or other countries might have considered assisting countries intent on testing nuclear weapons – as were both China and France before the conclusion of the Comprehensive Test Ban Treaty in 1996 – to develop the software and computer capabilities to simulate nuclear weapons tests. In this way, a country such as China could at least obtain the data it needs to determine the reliability of its current stockpiles, and thus remove that objective as an excuse for testing. The implications of such assistance to increase a country's capacity for developing new nuclear weapons would have to be weighed carefully, however.

A preventive approach could also help resolve regional security problems. There has been a case recently where several countries involved in ethnic and regional disputes have needed some relatively simple equipment and technical assistance that would help them work out their conflicts and foster regional economic cooperation. If American preventive defence efforts were broader and better funded, the United States could find more creative, low-profile ways to support local conflict resolution efforts.

Preventive measures are also a more effective and far cheaper alternative to strategic missile defence, for protecting the United States or other countries against the danger of ballistic missile attack. The United States does not have the technology today to deploy an effective ballistic missile defence of its national territory. It is better to prevent the proliferation of weapon systems in the first place, at the front end of the process, by providing incentives to other countries not to develop or deploy these weapons, or to dismantle them if they already have them, than it is to defend against the weapons once they are in place.

Another example of how preventive measures could be used to stem proliferation is the re-employment of weapons scientists on civilian projects. The development of nuclear weapons capabilities is sometimes driven or at least strongly supported by the military and scientific infrastructure of a country. If a country's weapons scientists can be given viable alternatives to weapons work, they may choose to change their focus. This approach might work with Indian or Pakistani nuclear scientists, as it has been utilized in Russia, Ukraine and Kazakhstan. And the same could be the case with a country's defence industry. If better alternatives are available to produce civilian goods, perhaps in joint ventures with American companies and with foreign investment, then the incentives to manufacture ballistic missile components or other weapons of mass destruction might diminish.

If we look at almost any international security problem, be it proliferation or regional conflict, we can see how this concept and combination of United States technical and financial assistance and our in-depth involvement in solving the problem could provide new, positive, creative ways of addressing security problems before they would require a military response. Analysing various types of security problems in different areas of the world, and considering how preventive measures could address these threats is a topic for further research and study.

Now, let us return to the unfortunate story of Commerce Secretary Ron Brown. What was he doing in Bosnia; and what did it have to do with United States and international security? In 1996 the United States was involved in IFOR, the peacekeeping effort in Bosnia under NATO auspices. The Pentagon desired to keep its involvement on the ground in Bosnia as short as possible, and to withdraw its forces as soon as possible. But the United States was clearly aware that its forces could not be withdrawn until a functioning civil, political and economic structure had at least begun to take shape in the former Yugoslavia, because war would break out again and nullify any positive effects that might have been achieved by the peacekeeping effort.

By travelling to Bosnia and taking a group of United States business executives with him, Secretary Brown was practising preventive defence. He was on the leading edge of United States engagement in trying to build economic interests and infrastructure in the region of the former Yugoslavia that would begin to transcend the ethnic and religious divisions, and in so doing prevent the resurgence of conflict in the area.

At the memorial service for Secretary Brown, Defense Secretary Perry said that the type of risk that Brown took was the 'price of peace'. Many people may not have fully understood what this meant. In today's world, given the nature of the threats and the new methods necessary for dealing with them, a planeload of business executives representing United States technology, financial commitment and direct involvement is a very important metaphor for pursuing national and international security.

Preventive defence is not well understood by the United States

Congress. It is a very non-traditional approach to security which requires a paradigm shift in understanding how we can best provide for our national defence. Preventive defence does not accord with the traditional concepts of weapons and forces, or the more recently and grudgingly accepted concept of arms negotiations as a way to solve international security problems. Congress has repeatedly tried to cut back and abolish the Nunn-Lugar programme, and the related programmes of the Overseas Private Investment Corporation and the Commerce Department which give the United States these new instruments of engagement and leverage which are so essential in dealing with new types of security problem.

The controversy over whether preventive measures should be a legitimate part of United States defence appears to be an entirely 'Inside-the-Beltway' debate, unique to Washington, DC. Based on non-scientific samples (this is a question which should be further explored through polling), the United States public seems to understand instinctively and supports this approach, for its economy and for its directness in solving problems. Public audiences are generally outraged to hear that it is not well supported in Congress.

To deal with the problem of lack of Congressional support, before leaving the Senate at the end of 1996, Senator Nunn sought to give the Nunn-Lugar programme a stronger political base, finding other allies in Congress such as New Mexico Senator Domenici and broadening it to deal with domestic terrorism issues. The Nunn-Lugar-Domenici bill, as it became for FY1997, included not only assistance to the former Soviet countries with dismantling nuclear weapons, but assistance to United States police and fire departments to deal with possible terrorism using weapons of mass destruction. This domestic political base may strengthen support for the effort.

But the strategies that Senator Nunn and the Clinton administration have been forced to adopt to protect this one programme show the fragile basis upon which the concept of preventive defence rests. This approach should not be a stepchild of United States strategy and policy. It is a major strategy for pursuing United States and international security in a new era in which military defences can only address certain kinds of threat but not others. The preventive approach should be expanding and not fundamentally questioned in the way it regularly is by the United States Congress.

In fact, so promising is this approach that each year the Defense Department should assess opportunities for prevention of threats in all regions and areas, and funds should be available in significantly greater quantity, with fewer restrictions, and more broadly for preventive measures worldwide. It is the responsibility of Congress to support preventive measures towards national security, the effectiveness of which has been demonstrated, and to make funds available for such programmes, if, for no other reason, than because their constituents support it.

NOTE

The author would like to thank the John D. and Catherine T. MacArthur Foundation and the Stanford Center for International Security and Arms Control for supporting the writing of this essay.

Nuclear Arms Control through Multilateral Negotiations

REBECCA JOHNSON

In August 1996, the sixty-member Conference on Disarmament (CD) concluded its negotiations on a comprehensive nuclear test ban treaty (CTBT) in Geneva.[1] Described by President Clinton as 'the longest sought, hardest fought prize in arms control history', the CTBT may be regarded as a major victory for multilateralism. However, although it negotiated the text, the CD was unable to adopt the treaty. The process of negotiations on the CTBT revealed political and structural problems which raise serious questions about the effectiveness of the CD – and by implication, multilateralism – for negotiating nuclear treaties.

The international community has already committed itself to further multilateral negotiations on a fissile materials production ban,[2] although it has to date proved impossible to overcome the obstacles and make a start. In December 1996, 115 states voted for a Malaysian-sponsored resolution in the United Nations General Assembly that called for negotiations leading to a nuclear weapon convention. While no one expects such negotiations to commence in the near future, the international pressure for a multilateral fissile materials ban ('fissban') or nuclear weapon convention make it necessary to examine the feasibility of further multilateral treaties.

This essay will analyse the dynamics of the 1994–96 CTBT negotiations, using the specific examples of entry into force and on-site inspections to illustrate how the conflicting interests of particular states dominated. The piece will then consider how the structure and context of negotiations could be improved to enhance the overall effectiveness of multilateral involvement, and discuss the prospects of CD negotiations on a fissban. A central question is whether and how multilateral negotiations can reconcile the perceived needs and national interests of the nuclear weapon states (NWS) and undeclared or threshold states (India, Israel and Pakistan, referred to as the 'T-3') with the political aspirations and international security interests of the non-nuclear weapon states (NNWS).

Arms Control Negotiations

With the exception of the 1968 Nuclear Non-Proliferation Treaty (NPT), nuclear arms control has been dominated by bilateral negotiations or by measures undertaken unilaterally. Recent examples of bilateral agreements include the 1987 Intermediate Nuclear Forces (INF) Treaty and Strategic Arms Reduction Treaties (START I and II) between the United States and Soviet Union/Russian Federation. The ending of the Cold War has also seen important unilateral withdrawals, such as the announcement in April 1995 that Britain's remaining tactical nuclear weapons would be phased out by the year 1998[3] and the removal of the Hades missiles from the Albion Plateau by France early in 1996. Plurilateral[4] negotiations among some of the possessor states have also been attempted, such as the unsuccessful nuclear test ban negotiations between the United States, the Soviet Union and Britain in 1977–80. These tripartite talks foundered partly because of verification difficulties, but more directly due to policy hardening when Margaret Thatcher and Ronald Reagan were elected in Britain and the United States respectively. The Soviet invasion of Afghanistan was also a factor in worsening East-West relations. Test ban negotiations in the 1950s were in response to international pressure, but in the end, the Partial Test Ban Treaty (PTBT) was achieved in 1963 with ten days of intensive negotiations in Moscow among the United States, Soviet Union and Britain. The recently signed CTBT was the first multilaterally negotiated nuclear arms control treaty for more than twenty-five years. For it not to be the last, the dynamics of multilateral negotiations need to be better comprehended.

The conditions which must pertain for states to engage in negotiations on arms control are the result of a complex interaction of domestic, regional and global interests. The success of those negotiations depends on the interplay of several related factors, including motivation, timing, commitment and stability of governments represented in the negotiations, degree of trust and tension between some or all of the parties, bargaining strategies, the diplomatic climate and level of public awareness and pressure. Of primary importance is each state's specific interests, such as possession of the weapons under discussion, hostile or allied relationship with another state which possesses the weapons, regional considerations, commercial trade in the materials or technologies related to the weapons under discussion, and so on. The authority vested in the negotiating team by its government becomes crucial in the final stages of negotiations when deals may have to be struck with little time for haggling with competing interests back home.

As the number of states participating in negotiations increases, so the variables multiply, complicating the process further. Multilateral negotiations are characterized by asymmetry of interests. Some states will participate because they no longer need the weapons or technologies under discussion, or because they fear that others will acquire them if they do not accept restrictions themselves. Others will have a broader ideological motive, such as the desire to see a class of weapon which they have eschewed put out of bounds for all. Interests may relate directly to security assessments or they may be indirect, such as economic and political gains. Examples of economic interests would be the benefits from enhanced trade or redirection of resources from military production. Alternatively, states could be reluctant to support arms control measures if they perceived them as closing off markets for certain materials or technologies. Political interests include closer relations with certain states and enhanced prestige or influence within a region or alliance. A particular government or regime may identify certain international relations gains with consolidation of domestic power or electoral prospects. Some arms control negotiations reinforce the hegemony of the powerful, freezing a particular *status quo* or enabling those with greater capability to rationalise their forces. While some hope that international measures will result in a kind of equalization at zero, arms control is generally undertaken only where the dominant states perceive a reasonable prospect of maintaining the power balances at lower levels of hardware.

To facilitate progress on future multilateral negotiations, it is first necessary to understand how the interplay of factors affected the course of the CTBT negotiations in the Conference on Disarmament. The CD is constituted as the sole multilateral negotiating forum on disarmament issues under UN auspices. As such the CD was intended to have a different function and purpose from fora such as the UN Disarmament Commission and the First Committee on Disarmament and International Security of the UN General Assembly, which discussed broader policy and inter-state relations. Aware of its shortcomings as an effective negotiating body, the CD has been attempting to update its agenda, structures and procedures. Reorganizing itself is proving a slow process, with no agreed solutions yet in sight.

Interests: Competing and Coinciding

Negotiations in the CD utilize formal groupings of states which represented the political affiliations of nations during the Cold War: the Group of Western States and Others, the Group of Eastern European States and Others, and the G-21 Group of Non-Aligned States. As became clear during the CTBT negotiations, the groups' usefulness in managing decision-making was limited because the level of nuclear development was a greater determinant of negotiating behaviour than membership of a particular group. This section looks at how coinciding and competing interests within two of these groups – the declared and threshold nuclear weapon states – dominated the CTBT negotiations, especially during the endgame.

Though there were some stresses, the groups functioned as required for two decades, with Soviet/Russian interests dominating the Eastern European states and the interests of the United States-UK Atlantic alliance directing the Western Group's positions. The G-21 comprised those countries in the CD which were members of the Non-Aligned Movement (NAM), i.e. which chose to remain 'neutral' and not ally themselves directly with either of the superpower blocs. Although it represents itself as the voice of the NNWS, the G-21 includes India and Pakistan, which have developed a threshold nuclear weapon capability. Depending on the personalities of their ambassadors as much as political factors, G-21 leadership tended to rotate among India, Sweden, Egypt, Mexico, Indonesia, and Nigeria. These groupings may have been a reasonably effective mechanism for coordinating decision-making and rotating Chairs of committees and other positions during the Cold War and when the CD was engaged in nothing more than debate, but they proved to be inadequate once negotiations had begun.

During the CTBT negotiations, the requirements of states within the three groups had become so diverse that the system failed to represent the interests of the majority of group members except in superficial ways. The G-21, due largely to the competing roles of India and Pakistan, was unable to decide on any matter of substance, restricting itself to declarations of principle on such issues as a CD committee on nuclear disarmament. In 1995 it was unable to provide a nominee to be Chair of the NTB Committee's Verification Working Group. In the end the non-aligned states agreed to Sweden, a former member of the G-21 which had left in 1993 and was not at that time in any other group. (Sweden was admitted to the Western group in early 1996.) Therefore, in 1995, both working group Chairs were held by European Union (EU) members, the Netherlands and Sweden, while the Chair of the NTB Committee itself went to Poland, an EU applicant, and as such, even less able to challenge EU positions.[5] This extraordinary situation negated the original purpose of the group system – to ensure balanced geographical and political representation at all levels.

With its European Union majority refusing to permit open opposition to French or British demands, the Western group stifled internal debate and succeeded in gagging or undermining some of its more committed advocates of nuclear disarmament, such as Australia and Sweden. The Eastern European group, with half its members wanting to join the EU and NATO, is no longer a cheerleader for Russian positions but has become little more than a passive adjunct to the Western group, with Russia going its own way. China forms its own group of one, with a virtual pact of no-criticism between itself and the G-21, in part because China maintains a policy of 'non-interference' in what it deems to be another state's national business.

If the inadequacy of the group system in the CD has been exposed by the exigencies of treaty negotiations, CD enlargement to sixty participating members has rung its death knell. It is now only a matter of time before the Cold War groupings are overhauled. The important question is: what will replace them? The present groupings were based on security interests as perceived under the East-West bloc system. A more sensible arrangement now might be for non-nuclear weapon states to be organized according to regional interests or alliances, with acknowledgement of the particular requirements, obligations and problems of those with nuclear weapons or nuclear ambitions.

Because of the nature of arms control, direct security-related interests would be paramount in the decision to engage in nuclear weapon reductions or disarmament negotiations. Nuclear weapons are possessed by only five declared states recognized under the NPT, also known as the P-5: China, France, the Russian Federation, the United Kingdom, and the United States.[6] However, nuclear weapon status is more complex than the two categories of haves and have-nots spelled out in the NPT. Three non-NPT states – India, Israel, and Pakistan – are known to have acquired a nuclear weapon capability, although the degree to which they have weaponized has been kept deliberately ambiguous and they are thought unlikely to have developed beyond first generation nuclear weapons. For this reason, they continue to be called 'threshold NWS' (the T-3). Additionally there have been persistent concerns raised about the nuclear weapon ambitions and capability of a handful of other states. These include NPT members Iraq, Iran and the Democratic People's Republic of Korea (DPRK/North Korea), which shall be classified as the 'wannabe NWS'. This term reflects the prevailing international perception of these states' nuclear ambitions and does not necessarily describe actual programmes or intentions.

There are also a small number of NPT members which have developed sufficient production capacity for plutonium and highly enriched uranium (HEU) and have the technology to build nuclear weapons. Though countries such as Brazil and Argentina turned back from the nuclear weapon option, South Africa publicly dismantled its nuclear bombs and facilities, and Germany, Japan, and South Korea have ruled out nuclear weapon acquisition for themselves, they may all be said to have maintained an insurance option for the future, which influences their approach to non-proliferation measures and nuclear materials control. They thus form a fourth group with particular interests distinct from the non-nuclear weapon states (NNWS), which we shall call the 'nuclear insurance states'.

The unequivocally non-nuclear weapon states also have specific characteristics depending on whether they have nuclear power facilities or participate in a nuclear-military alliance. Those states which have chosen to develop nuclear energy have interests different from the majority which have no nuclear infrastructure of their own. States which are part of NATO or a similar regional security arrangement with a nuclear power have policy perspectives which differ from those with no nuclear umbrella, especially those in regional nuclear weapon-free zone agreements.

Because of regional and international conditions, the P-5 and T-3 have competing interests among themselves as well as certain common interests attached to members of their grouping *vis-à-vis* the rest. During the CTBT negotiations the interests of the P-5 and T-3 dominated in all stages, becoming particularly acute as final decisions were taken on scope, on-site inspections and entry into force. During the first eighteen months of negotiations the P-5 had sought to maintain as many of their nuclear testing privileges as possible under the rubric of a CTBT. This was consistent with their view, clearly expressed by the three western nuclear powers, that a CTBT should curb horizontal proliferation. They were prepared to accept some restrictions, since preventing the spread of nuclear weapons was now a priority of foreign policy in the aftermath of the disintegration of the Eastern bloc. They did not intend a CTBT to diminish significantly the role of nuclear weapons in their own national security and political considerations.

From the beginning, France and Britain advocated exemptions for safety tests in exceptional circumstances. The United States had defined 'no threshold' as permitting hydronuclear tests up to 4 lbs (1.8 kg), the maximum set for one point safety tests. Russia had expectations of continuing testing up to a threshold of 10 tons under a CTBT, while China wanted to retain the right to conduct so-called peaceful nuclear explosions (PNEs). When Britain and France dropped the notion of exceptional tests they pushed for thresholds of 40-50 kg and 100–300 tons respectively. Non-nuclear weapon advocates of a CTBT such as Mexico and Australia called publicly for a *comprehensive* test ban treaty, but during 1994 their diplomatic representatives were prepared privately to say that they would turn a blind eye to very low level hydronuclear testing if that was the price of getting a treaty.

All that changed after the indefinite extension of the NPT in May 1995 and resumption of nuclear testing by France, which followed shortly thereafter. Having agreed not to rock the boat before the NPT Conference, sections of the US Department of Defense and nuclear weapon laboratories began pushing for a 500 ton threshold, regardless of United States endorsement of scope language proposed by Australia banning 'any nuclear weapon test explosion or any other nuclear explosion'.[7] President Chirac's decision to conduct a final series of nuclear explosions in the Pacific propelled the P-5 debate over threshold into the public arena. India responded with scope text of its own, intending to define and ban 'any release of nuclear energy caused by the rapid assembly or compression of fissile or fusion material by chemical explosive or other means'.[8] India's intention was to prevent the declared NWS from using their advanced technology in low yield and hydronuclear testing to continue qualitative improvements or develop advanced weapons after a CTBT. This was a legitimate aspiration of nuclear disarmament advocates, but India's underlying motivation was more complex. India had suddenly confronted the realization that the treaty would close off its nuclear options. Powerful sections of political and public opinion wanted India to keep all its options open; at the very least they wanted to prevent the treaty being used to reinforce the nuclear *status quo,* portrayed as a mechanism to freeze India's nuclear options while enabling the more advanced NWS to continue refining and developing their arsenals.

Indonesia, backed by many G-21 countries, proposed that the word 'explosion' be deleted from the scope altogether, so that it would prohibit all nuclear tests, including laboratory and non-fission testing and even (according to some) computer simulations.[9] Arguing that if the safety and reliability of weapons could not be assured without testing then they should be scrapped, the Indonesian formula also anticipated that if updated or improved designs could not be tested, it was likely that the military planners would lack the confidence to deploy them. In their view, the original objective of a CTBT (first called for by Jawaharlal Nehru in 1954) was to cap the nuclear arms race and prevent qualitative improvements and new developments.

By mid-1995, the P-5 discussions on scope were deadlocked. United States government departments and agencies disagreed over the merits of raising the threshold. Some doubted the possibility of finding a mutually agreed level that would win P-5 backing (whatever that might have been), while others feared that NNWS and the test ban lobby would reject another threshold treaty altogether, thereby diminishing the political pay-off. Recognizing that the credibility of the treaty hung on the outcome of the threshold debate, the Clinton administration announced on 11 August 1995 that it would support a 'true zero yield' ban. The decision was immediately endorsed by France, which had just decided to abandon its 100–300 ton demand, and received grudging acceptance from the United Kingdom the following month. Since it appeared to give in to China's original position, Beijing could hardly complain. Russia, however, was severely put out, and only accepted the *fait accompli* in May 1996, almost a year later.

The zero yield decision was widely welcomed and appeared to have reinvigorated negotiations, until the US Department of Energy announced in October 1995 that it would be undertaking a programme of sub-critical tests at the Nevada Test Site, beginning in June 1996. This caused furious debate over the function of the CTBT and the use and capabilities of sub-critical testing. Members of the Russian, Chinese and several non-aligned delegations accused the United States of seeking to circumvent the purpose of the treaty.[10] Fearing that this could derail the CTBT, senior Western diplomats intervened in Washington to persuade the United States not to conduct any sub-critical tests while negotiations were in progress.[11]

As a consequence of the fiasco over the sub-critical test announcement, the conflict between what the declared NWS wanted from a CTBT and what the NNWS wanted was not resolved, but merely shifted a few degrees. Although some observers regard the zero yield decision as a victory for the NNWS, the scope decisions exposed the degree to which the multilateral negotiations provided legitimacy for P-5 settlements. Each of the NWS wanted to retain the maximum possible design and development abilities under the treaty. They accepted the necessity for the treaty in non-proliferation terms, but not its disarmament purpose. The primary argument over threshold was one of technological capability at very low critical yields, sub-criticality and laboratory experiments. China opposed any low hydronuclear level because it suspected that this would widen the United States development gap. Russia was very unhappy with the zero yield decision for the same reason. France calculated that it could go to zero after a final series of real-size tests, and with some back-up from the United States on computer codes. Since the technology gaps among the P-5 were still significant, negotiations among them over permitted activities were unable to be resolved. The United States zero yield decision cut through this impasse. With the treaty under threat from the resumption of French testing and waning interest among non-aligned negotiators, Washington was prepared to compromise on the one-point safety threshold rather than lose the CTBT altogether. The United States, which had least to lose by dropping to a true zero, could make concessions to the NNWS and at the same time maintain its superiority in nuclear weapon design.

Had the NWS been united on a threshold, the story would have been different. The NNWS would have been expected to accept whatever threshold the P-5 agreed. G-21 states, which wanted the treaty to be fully comprehensive, were largely irrelevant in the decision-making process, although the outcome was better than they had expected at the start of negotiations. In view of the lack of P-5 agreement, it was possible for public pressure, inflamed by the French resumption of testing, to act directly on decision-makers in the United States and France, which ended up bypassing the P-5. Absent the public pressure, the non-aligned had no coherent alternative, having failed to improve or unite behind the more far-reaching scope proposals put forward by India and Indonesia.

The CTBT negotiations took place within a formally multilateral context, but the informal structures dominated decision-making on the key issues. The core negotiations were among the NWS, each seeking a way of maintaining its nuclear arsenals under a test ban treaty. India's belated attempts to do the same were stymied because the P-5 refused to deal directly with any of the T-3. However, India's pursuit of its interests as a threshold weapon state disrupted any attempts at unity among the non-aligned. Divisions among the P-5 intersected according to levels of nuclear sophistication and also reflected political alliances. The Western and Eastern European groups were rendered inactive in part because NATO and NATO applicants did not wish to offend the United States, and in part due to the dominance of France (and, to a lesser extent, Britain) in EU policy decisions. Major states such as Japan and Germany acted according to their interests under the nuclear umbrella rather than as NNWS. Many EU countries kept in the background of the CTBT negotiations because the economic and political relationships outweighed nuclear questions. The Australian delegation played as active a role as possible, even submitting a draft or 'model' treaty text in February 1996,[12] but was denied formal responsibility as a working group or committee chair, primarily because of French opposition in the Western Group.

Following enlargement of the CD to sixty participating members, future negotiations will have to take into account the inadequacy of the Cold War groupings in managing decision-making. Within the United Nations First Committee on Disarmament and Security cross boundary alliances are already beginning to emerge: in 1996, Brazil and New Zealand spearheaded a resolution on a nuclear-free southern hemisphere; NATO applicant states voted most often with the western nuclear powers, while the EU tended to divide along NATO lines, with Sweden, Ireland, and Austria joining the non-aligned, Australia and New Zealand on the most important nuclear votes. South Africa is emerging as one of the leaders of the non-aligned, but with a pragmatic approach on nuclear issues.

At present the CD is resisting any formal restructuring. However, hopes of successful negotiations on a fissile materials ban will depend on how the CD can respond to the challenge of competing P-5 and T-3 interests. At present Pakistan and India are ranged on opposite sides, with Pakistan (supported by leading G-21 members) demanding that stockpiles should be considered and India, like the P-5, insisting on their exclusion. In November 1996, India signalled a modification of its stance, arguing that stockpiles could be considered providing a fissban was undertaken concurrently with nuclear disarmament negotiations. This linkage is viewed as a not-so-subtle attempt to paralyse fissban negotiations by burying them in the larger picture. Israel was admitted to the Western Group, on attaining CD membership in June 1996. Despite the Group's strong advocacy of immediate negotiations on a fissban (without stocks), Israel has reserved its position, leaving open the option of refusing to enter fissban negotiations on the mandate adopted by the CD in March 1995, before it became a member.

To some extent the East–West confrontation of the Cold War has been replaced by a North–South separation of interests. In nuclear arms control, however, it would be more useful to organize decision-making on the basis of regional or nuclear-weapon-free zone affiliation, with the interests of states along a continuum reflecting different stages in nuclear development clearly acknowledged.

Continuity: Governments and Policy

Negotiations take time. An important factor in successful negotiations is the degree of commitment and clarity of objective exhibited by key or 'lead' governments. Continuity of government, personnel and policy in the key states during the negotiations greatly facilitates the development of negotiating strategies and enables trust and confidence to build among the negotiators at the table and capitals at home. In thirty months of negotiations the CTBT suffered from disruption and hiatus as changes in political leadership and the ensuing policy alterations took place within key countries. France, Russia, and India, for example, underwent elections in May 1995, May 1996, and June–July 1996 respectively and the Republicans took over the US Senate and House of Representatives in November 1994.

The election of Bill Clinton as United States President in 1992 provided a CTBT with policy backing at the highest level, enabling the CD negotiations to take place. Although the imposition by the US Congress of a nine-month moratorium on testing in October 1992 had obliged Republican President George Bush to join France and Russia in a temporary halt, Clinton's commitment to a CTBT removed the blocks.

French elections in May 1995 had a profound effect on that country's negotiating posture. From January 1994 to May 1995 France appeared mostly determined to hold its ground and delay any crucial decisions. François Mitterrand's position, despite his belated conversion to the test ban, was weak. France's negotiators hit the brakes whenever it looked as though other delegations, such as Mexico, the United States or Australia, would try to accelerate a CTBT to an early finish. The new President, Jacques Chirac, swept that away with a clear (if unpopular) decision to conduct up to eight further tests. He then dropped his country's insistence on a threshold of 100–300 tons, which paved the way for the zero yield decision. After agreeing to close down the Pacific Test Sites and sign the protocols of the Treaty of Rarotonga, France then became one of the strongest advocates for speedy conclusion of a CTBT, though less effective because of the transfer from Geneva of its most experienced negotiators.

A Cabinet reshuffle in London had elevated Malcolm Rifkind to the position of UK Foreign Secretary in the middle of the negotiations. As Secretary of State for Defence in 1992 and 1993, Rifkind had put his own personal prestige behind UK Ministry of Defence attempts to persuade Clinton not to renew the moratorium which had abruptly curtailed the British testing programme. Replaced as Defence Secretary by Michael Portillo, a young hawk eager to prove his credentials with the military, Rifkind and his Conservative minister of state, David Davies, have ensured that the British approach to the CTBT negotiations has been at best lukewarm; at worst, quietly obstructive. This led some negotiators to wish for a British election even as they feared the disruptive effect of elections in other key states.

While Boris Yeltsin renewed Gorbachev's 1991 moratorium and did not appear to dislike a CTBT, his attention was elsewhere during most of the negotiations. In the run-up to the NPT Conference, the Russian delegation worked closely with the United States and appeared to share its positions on most test ban and non-proliferation-related issues. After August 1995 the relationship became strained. Russia entered into its convulsive pre-election phase and it became almost impossible to obtain clear answers, leadership or even direction from Russia's representatives at the negotiations. Elections in 1996 therefore deprived the Russian negotiators of authority, direction and flexibility for much of the delicate endgame manoeuvres.

Elections in two of the threshold NWS have also been destabilizing factors in the negotiations. In Israel, the election of Binyamin Netanyahu and the return of a Likud-dominated government has not so much altered Israel's negotiating posture as affected its neighbours in the Middle East. As the Oslo Peace Process ran into difficulties and relations deteriorated, Egypt's increased anxiety translated into a renewed demand that the CTBT's scope should cover all nuclear tests. The text for this wider scope had just been abandoned by its proposer, Indonesia, on grounds that it was unverifiable and could hold up the CTBT's conclusion. Cairo's revival of the formula was related directly to Israel's return of a more hawkish government. Egypt's intention was to widen the prohibition to prevent Israel from conducting laboratory testing of its nuclear weapons. In the end, having failed to secure more than some vague preambular references on qualitative development, Cairo reluctantly accepted the treaty without further assurances on scope. At the same time, Egypt adopted an uncompromising approach to the treaty's conditions for entry into force, wanting to exert pressure on Israel by demanding that the CTBT should not become legally binding until all eight declared and threshold NWS had acceded to it. Britain, China, Russia, and Pakistan, at least three of whom focused particularly on India's accession, shared Egypt's position on entry into force. In the event, Israel signed the treaty early on. For India, the CTBT became a political football.

As India underwent the upheaval of a closely fought parliamentary election, the CTBT became the focus of a strident debate about its nuclear status in India's media, political and academic circles. United States intelligence leaks in December 1995 and January 1996 about possible test preparations at Rajasthan, where India had conducted a test (called 'peaceful') in 1974, fuelled the nationalists' arguments that India had a sovereign right to its own nuclear arsenal. The nationalist Hindu Bharatiya Janata Party (BJP) included opposition to a CTBT in its election manifesto. Forced on the defensive in the election run-up, the Congress I Party, headed by Narasimha Rao, began to sound an increasingly dogmatic note, reflected in Geneva by a series of proposals linking the CTBT with nuclear disarmament in a time-bound framework. Opinion in the CD was divided on whether India genuinely wanted a stronger treaty or whether it was merely preparing the ground to justify its refusal to sign. With China and Pakistan on its northern borders, there is some rationale to India's argument that its national security would not be served by constraining its own nuclear options without a commitment binding all nuclear weapon possessors to a programme for nuclear disarmament. Nevertheless, it appears that this was more a justification than reason for India's often contradictory approach to the CTBT negotiations.

Following the June/July1996 elections, the BJP became the largest party in the hung parliament, but was unable to form a government. The timing of Indian elections coincided with the submission of a clean draft text by NTB Committee Chair, Ambassador Jaap Ramaker of the Netherlands. India publicly declared that it could not sign the treaty in its present form. Yet there was still a sense that the new Prime Minister, H.D. Deve Gowda, was not so much taking a decision as hedging his bets, waiting for a better offer. That offer never came. The P-5 refused to negotiate directly with India. India refused to work with the rest of the non-aligned over strengthening the preamble, saying that it would negotiate only with the P-5. Consequently, without India, the non-aligned lacked leverage in pushing their demands. For the western NWS the pay-off for strengthening the preamble would have to have been New Delhi's unconditional acceptance of the treaty, and that was now unlikely.

If it was the election of a pro-test-ban President in the United States which opened the window of opportunity for a CTBT in 1992, the United States elections in 1996 were regarded by many as a deadline. Indeed there are indications that calculations about the likely outcome of the 1996 United States elections formed part of the early negotiating strategy of more than one country. China, for example, may have had initial hopes that delaying negotiations beyond 1996 could cause them to collapse if a Republican President were to be elected. China's relations with non-aligned countries and use of nuclear disarmament rhetoric meant that it did not wish to be perceived as the spoiler, but such calculations may have influenced its policy of delay during the first two years of negotiations.

The effect of pre-election rhetoric and paralysis of decision-making when a key country is awaiting election of a new government or president can be very destabilising during treaty negotiations. Other negotiating parties may attempt to calculate, influence or even manipulate election results. Representatives may be doubly cautious about pushing the envelope to get agreement, their uncertainty about their own future compounding the general uncertainty surrounding a change of government. Following the election (unless the government in power is re-elected with a renewed mandate) there may be power struggles and policy shifts. Depending on the relevance of the treaty to popular concerns raised during the elections, the new government may use the issue to pander to a particular interest group. Lack of attention, as was seen in Russia, can also have negative consequences. Instability during government transition in one key negotiating party may be destabilizing for the negotiations as a whole. If several participants have elections, as is likely if multilateral negotiations take several years, the disruptive effect on the process of bargaining and agreement becomes multiplied.

Continuity: Diplomatic Representatives

Classic negotiating theory regards continuity as important for building confidence and personal relations, deemed essential for successful negotiating strategies. In this regard, the CD suffers from a further structural drawback. As a standing body connected with (though not formally under) the United Nations, the CD's principal negotiators are career diplomats. While many western delegations are able to provide ambassadors for disarmament issues, together with a range of technical and policy specialists to cover the details of negotiations, the majority of delegations from developing countries have one ambassador in Geneva covering issues as diverse as trade and human rights in addition to their CD responsibilities. As ambassadors and their staff are subject to rotation every 3-5 years, and most foreign ministries work on the principle of diplomats as non-specialists, the likelihood of a significant proportion of ineffective representatives being engaged in the multilateral forum is high. There is also a demonstrated risk that effective personnel may be arbitrarily replaced regardless of whether negotiations are at a sensitive juncture. Just as a change of government can be positive if it results in greater commitment or a more constructive approach to the objective, so replacement of personnel during negotiations can occasionally be beneficial, particularly if personality clashes have developed or relationships have become hostile or suspicious. However, even in this case the transition is likely to provoke some disruption, causing realignments and taking time to establish a negotiating rapport.

The difficulties for some ambassadors of maintaining a continuous presence in negotiations because of other responsibilities may have several negative effects. Day-to-day representation is often put in the hands of junior diplomats who may either err on the side of caution or alternatively act as loose cannons, reluctant to sell positions with which they disagree, while lacking the authority or flexibility to make policy concessions themselves. If other delegations are headed by ambassadors, less senior diplomats representing their governments in meetings are not regarded as having equal authority. This imbalance of power can lead to circular debates and considerable wasting of time. Ambassadors with other responsibilities who are only semi-engaged in multilateral disarmament negotiations may also lack confidence on the issue. This may result in a more rigid approach and unwillingness to make concessions on their own position without direct authorisation from their government, which can take time.

Additionally, such ambassadors are more likely to see their job as reflecting and pushing their government's views in Geneva, whereas for treaty negotiations to succeed, they have at the same time to argue the case for compromise with their own governments. As negotiations reach their most intensive phase, ambassadors must be prepared to argue their government's case to opponents and the opponents' case to their government. This requires a certain degree of confidence, authority and freedom from a fear of reprisals if their advice is rejected. For reasons of ambition or even personal safety, some diplomats are unwilling or unable to facilitate this two-way process by presenting a full view of their opponents' case. While these problems do not necessarily arise in all delegations, the CTBT negotiations have had to deal with many incidents arising from a lack of continuity and attention, with consequences varying from delay and temporary confusion to a breakdown of agreement. Sometimes the only way to move negotiations forward is for intervention at the government level, bypassing the diplomats in Geneva, but that is usually reserved for treaty-breaking issues and exceptional circumstances.

The Diplomatic Climate

Many factors affect the diplomatic climate. These include: timing; public awareness and pressure; relations between the negotiating states in other arenas such as trade or regional security; the degree of trust or tension among the parties; and linkage between the issue under negotiation and other questions of arms control or security, including other fora.

Public interest has been historically high in the case of the CTBT. It played a role in Mitterrand's decision to initiate the French moratorium in April 1992 and helped push the United States to adopt its own moratorium in October of the same year. Once negotiations started, however, attention seemed to fade. This was partly the effect of minimal media coverage and partly the result of activists turning to other issues. Media coverage and activism tend to be related. Both were low because of a perception that the issue was being dealt with and that a test ban was under way. The complexities of negotiations made it difficult to find a hook for stories in the mass media. When French testing sparked widespread public and international opposition, the renewed attention had a positive effect on the CTBT negotiations, influencing the zero yield decision and reminding some leaders of the popular appeal of a comprehensive test ban treaty.

France had calculated that there would be adverse reaction to its decision to complete a series of tests before joining a CTBT, but it seems to have underestimated the scale of opposition. Though it had undertaken a canny PR approach in announcing the number of tests and the date of completion (and in leaving itself a margin for stopping earlier), France still faced direct action and boycotts of its wine and cheese products. Condemnation from public opinion and governments was most notable in the Pacific and Japan, although there were also demonstrations and boycotts in Europe. France maintains that the further tests enabled it to drop its 100–300 ton threshold, making possible the announcement on 10 August 1995 that it would support the Australian proposal for a comprehensive scope covering 'any nuclear weapon test explosion or any other nuclear explosion'. The timing was clearly designed to deflect criticism, and appears to have been coordinated with the United States.

Bill Clinton is reputed to be influenced by public opinion more than any previous US president. The protests against French testing – with their implied demand for a complete and total ban on nuclear tests – convinced the Clinton administration that important sections of American public opinion would never accept another threshold treaty, however small the yield level. A report from the JASON group of 14 nuclear and policy experts commissioned by the DOE provided Clinton with the arguments to go to zero, while also claiming the moral high ground above those in the other NWS who wanted a higher threshold. France's softened position was vital to the timing and effect of Clinton's decision, announced on 11 August.

Timing for negotiations is a function of several factors, the most important of which reflects the power dynamic of the participating states.

The CD had included a CTBT on its agenda for twenty-three years before the timing was considered 'ripe' for negotiations. Taking into account technological advance, proliferation concerns, domestic and international pressure, the United States decided that the time was right in 1992–93. It withdrew its objection to a mandate for negotiating a CTBT, which was then internationally codified by the consensus decision in the UN General Assembly. As the most powerful among the NWS, the United States was able to carry the others into the negotiations, although China and Britain were markedly reluctant. China continued testing, at a rate of two per year, during the negotiations. Britain had planned at least three more nuclear tests. Denied use of the Nevada test site by the United States moratorium, the British government gave in, but with ill grace.

The US Senate moratorium had identified September 1996 as a target date for the CTBT. This was taken up by many negotiators. Especially when the November 1994 elections returned a Republican Senate and House of Representatives, many feared that United States voters in November 1996 might elect a President who would slam the window of opportunity shut. Some non-aligned states pushed hard for conclusion of the CTBT before the Review and Extension Conference of the NPT in April/May 1995. They were afraid that the P-5's interest in the CTBT would wane once the NPT was extended. France and Britain reversed the implied linkage by arguing that indefinite extension of the NPT would make them more amenable to concluding a CTBT.

Because of the proximity of the decision on extending the NPT, the relationship between the CTBT and the NPT was pivotal. The preamble of the NPT had expressed the determination of Parties 'to seek to achieve the discontinuance of all test explosions of nuclear weapons'. When Mexico led the non-aligned states to prevent agreement on a final declaration at the NPT Fourth Review Conference in 1990 unless the United States, the Soviet Union, and the United Kingdom would commit themselves to begin negotiating a CTBT, it was a clear signal that without some movement on Article VI – and particularly a CTBT – there could be problems over renewal of the NPT in 1995. Determining that the indefinite extension of the NPT was a central objective of their foreign policy constituted a major factor in the decision of the western nuclear powers and Russia to allow the CD to start working on a CTBT in earnest.

For the first part of CTBT negotiations, in 1994–95, the diplomatic climate seemed generally favourable. The Cold War was over and relations among Eastern and Western states were shifting into new alignments. None of the major players became embroiled in a war, a frequent cause (and excuse) for breaking off negotiations.[13] Concern about nuclear weapons focused on the dangers of too many, so testing new designs was seen as an expensive and unnecessary luxury. When the United States decided the time was right, others followed, permitting negotiations to get under way. During the negotiations each of the P-5 made the political and structural adjustments to enable it to join a CTBT. Some were behind closed doors, as with the zero yield decisions and commitments on stockpile stewardship. Others, like the French decision to conduct a final testing series, evoked public reaction, which in turn had impact on the context of decision-making. Timing did not work completely in the treaty's favour, however. As a CTBT became a closer reality, some states began to exhibit anxiety. India, realizing that a CTBT would prevent it weaponizing beyond first generation warheads, dressed its reluctance in calls for timebound nuclear disarmament. Fuelled by the stockpile stewardship programme, sub-critical tests and leaks about information exchange among some of the NWS, non-aligned countries such as Egypt, Nigeria, Pakistan, Indonesia, and Iran began to view a CTBT as a measure whose time had passed. As the traditional leadership in the G-21 lost interest in pushing for the treaty, India was quick to seize on their concerns. In 1996 India's Ambassador Arundhati Ghose proclaimed that 'as the PTBT drove testing underground, we do not wish the CTBT to drive testing into the laboratories by those who have the resources to do so'.[14]

A number of non-aligned countries shared India's scepticism, despite the statement from John Holum, US Director of the Arms Control and Disarmament Agency (ACDA), that the CTBT would mean that the NWS 'will not be able to pursue confidently such technologies as the nuclear explosion pumped X-ray laser, the so-called nuclear shotgun, enhanced electromagnetic pulse weapons, microwave weapons and enhanced radiation weapons ... The true-zero test ban will also place out of reach new "mini-nuke" and "micro-nuke" concepts.'[15] If negotiations had stretched beyond 1996, there was a growing risk that it would lose out to a growing cynicism and apathy as the NNWS came to believe that advances in nuclear weapon research and technology had made the test ban treaty an irrelevance, fit only to curb horizontal proliferation and maintain the nuclear status quo.

The diplomatic context is important, but the CTBT experience reveals that it is also malleable and can be manipulated by the more powerful players. The United States largely determined the start and finish of the CTBT negotiations. An attempt by Mexican Ambassador Miguel Marín-Bosch in June 1994 to speed up negotiations with a Chair's vision text failed due to vigorous opposition from France. The other Chairs adopted the pace dictated by the 1994–96 window which had been reinforced in the Programme of Action adopted by NPT Parties in May 1995.[16] In terms of the relationship between key states, the CTBT benefited from the post Cold

War shifts. However, the negotiations suffered from being accorded a lack of importance or priority in the relations among participating states.

The CTBT mandate, agreed in 1993, was perceived by many as setting the tone for the negotiations. It referred both to the 'prevention of proliferation of nuclear weapons in all its aspects' and to 'the process of nuclear disarmament'.[17] However, subsequent negotiations revealed a chasm between the P-5, India and the majority of non-nuclear-weapon states. The P-5 prioritized the treaty's non-proliferation role but resisted linking it with any explicit commitment on qualitative improvements of nuclear weapon design. While most non-aligned countries sought to ensure that the CTBT would also contribute to nuclear disarmament, India resented any non-proliferation measure which would freeze its capability at a level inferior to China's. The sidelining of the interests of states without a testing capability was most clearly revealed during the final stages of negotiations on on-site inspections and entry into force.

Protecting Interests: On-site Inspections

Achieving agreement on the procedures and decision-making for on-site inspections (OSI) became one of the most difficult issues to resolve. As the most intrusive component of the verification regime, at the interface between national security and the verifiability of the treaty, OSI are historically one of the most sensitive issues and have contributed to failures in the past. For two years the negotiations considered the various kinds of phenomena that might provide evidence of a clandestine nuclear explosion, without really addressing the two central political questions: what kind of evidence would be admissible in supporting an OSI request; and what level of decision-making would be required before an inspection went ahead.

With regard to the first question, the United States, supported by Britain and France, argued that any kind of relevant information should be permissible. These three countries also argued that the Technical Secretariat of the CTBT Organisation should be able to proceed automatically with an inspection unless countermanded by a majority decision of the Executive Council (the so-called 'red light' process). Russia supported incorporation of national technical means (NTM) as a cost effective supplement to the international monitoring system (IMS) but ruled out human intelligence or espionage. Russia also maintained that the Executive Council should be required to give majority approval before an OSI request could proceed (the 'green light'). Israel's position was similar to Russia's, also backing Moscow's attempts to restrict access to buildings or facilities not directly connected with a suspected nuclear test, allowing the inspected state to deny or provide strictly 'managed access' during an OSI. China, India, and

Pakistan went even further to restrict inspections. With some nuanced differences among them, their initial position was for NTM to be ruled out and for the Executive Council to approve an inspection by a two-thirds or three-quarters majority. Towards the endgame, they indicated acceptance of some NTM information, especially 'IMS-type data' and satellites, but under strict control and only if corroborated by the IMS.

Multilateral negotiations proceeded during the first two years with various Friends of the Chair and convenors (including Russia, the United States, Germany and Canada) but only dealt with the techniques, indications, tools and timelines. As decision-time neared, the P-5 entered into negotiations among themselves, with some additional talks in informal groups, bilaterally and plurilaterally, with representatives of Israel, Pakistan and India. The United Kingdom and France could afford to be flexible, since the UK had no test site on its territory and France had promised to close down its facilities in the South Pacific. The United States appeared less concerned about abusive requests than to ensure that its intelligence and military establishments had what they wanted, since their approval was necessary for Senate ratification.

As the P-5 struggled to agree on a package comprising PNEs, inspections and entry into force, it was clear that if they could come to agreement this would be presented to the NTB Committee on a take-it-or-leave-it basis. At one point the United States delegation appeared ready to give China its desired Article 2 on PNEs and adopt the entry-into-force condition pushed by Russia, China, and the United Kingdom if it could only have China accept the general admissibility of NTM and a simple majority decision-making requirement. Although Pakistan and Israel had very strong positions of their own, and many non-aligned countries had publicly echoed the Pakistan/India/China position opposing NTM and requiring a two-thirds majority of the Council to decide, it was clear that the P-5 considered that if they could agree, everyone else would go along with it. In the end, the P-5 were able to resolve some of their differences, but could not agree on the whole package. This forced China to 'go it alone' on PNEs, securing much less than it had hoped for.

Notwithstanding its declarations against reopening the Chair's 'final text' of 28 June, the United States agreed to China's demands for further discussions on OSI. After hard bilateral bargaining, during which Beijing's support for the treaty appeared to hang in the balance, the United States in mid-August accepted China's proposal that at least thirty of the fifty-one-member Executive Council of the proposed CTBT Organisation would have to approve (give a 'green light') before an OSI could go ahead. Ambassador Ghose was furious that the treaty text had been amended at the behest of the United States and China, since no one was prepared to reopen negotiations on India's disarmament or entry into force proposals. An unguarded comment from a senior United States official who reportedly explained the accommodation to Geneva journalists by saying that 'China was a nuclear weapon state' was widely reported in the Indian press. In consequence, many articles and editorials argued that India should test and weaponize its nuclear arsenal in order to be taken seriously.

The only countries with real interests in the provisions for OSI were those with sensitive military sites which might be the subject of an inspection request and those which suspected their neighbours or rivals of clandestine activities. The multilateral negotiations on OSI were slow moving and insubstantial during the first two years because they lacked real interest. Technical questions were addressed, but the central political differences of approach were avoided. In the final year at least two sets of negotiations ran in parallel. The P-5 negotiations determined the outcome, reducing to a final bilateral trade-off between the United States and China once the concerns of Russia, Britain and France had been met. India, Pakistan and Israel put in their requirements and engaged in some informal consultations with the P-5. The T-3 were able to be indirectly accommodated, but only to the extent that their preferences coincided with the concerns of China and Russia, for a restricted OSI regime with some protections for sensitive facilities. The United States was under pressure from the Pentagon and intelligence agencies to push hard for open access OSI and unrestricted NTM. Though the United States won much of what it wanted, the price was high in other areas, especially the treaty's entry into force.

Treaty Targets: Entry into Force

Negotiations on the conditions which would have to be met before the CTBT became legally binding were only desultorily conducted in the NTB Committee and in consultations with various Friends of the Chair until the final stage of negotiations, when the issue emerged as a treaty-breaker. Once again the territory of conflict was almost exclusively occupied by the P-5 and the T-3.

Early in negotiations Russia had proposed a condition based on the sixty-eight states listed by the International Atomic Energy Agency (IAEA) while Britain, France and China wanted all sixty-one states of the expanded CD to accede before entry into force. The United States, on the other hand, preferred accession by forty states, specifying only the P-5, arguing that the other lists would give a veto to too many countries. By March 1996 the United Kingdom had suggested making implementation dependent on the ratification of only the eight countries without full-scope safeguards on their nuclear facilities, thus exposing the underlying purpose of the more elaborate lists. This '5 plus 3 formula' was rejected by countries such as South Africa and Brazil, which argued that it gave special status to the threshold NWS, appearing to reward them for staying out of the NPT by giving them veto power over the CTBT. With India's early signature on the treaty looking less and less likely, Ramaker sought a formula that would appease the hard-liners such as Russia and Britain. On 20 June, just after India's declaration that it would 'not accept any language in the treaty text which would affect our sovereign right to decide, in the light of our supreme national interest whether we should or should not accede to such a treaty'.[18] Ramaker issued a working paper on entry into force. It included a very complicated procedure offering a series of options to be tried in turn if the initial condition, a list of 37 including the P-5 and T-3, was not met within five years. This proved unacceptable to Russia, Pakistan, and the United Kingdom, although there is some evidence that the timing and tactics of its introduction were instrumental in its speedy and unconsidered rejection. In particular, the United Kingdom objected to being 'jumped' by France and the United States. Many other states considered the new proposal too complicated. Some felt that support could have been possible if more time had been devoted to explanations and wider consultations before it was presented.

Ramaker subsequently introduced a new and untried proposal in his final text on 28 June. According to this draft, the treaty would take effect after two years and upon ratification by forty-four specified states which are CD members and also on the IAEA list as possessing nuclear research or power reactors. After three years, if India or others on the list had still not joined the treaty, the states which had ratified would be able to hold a conference to discuss accession and possibly even agree on provisional application. By current interpretations, Article XIV would not permit parties to waive the original conditions. Afraid that the powers are too weak to bring about entry into force, some negotiators dubbed the provision a 'handwringing conference'.

No one disagreed with the principle that the treaty should aim to bind all the states with the capability of conducting nuclear explosions, but the vast majority favoured a more flexible approach to entry into force, arguing against conditions that could be used to hold the treaty hostage. Many countries had a vested interest in ensuring that the treaty be implemented as early as possible, and thus preferred a simpler condition. These countries seemed to lack the power to intervene in the bargaining conducted among the P-5. The intentions of India and Pakistan may have been pivotal factors, but neither country was treated as a full negotiating partner. The views of other states, including Germany and Japan, were virtually ignored. During a heated debate on entry into force, stretching to midnight in the final week of negotiations in June 1996, the United Kingdom's ambassador spelled out his view that the treaty was only for the eight declared and undeclared nuclear weapon states, all others being there just to share the financial burden of verification.[19]

Even without the UK ambassador's explicit statement, this issue more than any other demonstrated the fallacy of multilateral CTBT negotiations. The P-5 with varying degrees of reluctance decided to agree to a CTBT as a non-proliferation measure with two objectives: to convince the majority of non-nuclear weapon states that the NPT was worth making permanent; and to bring the threshold NWS into the multilateral non-proliferation regime. They perceived negotiations on a CTBT as able to deliver both these objectives and were prepared to pay the price of limiting their own nuclear explosive testing. With the first objective achieved in May 1995, the second objective became the bottom line for Russia and Britain. Although advocating a condition that would bind the T-3 along with the P-5, China appeared to signal more flexibility on this issue than over on-site inspections. (It cannot be inferred from this that China *was* more flexible, as China frequently expresses a 'flexible' approach when another state is in front holding down a position that China actually wants.) Although Pakistan and Egypt both advocated the same stringent conditions, their objections were not perceived as treaty breakers to the same degree as Russia's and Britain's. Britain had cited Pakistan's needs in support of the '5 plus 3' formula, but miscalculated Pakistan's ability to deliver: even after the final treaty contained its preferred entry into force condition, Pakistan refused to sign, citing the need for improvement in its regional security. Regardless of the entry into force conditions, Pakistan was unlikely to join without India.

Inept handling of the entry into force negotiations, combined with India's frenzied search for a way out of the CTBT's closing grip, nearly caused loss of the treaty. China shares a long border with India and has direct security rationale for wanting to prevent India from developing a more sophisticated, missile-deliverable nuclear arsenal. Neither Russia nor Britain can claim that the threshold states pose any kind of direct nuclear threat. Their rigidity over entry into force only makes sense in terms of their perspective that the primary purpose of the CTBT is non-proliferation. The implication is that the major nuclear powers will not accept constraints unless they are legally binding on minor rivals, including those which are far behind in the nuclear arms race. However, in their heavy handed determination to bind the T-3, the NWS may have driven India into the arms of its nuclear hawks. India's ambassador responded that her government 'cannot accept any restraints on its capability if other countries remain unwilling to accept the obligation to eliminate their nuclear weapons'.[20]

India's attempts to have the CTBT incorporate a commitment to time-bound nuclear disarmament were doomed from the start but provided the grounds for declaring on 20 June that it could not sign the CTBT 'in its present form'. Moreover, Ghose warned against making ratification by India (among others) a requirement in the treaty, claiming that this would be an infringement of its sovereignty.

Although the majority of delegations preferred a more flexible provision, they failed to become involved. Lacking sufficient pressure for a credible alternative, Ramaker's finalised treaty listed India among the forty-four states required for the treaty to take effect. Following through its threat, India vetoed the treaty's adoption by the CD. This meant the treaty had no authority beyond that of a NTB Committee working paper. It was rescued by Australia, who took it directly to the UN General Assembly on 10 September 1996, where it was endorsed by 158 votes to 3, with 5 abstentions. By early December it had been signed by 135 countries. Of the forty-four states required by Article XIV on entry into force, all but India, Pakistan and DPRK have signed. Close observers of Indian politics are concerned that the heavy handling of the endgame negotiations, especially on entry into force, have made it more difficult for a future Indian government to accede to the CTBT, even if India backs away from further testing.

Making the treaty hostage to the decision of a state which declared it would not join the treaty increases the prospect of the CTBT sitting in limbo for a long time, perhaps indefinitely. If no one attempts any nuclear explosions, the treaty's norm against testing may be sufficient. However, if there are accusations of low-yield testing or other compliance ambiguities, the treaty regime could be weakened and discredited, lowering the penalties of break-out. For the foreseeable future, funding and verification will be on a voluntary basis, though managed by the CTBT Organisation in Vienna.

The saga on entry into force reveals many of the dilemmas of multilateral negotiations. The NWS, having come to the decision to constrain or halt a particular activity, are not content with mutual agreement among those who have engaged or benefited most from the activity in question. They are not willing to accept restraints because the rest of the world has long been advocating a halt. They want an additional pay-off, and seek to use multilateral negotiations to extend legally binding curbs to the lesser or threshold nuclear states. Britain, France, and Russia have again utilized this argument when insisting on the need for multilateral negotiations on a fissile materials ban or cut-off. Yet the CTBT problems over entry into force and the role of India and Pakistan in the negotiations show that multilateral procedures *per se* are no guarantor of accession by participating states.

Fissban or Cut-Off

The next item scheduled for multilateral negotiations in the CD is a treaty banning the production of fissile material for nuclear weapons or other nuclear explosive devices. The history of the fissban issue has paralleled that of the CTBT. By 1992 Russia and the United States had decided to halt production of plutonium and highly enriched uranium for weapons purposes. They brought Britain and France on board and got consensus for a UN General Assembly resolution in December 1993.[21] The CD itself decided that it was the most appropriate forum to negotiate a fissban. In order to present progress on this issue before the NPT Conference in April 1995, the CD made a hurried agreement to fudge the central issue of contention when adopting its mandate for negotiations: whether or not existing stockpiles should be included for consideration. The fissban subsequently became tangled in the politics around establishing a nuclear disarmament committee. At time of writing, the CD has still failed to convene a Fissban Committee and begin negotiations.

As with the CTBT, the NWS are responding to a long-sought demand by the non-nuclear weapon states, but at a time of their choosing. Awash with plutonium and highly enriched uranium (HEU) from post-Cold War weapons dismantlements, the major NWS decided they no longer needed to keep producing fissile materials for weapons purposes. They sought to codify this by a multilateral treaty not only to get China on board but also to bring the nuclear facilities of the non NPT threshold states under full scope IAEA safeguards. However, Pakistan has spearheaded the demand by some non-aligned countries for existing stocks to be brought into negotiations, for declaration, control and even elimination. This has been unacceptable to the P-5 and India. Then in November 1996 India echoed its CTBT stance by claiming that it would be willing to undertake a fissban including stocks providing that negotiations were concurrent with time-bound progress on nuclear disarmament. Israel, which was not a member of the CD when the March 1995 mandate was adopted, has expressed reservations and may withhold participation if negotiations on a fissban go forward in the CD.[22]

Depending on the stringency of the prohibition, a fissban could be a minor step towards non-proliferation or a significant measure of nuclear arms control and disarmament. Conceptually there are four options. From least to greatest impact on nuclear proliferation and materials control, they are: a basic 'cut-off' of future production of plutonium and HEU for weapons purposes; a ban on the production and stockpiling of plutonium and HEU for weapons purposes; a ban on the production and stockpiling of plutonium, HEU and tritium for weapons purposes; and a ban on the production and stockpiling of weapon-usable fissionable materials and tritium. Each of these options has advocates and detractors. At present the politically feasible choice is between the first two. Until 1993 the majority of states had supported resolutions in the UN General Assembly calling for a ban on the production and stockpiling of fissile materials for weapons purposes. This was opposed by the nuclear weapon and some threshold states. To obtain consensus, the resolution of December 1993 referred only to a ban on production. But the issue of stockpiles became contentious as soon as consultations in the CD opened. In particular, Pakistan, Iran, Egypt, and Algeria wanted the negotiating mandate for a fissban to permit consideration of stocks, while the P-5 and India insisted that it should not. There was a fifteen month stand-off until the Special Coordinator, Ambassador Gerald Shannon of Canada, came up with a solution that utilised the UN General Assembly resolution's formula without stocks for the three-point mandate, but also referred to the desire of some states to consider not only future but 'past production'. Shannon's report stated that 'it has been agreed by delegations that the mandate for the establishment of the ad hoc Committee does not preclude any delegation from raising for consideration ... any of the above noted issues'.[23] France and Britain immediately put on record their interpretations that the mandate was for negotiating a cut-off without stocks. This prompted Pakistan and others to revive their insistence on explicit agreement that stocks *would* be considered. The issue remained deadlocked throughout 1995 and 1996, and is unresolved at time of writing.

Even more than the CTBT, negotiations on the proposed fissban will become bogged down in the CD unless the purpose and the different capabilities, concerns and obligations of the P-5, the T-3 and the rest of the world are clarified in advance. In practical terms, the first step could be taken by the P-5. A verified halt to fissile materials production undertaken by the five major nuclear weapon states could be done by a convention in which each would sign legally binding verification agreements with the IAEA for fullscope safeguards. Alternatively, a plurilateral treaty could be negotiated, with five original signatories. Such a treaty could then be opened to other states for signature, like the 1963 PTBT, with the hope of establishing a norm that would soon encompass the T-3. Resourcing the IAEA for the additional tasks of verifying a cut-off makes more sense than establishing some independent implementing organization.

In view of the difficulties being thrown up by Israel, India, and Pakistan, a P-5 cut-off would be the most immediate and practical solution and could be accomplished within a year. But most of the P-5 insist on multilateral negotiations, arguing that the T-3 must be on board. They complain that a P-5 measure would not serve non-proliferation, but only nuclear disarmament. Given the disparities in the production capacity of the T-3, as compared with the fissile materials which would continue to be available to the P-5 after a cut-off (confirmed by the voluntary cessation undertaken by all the P-5 except China), this argument appears disingenuous. But the smaller nuclear weapon states are adamant. They are not prepared to enter into legally binding restraints without the T-3. France and Britain appear worried that the threshold states might make rapid moves to narrow the gap, although there is no real evidence for this. The domino theory also seems to operate. China says little; it is the only country which has not announced a voluntary halt, although observers believe that China has now made the decision to cease production of fissile materials. Russia, which has entered into bilateral arrangements with the United States, wants China to be equally bound by any verified ban; Russian diplomats then argue that China will not stop without India, thereby making an argument for a 'five-plus-three' fissban.

Some of the NNWS call for the CD to begin work immediately on a fissban, hoping that the question of stocks will be resolved during the negotiations. Others, particularly among the non-aligned countries, are concerned that the cut-off issue will be used to tie up the resources and work of the CD for a long time, making further negotiations on nuclear disarmament impossible. Their anxiety could be alleviated if the P-5 were willing to put a target date on a cut-off, in return for agreement that stocks will be addressed in further talks once a basic cut-off has been established. Such a trade-off might win the support of many non-aligned countries, including Egypt, which is particularly keen to involve Israel in the process of negotiating fissile material controls of some kind. However, considerable diplomatic finesse may be required to overcome the opposition of Pakistan to a cut-off without stocks or the political hostility of India to a cut-off without timebound nuclear disarmament. Agreement on establishing an *ad hoc* Committee on nuclear disarmament may be the price they set for allowing the fissban to go forward. On present indications, the United States, France, and Britain are not yet willing to pay that price, fearing a 'slippery slope' into disarmament.

If the CD begins negotiating a fissban under the terms of the mandate of March 1995, the issue of stockpiles will polarize states over its objective and context. Questions of equality, non-proliferation, freezing of the nuclear *status quo*, and nuclear disarmament will be manipulated by the P-5, T-3 and some of the non-aligned states for their own political ends. In the case of the CTBT, the majority of NNWS had a vested interest in ensuring a complete halt to all nuclear testing. The limitations of the CTBT as a nuclear disarmament measure became more apparent to the NNWS during negotiations, as the P-5 sought to retain activities for maintaining the 'safety and reliability' of their arsenals. In the case of a fissile materials ban, the limitations are a source of deep conflict even before negotiations begin. If the P-5 are unwilling to go further than a basic cut-off, they should seriously consider alternative ways of making it legally binding among themselves. Refusing to do so implies that they do not regard a cut-off among the five most advanced nuclear weapon states to be intrinsically valuable.

Assessment

The experience of the test ban negotiations have pointed up some major shortcomings in the ability of the CD to deliver genuinely multilateral negotiations on nuclear arms control. At the root is the imbalance of power, with the P-5 able to control the timing, pace and parameters of the negotiations. The nuclear possessor states can veto any progress on multilateral arms control until they are ready to engage. Once negotiations begin, their interests are paramount. When placed under pressure by the demands of non-nuclear weapon states, they may threaten to pull out, as when a senior United States official warned those who sought a timetable for nuclear disarmament that the United States 'could very well abandon the negotiations and if it wanted to get a test ban just work it out with the P-5'.[24] However, that threat was empty. The P-5 had no intention of negotiating a CTBT solely among themselves, as that would have defeated one of its main objectives in their eyes: to bind the threshold states and bring them inch by inch into the nuclear non-proliferation regime.

As became increasingly clear in the CTBT endgame, the P-5 were not interested in the views of the majority of negotiating parties: Germany and Sweden failed in their bid to have 'imminent test preparations' covered by the treaty; Indonesia and the G-21 were accorded only a very weak preambular reference to qualitative development of nuclear weapons; and the majority wish for a flexible provision that would enable early entry into force was over-ruled. If China had conceded to United States demands on verification, the P-5 had been prepared to impose a package deal with greater concessions to China on PNEs than acceptable to Japan, Canada, Australia, and the rest of the CD. Though it offended at the time, the British ambassador's remark about the majority of participants being relevant only insofar as they shared the costs and burden of verification was a true reflection of the P-5 approach to multilateral negotiations.

Following its expansion to sixty members the CD needs to rethink its ways of working and decision-making. Is it feasible to retain the principle of decision-making by consensus? Since the treaties it negotiates will directly affect states' national security, no decision of the CD could be binding unless accepted by the states themselves. Consensus is an important principle of negotiations among parties with an equal interest and responsibility in the outcome. But it is also vulnerable to manipulation and hostage taking. Attention needs to be given to ways of bypassing vetoes exercised for extraneous political reasons rather than serious objections to the provisions under negotiation. The Australian initiative of taking the vetoed CTBT to the United Nations General Assembly for adoption should not be regarded as a threat to the CD. The CD works under the auspices of the United Nations and is funded by its members, even though it is 'formally autonomous'.[25] UN General Assembly resolutions have long been used to indicate priorities for the CD, with consensus resolutions sometimes acting as 'instructions' for the CD to initiate negotiations.

Instead of being viewed as bypassing the CD, oversight of the CD's agenda and priorities should be regarded as the proper business of the UN. The General Assembly should not be used merely as a rubber stamp once the CD has reached consensus. It would be preferable for the United Nations to have an acknowledged role if and when the CD becomes badly deadlocked or a completed treaty is vetoed. While all attempts should be made to reach consensus on CD decisions, the jurisdiction of the wider international community should be available as a recognized mechanism if a blockage is intransigent, unreasonable or reflects only the special interests of one or two states. The international community has a legitimate interest in CD outcomes, which should be fully recognized and incorporated in CD procedures. This would not violate the sovereign right of a state not to accede to any agreement or treaty, but would deny individual governments the power to veto measures which are sought by the great majority. Even then, an opposition vote by the most powerful states (especially the P-5) would carry greater force and might stymie adoption or implementation of a measure despite a majority in favour. In such a case, the United Nations need not be limited to acceptance or rejection; it could send a draft treaty back to the CD for its negotiators to try again to reach consensus.

The present system of dividing countries into three groupings distorts rather than facilitates the communication of interests and requirements necessary for effective decisions to be taken. The initial response to expansion has been for the existing groups to absorb the new members according to old criteria. Yet the schisms within the groups are growing more obvious. The interests of the western nuclear powers are not necessarily those of the majority of western countries in the CD, although states in NATO or under the US nuclear umbrellas may be expected to back US positions. As France moves closer to the United States and the United Kingdom on defence and security policies, a form of nuclear umbrella coalition based around an EU core may well emerge as a backing group for the western nuclear powers. Tension between the interests of this NATO core and non-NATO countries in Europe and the Pacific may increase. Since the latter are relatively powerless within the Western Group, they will either remain on the margins of decisions or they may form practical alliances with moderate members of other groups and regions. The decisive factor in this choice is likely to be the nature of the governments in power in the relevant states, with conservative administrations more likely to stay close to the United States/NATO core.

With regard to the Eastern European group, it is absurd now to expect representation of a common position from a group that includes both Russia and the former Soviet satellites from Eastern Europe who wish to join NATO or the European Union. The ever expanding list of 'associated states' which attach themselves to EU statements is an illustration of this. The Mason and Barton Groups are utilized more frequently now, enabling eastern European and western countries to discuss common approaches on disarmament and security issues. The Western Group may be reshaped along these lines, with an appropriate name change. With NATO expansion still unresolved, it is not yet apparent how Russia will choose to position itself politically and diplomatically in the future. It is unlikely to copy China and become a 'group of one'. Russia retains some close allies, but not enough to form a stable and coherent group on a par with the others.

Thirty states – half of the expanded CD – belong to the G-21 Group of Non-Aligned States. Attempts to paper over the conflicting interests of India and Pakistan and represent anything but the lowest common denominator of nuclear disarmament rhetoric in the G-21 have been increasingly unsuccessful. A Mexican initiative for a 'Programme of action for the elimination of nuclear weapons' was unable to be put forward by the G-21 because of opposition from South Africa and Chile, principally over Indian insistence on linking negotiations on a fissban with negotiations on nuclear disarmament.[26] Alliances between states within nuclear-weapon-free zones in the Pacific, Africa, Latin America and possibly South-East Asia could perhaps give the 'nuclear disarmers' a more coherent and effective voice in negotiations. However, it is difficult to see how India, Pakistan, Israel, and the Middle Eastern and North Asian countries would coordinate their representation to have an effective voice in the expanded CD.

The CTBT negotiations exposed parallel negotiating levels. Within each level there were distinct patterns of common interests and strategies, but these could never form the basis for coordinating decision-making in the CD because the involved states were also principal political and military opponents. The P-5's differences and interests determined the course of the negotiations. The T-3 had no mechanism for resolving their difficulties in relation to each other and were seldom brought into direct negotiations with the P-5. Provision of any mechanism for explicitly addressing T-3 interests is opposed by NPT states. South Africa has been particularly vocal in rejecting any special treatment for the T-3 which might be seen as conferring privileged status, while India, Israel and Pakistan themselves object whenever they think they are being singled out. However, the continued participation of Pakistan and India in the G-21 or its successor distorts the role of the non-aligned, resulting in manipulation of nuclear disarmament positions to delay or frustrate actual steps towards nuclear arms control and disarmament.

If further multilateral negotiations are to avoid some of the problems that beset the CTBT, a way must be found to address the capabilities and concerns of the T-3 without providing them with undue status. The desire not to confer preferential treatment on states which have violated the non-proliferation norm is legitimate; ignoring them or lumping them in with the non-aligned, non-nuclear weapon states does not work as an alternative. The familiar argument that the G-21 or NAM apply moral and political pressure within the group is not convincingly borne out by empirical study. Though India suffered some isolation following its veto of the CTBT, it continued to benefit from its 'leadership' role within the non-aligned groupings. Unless alternative mechanisms for participation by the threshold and non-aligned states are found, the distortion of decision-making by the dysfunctional G-21 could spell disaster for the fissban negotiations or any future nuclear arms control initiative.

Conclusion

Multilateral negotiations on nuclear arms control are in essence a fiction to enable the P-5 to negotiate with the threshold nuclear states without appearing to give them special status. It is neither new nor surprising that the powerful states dominate multilateral negotiations. The disparity of interests and resources among states would inevitably cause some imbalance. However, this becomes seriously counter-productive if the multilateral negotiations are not structured effectively to address the concerns of target countries. The CTBT negotiators tied themselves in knots to find an entry-into-force provision that would include the nuclear test capable states without identifying them. The resulting entry-into-force requirement may undermine the CTBT and prevent it from taking effect. Similarly, the effectiveness and credibility of the CD in negotiating nuclear agreements may be undermined unless the interests and concerns of states at different places along the continuum of nuclear development are openly acknowledged.

Insistence by the P-5 on multilateral negotiations for certain measures will not necessarily ensure T-3 signatures or compliance. If involving the T-3 in the multilateral process is of compelling importance, there are two ways to avoid undermining the CD: provide a target date for conclusion of the prioritized negotiations, so that the CD is not indefinitely tied up if the talks become hopelessly deadlocked; and/or provide mechanisms for bypassing the veto conferred by the CD practice of consensus. Such an approach could enable progress to be made on the fissban issue. It would require that Pakistan, Egypt and others would agree to negotiate as a first step a basic cut-off without consideration of stockpiles, in return for P-5 acceptance of a reasonable and specified target date. The CTBT target date of 1996 has set a precedent for this. India would have to be persuaded to abandon its linkage and Israel would need to agree to join the talks.

Even if negotiations on a cut-off were started, it is likely that the endgame would reproduce the conflicts that nearly caused the collapse of the CTBT. The P-5 may well insist on binding the T-3 as part of the entry into force requirement, with more cause than in the CTBT, since all the threshold states are continuing to produce fissile materials (whereas none had tested for over twenty years). If New Delhi has not resolved its internal argument over keeping India's nuclear options open, India may again refuse to sign unless and until it is satisfied that nuclear disarmament is irreversibly underway. The CD should be prepared for consensus to be blocked on the final draft. It would be better to consider that possibility now, and make it politically and structurally more acceptable to take the treaty directly to the UN General Assembly, if the CD considers it has achieved the closest degree of agreement possible.

The group system is not merely a dysfunctional relic of the Cold War; it impedes rather than facilitates decision-making based on the genuine interests of the participating states. Though viewed by some as consigning the multilateral process to a subsidiary role, the sidebar negotiations among the P-5 helped to resolve their differences and difficulties and thus contributed to conclusion of a treaty acceptable to the NWS. Where relevant, in future negotiations such as the proposed fissban, sidebar meetings involving the P-5 and T-3 should be considered. These could take place informally or under the auspices of the Chair of the negotiations. Keeping the meetings strictly informal might be more acceptable to the NNWS.

As a counterweight, a group of moderate western and non-aligned states need to break free of the present group system and form cross-group alliances to provide more coherent and effective representation of the interests of NNWS. The alliances could be formally established, but again it might be better if they were initially informal, with membership determined by attitudes to the particular measure under consideration. A separate mechanism for rotating formal positions such as Committee Chairs could be established, based on geographical distribution. This would at least provide wider representation and more balanced choices than the present system. To maximize effectiveness, the alliance of like-minded NNWS should cut across regions. Its primary function would be to act collectively to coordinate NNWS demands and juxtapose them against the dominant negotiating postures of the P-5. It would also undercut the manipulation of nuclear disarmament aspirations by some of the NWS or threshold states for their own purposes.

Although the sole multilateral negotiating forum, the CD should not be regarded as the only valid mechanism for international influence to achieve agreements and progress on nuclear arms control and disarmament. The first review PrepCom of the NPT enhanced review process, initiated in conjunction with the decision on indefinite extension last year, will take place in April 1997, and in subsequent years, leading up to the Sixth Review Conference in the year 2000. While this has no negotiating powers as such, NPT parties could identify steps to be undertaken by the P-5 through updating the principles and objectives agreed in 1995. With the capability of reviewing their progress on an almost annual basis, the NPT regime could thus constitute a very important multilateral mechanism to maintain pressure for unilateral, bilateral and P-5 arms reduction and elimination. If nuclear weapons were reduced among the P-5 with enhanced monitoring of their nuclear activities, it would increase the pressure on the hold-outs to sign multilateral agreements such as the CTBT or a fissban and place their facilities under appropriate international safeguards. This in turn could help develop momentum for the elimination of nuclear weapons, which could be codified in a nuclear weapon convention or similar treaty.

However, the NPT review process and principles and objectives are not legally binding, so their effectiveness will depend on the political will of the NPT parties to make them work. A symbiotic relationship between the NPT enhanced review process and multilateral negotiations in the CD could mitigate the structural short-comings of each, providing a pincer action to propel the declared and undeclared NWS towards the elimination of nuclear weapons.

NOTES

The author would like to thank Marie Chevrier and Amy Sands for helpful comments and suggestions.

1. Following its enlargement in June 1996, the CD now has sixty-one official members, but with Yugoslavia's seat under dispute, only sixty have the right to participate.
2. A fissile materials production ban ('fissban') was the subject of a consensus resolution of the United Nations General Assembly in Dec. 1993 (UNGA 48/75L). A mandate for this was

adopted by the CD in 1995 (CD/1299, 24 March 1995), and it was further endorsed as the second measure identified in the programme of action on nuclear disarmament, in the 'Principles and Objectives on Nuclear Non-Proliferation and Disarmament' adopted by NPT parties on 11 May 1995 (NPT/CONF.1995/L.5).

3. Nicholas Soames, Minister of State for the Armed Forces, Hansard 1097, 4 April 1995.
4. The term 'plurilateral' is used when a small number of states participate in negotiations which relate to weapons or technologies which they all possess. The term 'multilateral' denotes negotiations among a number of states representing the 'international community', when some but not all participants possess the weapons or technologies under discussion.
5. For the crucial first six months of 1995, the EU Presidency was with France, a nuclear weapon state, which made all significant public statements on behalf of the fifteen states and associated Eastern European applicant countries.
6. The declared NWS are called 'the P-5' because of their permanent seats on the UN Security Council, which predated nuclear possession by all except the United States.
7. CD/NTB/WP.222, March 1995.
8. CD/NTB/WP.244, June 1995, updated March 1996.
9. CD/NTB/WP.243, June 1995.
10. Off-the-record conversations with the author, 1995–96.
11. The sub-critical tests were subsequently postponed beyond 1996. Although 'technical reasons' were cited by the DOE, political considerations were probably the decisive factor.
12. Australia, Comprehensive Nuclear Test Ban Treaty, Model Treaty Text, CD/1386, and Explanatory Notes, CD/1387.
13. The conflict in Chechnya was treated as a civil war and an internal matter for Moscow.
14. Arundhati Ghose, Ambassador of India, 25 Jan. 1996, CD/PV.722.
15. John Holum, to the CD Plenary, 23 Jan. 1996, CD/PV.721.
16. 'Principles and Objectives on Nuclear Non-Proliferation and Disarmament' adopted by NPT parties on 11 May 1995 (NPT/CONF.1995/L.5).
17. 'Mandate for an ad hoc Committee on Nuclear Test Ban' adopted by the CD on 25 Jan. 1994, CD/1238.
18. Arundhati Ghose, Ambassador of India to CD plenary, 20 June 1996, CD/PV.740.
19. Sir Michael Weston, Ambassador of the United Kingdom, to the NTB Committee, informal discussions on 26 June 1996, reported to the author by several delegates on leaving the meeting, and subsequently confirmed with the principals.
20. Arundhati Ghose, 20 June 1996.
21. UNGA Resolution 48/75L.
22. Off-the-record clarification to the author made by a senior Israeli official at an international Conference on Non-Proliferation in Dec. 1996.
23. Report of Ambassador Gerald E. Shannon of Canada on 'Consultations on the Most Appropriate Arrangement to Negotiate a Treaty Banning the Production of Fissile Material for Nuclear Weapons or Other Explosive Devices', CD/1299, 24 March 1995.
24. Philippe Naughton, 'US officials pessimistic over test ban', Reuters, 9 April 1996.
25. Jozef Goldblat, *Arms Control: A Guide to Negotiations and Agreements* (Oslo: International Peace Research Institute, 1994), p.8.
26. CD/1419, 7 Aug. 1996. For more on this, see Rebecca Johnson, Geneva Update No.30, in *Disarmament Diplomacy*, No.7 (July/Aug. 1996).

The Impact of Governmental Context on Negotiation and Implementation: Constraints and Opportunities for Change

AMY SANDS

Introduction: A Holistic Approach to Governmental Decision-making

As new arms control and non-proliferation challenges emerge, the governmental process used to develop and implement strategies to address them will be critical for achieving success.[1] The ongoing attempt to develop and effectively implement appropriate policies is the crux of what governments do. Despite the many bright, well-intending souls in government, however, the strategies that emerge from this process are often ambiguous and poorly thought out. While these problems are not unique to arms control and non-proliferation initiatives, the particular reasons for their continual presence may be.

The case of the Chemical Weapons Convention (CWC) provides a clear example of how arms control treaties that appear to be non-controversial and to the benefit of all concerned can have trouble being ratified because of governmental context. Early in its first term, the Clinton administration's efforts to get the CWC ratified suffered from insufficient priority, inadequate interagency coordination, and overconfidence; later, it became entangled in partisan politics and continued to receive insufficient high-level attention until the final weeks before the ratification vote. The near failure of CWC ratification demonstrates not only the significance of 'governmental context' in the pursuit of arms control objectives, but also the lack of appreciation by the Clinton administration of this significance. All of the problems that besieged the CWC embody different aspects of the environment in which the government functions as it pursues arms control initiatives.

The governments' decision-making processes have long been a focus of research that has resulted in a wide array of theories, models, and case studies.[2] The generally employed decision-making models (the rational actor model, the organizational model, and the bureaucratic politics model) have pursued single-factor explanations that oversimplify a very complex, multifaceted process. Focusing on only one aspect of the overall environment eliminates or downplays other factors.[3] Because alternative decision-making models are derived from diverse theoretical conceptions about society, attempts to integrate them can be problematic. Yet, the failure to consider interconnections between factors identified by different types of model weakens the practical application of such approaches to policy-making.

Decision-making has always involved numerous factors that are interwoven in an intricate web of activities, events, bureaucracies, and personalities. Today, though, the issues to be decided are more complex and involve multiple, diverse parties. Conceptual frameworks need to move beyond single-factor analysis to provide a better understanding of how these new complexities affect decision-making. What is needed is a more synergistic, holistic approach to the study of decision-making, one that deals with not only all of the parts, but also the integration of the parts and their dynamic interface.

In an attempt to promote a more holistic approach, this essay delineates both the complexities of the current governmental context and the dynamic of interaction among the various factors. The examination will focus on the process as experienced while the author was an Assistant Director at the Arms Control and Disarmament Agency (ACDA) in an effort to provide a 'practical' building block for the development of an integrated theory of decision-making. The first step towards developing an enhanced conceptual framework will involve a general discussion of actors (their major features and those factors affecting them) and the process of arms control decision-making (planning, policy decision, implementation). Second, the essay will examine the United States arms control decision-making process, describing systemic problems and new challenges that emerge as issues play out within an American governmental context. Finally, the essay will provide recommendations designed to enhance United States government decision-making and to encourage more cooperative research. While the focus of these concluding comments is on leadership and constancy, underlying all of the suggestions is a need for revitalizing and rethinking how arms control and non-proliferation treaties are pursued and implemented.

Complexity of the Current Governmental Context

Actors

A critical 'block' in any decision-making theory must be the various organizational actors that play a role and have responsibilities in the arms control arena. While the arms control decision-making process in the United States is evolving, it currently contains the following actors:

1. National Security Council, the President's primary agent for ensuring the effective pursuit of his foreign policy agenda.
2. State Department, the principal foreign policy agency.

3. Arms Control and Disarmament Agency (ACDA), with the specific responsibility for advising and negotiating arms control and non-proliferation agreements.
4. On-Site Inspection Agency, with operational responsibility for implementing many arms control agreements.
5. Parts of the Defense Department and Energy Department, with the tasking and resources to develop enabling technologies and provide the expert personnel needed to implement many agreements.
6. Department of Defense military services, with the task of deterring, and where necessary countering, threats to national security.
7. Commerce Department, with the primary responsibility for dual-use export control policies and implementation as well as promotion of US trade and industry.
8. Intelligence Community, with its extensive network of intelligence organizations responsible for monitoring requirements and providing critical information about other states, capabilities and potential threats.
9. Congress, providing not only budget appropriation and authorization for initiatives, but also 'advice and consent' required for formal treaties to become the law of the land.
10. International actors, including allies, agreement partners, organizations, and individual leaders.
11. Special interest groups, including non-governmental organizations (such as the Nuclear Control Institute), academia, or defence contractors.
12. The media, including journalists, newspapers, freelance writers, and radio and TV newscasters.

As the list above reveals, the United States process involves an extensive number of diverse actors. Thus, determining who should be engaged in any one issue is a complex challenge, even without including the greater question of whose views should dominate discussions. Traditionally, the critical participants outside of the White House have been State, Defense, Energy, the Intelligence Community, and usually ACDA. The continuing battle between ACDA and the State Department over whose 'turf' covers arms control and non-proliferation continues, even while the Department of Defense increasingly has carved out a larger role for itself. Because many treaties affect United States military facilities and require significant resources for implementation, the Department of Defense currently plays a significant role via the On-Site Inspection Agency, the Defense Special Weapons Agency (formerly the Defense Nuclear Agency), and direct military-to-military activities. Meanwhile, initiatives such as the Cooperative Threat Reduction Program, the United States-North Korea Agreed Framework, and counter-terrorism have drawn the Commerce,

Treasury, and Justice Departments into the already complex arms control discussions. The chaos created by so many organizational actors is exacerbated because several organizations are often represented by more than one person at inter-agency meetings. Moreover, each of the government institutions mentioned above creates its own intricate microcosm with senior-appointed officials, civil service staff, organizational legacies and procedures, and overlapping internal and external jurisdictions.

The playing field is anything but level. The variance among agencies concerning available resources, access to the President, internal cohesion, effective leadership and management, and arms control expertise is extensive. Finally, except for ACDA, all of the other actors have responsibilities beyond arms control that affect the resources available and attention allocated to arms control activities.

All of these agencies vie for control of the arms control agenda. In the first Clinton administration, this conflict provided opponents of arms control with ammunition, and at times made reaching and implementing decisions more difficult. Given the number of actors and the complexity of the interrelationships, it is a testament to the foresight and dedication of those concerned that this arms control paradigm has yielded the many treaties, agreements and confidence-building measures in effect or currently under negotiation.

Outside of the Executive Branch, individuals and non-governmental activists lobby officials in the Executive Branch as well as in Congress. During the final year of negotiations on the Comprehensive Test Ban Treaty (CTBT), representatives from non-governmental organizations (NGOs) sought out ACDA officials, formally and informally, to press for specific positions and continued, intensive negotiations. Moreover, it is not only the Executive Branch that is lobbied. Congress' role in authorizing and appropriating funds and the Senate's special responsibilities for approving international treaties provide the legislative branch with influence in the arms control decision-making process, thereby opening it to lobbying attempts as well. During the week prior to the scheduled votes on the CWC, outsiders actively lobbied senators and their staffs in an effort to prevent the treaty's ratification.

A final actor is the news media. This element of the political environment rarely acts in a proactive way. In fact, since the news media can only react to events, treaty negotiations, issued reports, policy discussions or statements, it may be manipulated by the actors involved directly in arms control activities. One of the major ways the news media plays a role is by leaking classified or confidential information relating to discussions/negotiations. William Gertz of the *Washington Times* often appeared to be on the distribution list for classified cables relating to the negotiations with the Russians about the Anti-Ballistic Missile (ABM) Treaty. His publication of these materials made negotiations more difficult in the following three ways:

1. the Russians were wary of exchanging confidential information for fear it might end up in the public arena prematurely;
2. the number of actors involved in any discussions where leaks regularly occurred had to be severely limited; and
3. key officials became overly sensitive to press reactions.

These reactions to press leaks weaken national security decision-making, specifically as it relates to arms control issues. Critical experts may not be brought into discussions, there may not be much discussion, and what little discussion there is may focus on how the media will 'misuse' the decision, rather than how national security objectives are affected.

Factors Affecting the Actors

The role and significance of the organizational actors described above are determined by a variety of factors whose impact will differ according to time and organization. A good example of this phenomenon involves ACDA, which was severely hamstrung during much of FY 1996 because of the uncertainty over its budget. The Department of Defense with its much larger revenue pool was less affected. While some portion of an organization's power is the result of its size and resources, its access to the President and/or Congress, as well as the quality of its leadership, are equally important. Since these factors do not normally function in an isolated context, the dynamic between them is an important piece of the governmental context. In the brief discussion that follows, some of these factors, their interactions, and their effects on the decision-making process are highlighted.

Resources and Time Pressure. Resources and time significantly impact decision-making capabilities and quality. They can be independent factors, but more often are intertwined. Organizations with substantial resources can more easily overcome time constraints. When time becomes a critical factor, the organizations with greater resources can be more effective because of their ability to put on a 'full court press'. Smaller organizations tend to be more adept at reacting to changing circumstances, but they may not be able to maintain their involvement. Arms control negotiations and implementation efforts may be more affected than others by time and resource constraints because of the centrality of substantive experience and technical expertise to success.

Recognizing that few senior officials have the time to be involved directly in the planning phase, it is worth discussing how resources and time affect what little is done. For the best results, an effective leader should assign to a trusted staff member the responsibility for drafting a strategy once the overall objectives have been defined. Unfortunately, senior officials, and especially the President, may not find it helpful to have clearly articulated objectives; therefore, a staff member may be working with ambiguous directions. If planning is meant to examine issues such as:

- what kind of decisions are needed,
- what changes might have to be considered,
- what decisions to avoid,
- what are the outer bounds for discussions, and
- what compromises should be prepared for,

then a lack of time and resources may result in insufficient planning for contingencies and inadequate substantive grounding. In addition, if time pressures do not permit adequate consideration of alternatives, then an arms control negotiator may find himself without the proper materials or preparations to craft a response or initiate new venues for agreement.

Resources play a critical role in determining how much power organizations bring to the table and how much effort they can put towards pushing their views. Just being able to send participants to most inter-agency and/or international meetings requires a large number of trained personnel. During much of 1995–96, when ACDA suffered without a budget, its ability to fulfil its arms control responsibilities was endangered. Several trips and activities were postponed and participation in international meetings was significantly reduced. At one point ACDA decided not to send its representative on a critical visit to Moscow and Europe for discussions about Conventional Armed Forces in Europe Treaty (CFE) compliance issues, leaving it on the margins of these discussions for some time.

Decisions involving physical activities and the commitment of physical resources, such as those relating to on-site inspections or other forms of monitoring of arms control agreements, give an edge to the Defense (DoD) and Energy Departments (DoE) that have operational resources. When decisions involve policy strategy in general terms, then players with substantive credibility, political links, and arms control experience will be more likely to dominate a decision-making process. Individuals such as Paul Nitze, Jim Timbie (a senior State Department official), and Jim Goodby exemplify this type of influential arms control expert.

Personality. Another factor which affects organizational actors is the personalities of key individuals. The influence of personality changes considerably over time, as the key players change or mature in their positions. When linked to organizational power, bureaucratic setting, and Presidential access, personality can be a central determinant of an individual's effectiveness in the arms control decision-making process.

The effect of personality on the decision-making process was evident in the diverse styles and resulting tensions between the National Security Advisor and the Secretary of State under Presidents Nixon and Carter.[4] Personalities clearly played a major role in these conflicts, and probably limited the role of Secretary of State Rogers. As Henry Kissinger himself described it, 'Upon reflection [Secretary of State William] Rogers was too proud, I intellectually too arrogant, and we were both too insecure to compose personal differences.'[5] Paul Nitze provides a more positive example where personality was central to the successful development and negotiation of arms control initiatives.[6] His strength of commitment, attention to detail, clear strategic vision, and perseverance gave him credibility and access to several American presidents. These personal traits secured him a central role in most of the strategic arms control negotiations during the Cold War. The force of personality was also crucial to Assistant Secretary of State Richard Holbrook's successes in transforming the Bosnian conflict from a military engagement into an arms control and political process. His aggressive and dogged nature combined with an unyielding and personalized involvement were clearly vital ingredients during the negotiations in Dayton, Ohio.

Leadership skills must also be recognized as an important aspect of an individual's personality. Substantive and managerial expertise are critical to effective arms control decision-making. Unfortunately, most political appointees do not come with all of the skills needed to succeed as both substantive and managerial leaders. In fact, many have little managerial expertise or appropriate experience, such as congressional staffers or academics. In addition, most senior officials are not very interested in managing an organization, much less a process. This is not what drew them into the government, and it is not what will be remembered. Finally, many do not stay long enough to develop the credibility within the critical bureaucratic and political circles required to be an effective manager. The average stay in government is eighteen months, just enough time to learn the job and gain some experience, but not enough to become a skilled bureaucratic player and substantive expert.[7]

Participation. As the decision-making process evolves and the arms control activity is developed, players' involvement may also evolve. Organizations as well as their leaders may decide to opt in or out of an arms control decision process. The decision whether or not 'to play' will revolve around:

1. time and energy required,
2. effect on reputation with the President or other significant political players, such as Congress or even the news media,
3. cost to personal relationship with the President,
4. possibility of alienating other organizations, and
5. concept of the organization's and/or one's own role.[8]

In some cases, organizations may not be given a choice about their participation: they may be excluded purposely because of concerns about too much bureaucratic politicking, news media leaks, or policy resistance.

The involvement of organizations and individuals may also reflect shrewd calculations about the optimal time to weigh in. Bureaucrats often believe that decisions need to work their way through various traditional phases of deliberation before senior officials become engaged. Senior officials may be advised not to compromise too early in the process for fear of giving up too much. As an Assistant Director at ACDA, this author was more than once told it was too soon to weigh in with a possible compromise. Thus, decisions that would appear clear-cut if political appointees all met can languish in junior inter-agency manoeuvring. Staff at these lower-level meetings have insufficient authority to resolve thorny problems and have little incentive to develop constructive compromises. This approach to decision-making, which seems to mimic the way the United States and the Soviet Union/Russia negotiate arms control agreements, is not efficient. While the delay caused by such tactics may be deliberate, it may also reflect an organization's overload or indecisiveness about how to proceed, just as it often does in international arms control negotiations.

Characteristics of the Governmental Context

While the actors and the factors which may be affecting them remain at the core of the arms control decision-making process, there are other aspects of the governmental context that intervene, such as the flow of information and the timing of events. Each of these features can play an important role, but rarely do situations call into play only one of them. Thus, these intervening variables, which are constant aspects of the environment in which arms control decision-making takes place, may be critical throughout the decision-making process. A skilled decision-maker may use them to push the process towards his desired outcome or to impede progress. These features, though basically embodying the trends of the larger societal context, may play a more significant role in arms control because they can impede a thorough, expert examination of issues and options.

One extremely important feature of the environment is information flow. Information overload is a basic characteristic: there is always more to read, analyse, and comment on than can be considered effectively. There is a well-known quip about the number of trees that have fallen in the service of the country because of the paperwork generated to support new initiatives or pursue old ones. Consequently, the challenge for decision-makers is to ensure that they not only do not drown in this flood of information, but that they see what is needed.

Another challenge emerging from the excessive information flow involves being able to absorb effectively and efficiently information. Since a senior official relies on staff, it becomes critical to work with the staff to define goals clearly; to assign responsibility for information acquisition, evaluation, and organization; and most importantly, to take the time to provide feedback on materials developed. With proper management and substantive expertise, a senior official can organize himself and his staff so as to present the information constructively, filter out unneeded materials, and provide a coherent, focused packet of information. When I first arrived at ACDA as an Assistant Director, I had never had such an extensive staff available to me. Several awkward, and at times painful, months passed before I understood what I wanted from this staff and what they could realistically provide. A related problem involves ensuring access to information in a timely way. It is not uncommon for agencies such as ACDA to hear about critical papers second-hand and to have to use 'under-the-table means' to obtain them. Talking points and associated papers for presidential summit meetings or other senior meetings provide opportunities to cut or be cut out of the information loop until it is too late to influence the outcome. Having some way to obtain and consolidate information, then evaluate its significance is a critical skill for effective decision-making.

A second feature of the governmental context is domestic politics, whether it be election-year concerns or the continual wrestling with domestic priorities for attention. Within the first Clinton administration, it was recognized that the President had campaigned and won the 1992 election on domestic issues and that his experience in dealing with foreign policy, especially arms control, was limited. Clinton's closest advisers and inner circle tended to consist of people whose focus and own experiences were in domestic politics. Thus, it was hard to win and then maintain presidential attention for an issue beyond a given meeting, speech, or event.

Another aspect of the domestic political context which influences the outcome of decisions is the context at the time of an event. If a critical vote on the Cooperative Threat Reduction Program were about to happen, the key to winning that vote may be reaching some agreement with the Russians on Strategic Arms Reduction Treaty (START I) implementation or inspections involving chemical weapons production facilities. In addition, the advent of domestic elections may affect the type of negotiations that are pursued and the intensity of the commitment to finding an agreement. During 1996, when the Russians and the United States had presidential elections, few controversial issues were put on the table after the American primaries ended in the Spring. On the other hand, many felt that the Clinton administration pressed to reach agreement on the CTBT so it could be used as part of Clinton's re-election campaign.

Efforts can be made to control the timing of such events so that external events have minimal effect or are exploited to the fullest degree possible. Unfortunately the CWC was initially scheduled for a vote near the end of the American presidential elections. It clearly ran foul of presidential politics. Bob Dole's statement that he did not endorse the current version of the CWC – despite it being a treaty promoted and drafted by previous Republican administrations – forced the Democrats to delay the Senate's vote for fear of a defeat. Apparently, the Dole campaign could not afford to give the President such a 'foreign policy' victory so close to election day.[9] Perhaps with better management of the CWC ratification process in its earlier stages, this regrettable timing problem might have been avoided. What the CWC demonstrates, though, is that taking care of timing requires continuous and extensive managing of the decision-making process, a feat that is increasingly hard for senior leaders already overwhelmed by the burden of daily schedules.

The Dynamics of the Decision-Making and Implementation Process

The nature of the process is rarely clear-cut, and it does not unfold very precisely. Thus, while an initiative might have begun because a President mentioned it during a speech, its chance of success depends on continued high-level attention and a supportive organizational infrastructure. As the decision-making process moves from planning to deciding, organizational and bureaucratic issues can become predominant. In the planning phase, the key players may have been a small group or even an individual – perhaps selected to do the planning because of organizational, bureaucratic or political ties. During the decision phase, the numbers of players increase and the structure and procedures of involved organizations come into play, thereby opening the way for 'politicking' between various bureaucratic players. As Dr Steve Miller of Harvard University's Center for Science and International Affairs explained:

> ... arms control proposals are usually the result of internal bargaining. Consequently, deliberations are slow and changing proposals can be difficult. Considerable time and effort must be spent overcoming bureaucratic stand-offs and adjudicating internal disputes. Second, in

these internal negotiations, some participants often have to be bought off – their positions accommodated [in the proposal] or their sacrifices in one area made up in another. Third, losers in the process need not give up. They can oppose or circumvent restrictions, take their case to the public, or air their disagreements before Congress – in short, broaden the fight to the ratification phase, having lost it internally. Such tactics will inevitably obstruct the smooth passage to a signed and ratified agreement. Fourth, internal critics will usually have to be paid for their public support of the treaty, as was the case, for example, with SALT I, where Secretary of Defense Laird and the Joint Chiefs of Staff made administration support of a broad program of strategic modernization the fairly explicit condition of their support of the treaty.[10]

Decision-making in the Executive Branch is by nature a 'composite' of many sources. President Franklin Roosevelt, perhaps one of the best leaders to understand the complexity of decision-making, was 'forever weighing questions of personal force, of political timing, of congressional concerns, of partisan benefit, of public interest'.[11] Organizations will be more or less influential because of their abilities to integrate simultaneously many key elements, such as: gaining the confidence of the President or his key advisers; accepting responsibility for action; threatening negative results, resignation, or leaks of information; skills of their supporting staff; and organizing support outside of the government. These items reflect a combination of many factors including: personality, personal capabilities, organizational resources, political connections and skills, and bureaucratic positioning.

The chaos of the process provides both its strengths and weaknesses: it is sensitive to strong leadership, vulnerable to assertive personalities and stubbornness by individuals and organizations, and open to potentially unending decision-making. Strong leadership may involve the guiding hand of a president over all or some aspects of the decision-making process, or it may involve his delegation of authority to a close advisor. Ongoing senior-level attention ensures that initiatives do not get off-track, derailed, or lost amongst other priorities. One of the reasons for the first Clinton administration's inconsistent record on arms control (strong on treaties such as the Non-Proliferation Treaty (NPT) and CTBT but weak on chemical and biological weapon issues) was its inability, or unwillingness to deliver continuing high-level attention and direction. Despite its recognized significance to the non-proliferation efforts, even the effort to get the NPT extended indefinitely initially did not have the span of activities and senior level involvement needed to succeed. Until the final six months before the

Review and Extension Conference, a small group of dedicated government officials at ACDA had to carry the load of extensive foreign travel, development of position papers, and coordination of inter-agency, non-governmental, congressional, and international activities. Only once it became apparent that a concerted, well-coordinated effort would be necessary to save the treaty, much less indefinitely extend it, did the State Department and the White House seriously join ACDA's efforts with both resources and focused attention. The result was a resounding victory.

The process itself, however, works against rewarding clarity. Especially early in a process, it is not advantageous for decision-makers to make clear their goals and methods. Such information can be used by bureaucrats or outsiders to delay or derail their efforts. Although clarity of purpose is always important when trying to implement a decision, it may prevent various parties from reaching agreement on a decision.[12] Thus, a bit of ambiguity and lack of detail may be the only way to make progress; the battle over the specifics will be re-engaged when the agreement is being implemented.

Once a decision has been agreed, implementation becomes crucial if a hard-fought policy battle is ever to reach its objectives. The dichotomy that may have existed at one time between decision-makers and implementers does not exist in today's world. The two roles are intertwined by necessity: the decision-maker needs to ensure that a policy is not only decided upon, but also is accurately implemented. Once again the forces of personality, leadership and management, organizational structure and procedures, and bureaucratic politics come into play. Faithful implementation may be hindered by uncertainty about what was agreed to, a lack of resources, or the resistance of bureaucrats or even senior leaders to do what they were ordered to do. If such problems are not addressed, the original decision may never be implemented or may be delayed until it is altered or reversed.[13]

Many are concerned that as arms control treaties are being implemented they will be altered or weakened. For example, as the signatories to the CWC have discussed the details of verification activities, several countries appear interested in diminishing the intrusiveness of the CWC's obligations as they negotiated the specifics of verification procedures, equipment and protocols. The implementation of START I by the United States also has revealed some of the problems that must be resolved both within the United States government as well as negotiated with treaty signatories, in this case the Russians. Organizations with aggressive leaders or substantial responsibility for implementation will dominate this process. Thus, despite its legislative responsibility for overall treaty compliance, ACDA cannot require the Defense Department to provide it with access to the DoD's decisions and plans concerning compliance with arms control agreements. ACDA's only hope is to obtain strong and extensive help from the National

Security Council as well as the State Department. Currently, when Russia objects to how the United States permits access to Russian inspectors during on-site START I inspections, the DoD is the only source of information and its evaluation tends to dominate any inter-agency meetings held to discuss Russian official complaints. Review of procedures for such inspections is limited to DoD, so problems that might be foreseen are not discussed outside of DoD until after a Russian objection is lodged.

The continuing inter-agency discussions over Intermediate Range Nuclear Forces (INF) and START I implementation and compliance issues are really internal 'negotiations'. Some have described such a process unfortunately as 'satisficing',[14] in which the lowest common denominator becomes the solution. These internal discussions, while often bitterly fought, result in a thorough review of options and an evolutionary process that eventually develops a realistic approach. Thus, answers reached may not be perfect, but they do reflect what is achievable within the United States government (and often include congressional concerns) and thought to be reasonable to foreign counterparts. While it would be tempting to press for the ideal decision, often time, resources, and other issues require decisions to be made even when they are acknowledged to be incomplete or less than perfect.

How smoothly and effectively players reach decisions may be significantly influenced by the force of presidential leadership either directly or through his ability to control his senior political appointees. Presidents have employed many leadership styles,[15] as they struggled to control their bureaucracies.[16] The President, however, may not be able to impose, untouched, his plans on the Executive Branch except in times of crisis. Without a strong presidential hand (directly or indirectly), the process may be dominated by the 'heavy hitters' in the bureaucracy, may bog down, or get off-track. Moreover, attention to implementation of issues usually comes only after an embarrassing event occurs, such as when Russia issued high-level objections to United States interpretations of on-site inspection protocols. Because these issues may cause tension in United States-Russian relations, the focus is on solving the immediate issue and putting aside until later the underlying problem. Once the crisis is passed, there is neither time nor inclination to examine the larger issue, because the next crisis needing attention has already emerged.

The Governmental Context and Future Arms Control Challenges

Determining how the components of the decision-making framework discussed above fit with the current arms control paradigm involves a brief review of the evolution of arms control and its current characteristics. Prior to the Second World War, arms accords had, for the most part, been gentlemen's agreements in which signatories pledged to abide by provisions without intrusive monitoring and verification. Implementation was simpler, since it did not involve much more than declarations with each party being responsible for fulfilling its obligations. Parties to agreements relied on the political ethos of the times that stressed sovereign rights and diplomacy, not extensive, intrusive verification efforts.

After the Second World War, two changes emerged in thinking about arms control. First was the change symbolized in the 1946 'Baruch Plan' to control nuclear weapons and the development of atomic energy. It changed 'trust' to 'verify' by proposing an international authority with power to license, control, manage, and inspect and by providing for production termination, weapon destruction, data sharing, and sanctions. More importantly, as the Cold War set in, and states no longer trusted each other to comply with agreements, the political context required more than a gentleman's agreement if arms control efforts were to proceed. Progress was needed both in technical and political arenas for effective arms control to be feasible.

At the beginning of the post-Second World War era of arms control, on-site inspections, local monitoring, or cooperative measures were unacceptable to one or other of the parties. Significant progress on arms control issues stalled until the level of technological capabilities for national technical means (NTM) permitted some verifiability for limited arms control objectives. Until the 1980s, the United States and the Soviet Union based arms control verification on NTM, but it was increasingly apparent that future arms control agreements would require more intrusive means of verification if they were to provide the security guarantee required.

What has changed in the arms control equation in the last decade is the diversity and complexity of the threat. No longer is it principally one of bilateral nuclear confrontation. Countries, once sure of security arrangements developed to counter the threat of Soviet expansion and ideology, are making the transition to a more fluid and uncertain security context. Now the threat may be multifaceted and multinational, and may emerge from multiple, varied sources that include states as well as sub-national terrorist groups. The technological sophistication and physical dimensions of the threats to global and national security appear to have multiplied at the same time as societal vulnerabilities increased. Fortunately, the technical precision, accuracy, and capabilities to counter these threats are also multiplying.

Those technological changes, however, have not been the only factors to change in the equation. The parties have undergone a concomitant change in attitude. As the Cold War began to wane, more intrusive arms control agreements became possible. With the advent of INF, CFE, and START, on-site inspection and cooperative measures became integral components of arms control discussions and negotiated verification regimes. These agreements also reflect the shift from bilateral to multilateral arms control agreements. Agreements such as CWC, CTBT, and START II continue this trend towards responding to an increasingly complex and diverse threat with complex and diverse arms control agreements.

Broad-based multilateral agreements addressing the global threat of proliferation face at least five new complications compared to the US-Soviet agreements of the Cold War. First, the technology base of the participants is radically disparate, so multilateral arms control cannot rely exclusively on NTM or on the advanced technological capabilities of institutional multilateral verification. Second, because these agreements rely more on 'transparency' and a panoply of political pressures to secure the cooperation of states, they require constant attention and an intrusive openness that most states see as challenging their sovereign rights. Third, the strategic views, positions, and needs of the participants vary widely. Fourth, the agreements must ensure that the inherent intrusiveness of the agreement does not undermine the political will to follow through with the commitments made to vigorous implementation. Expanding verification capabilities must keep ahead of evasion methods through the appropriate combination of on-site inspections, data exchanges, cooperative measures, NTM monitoring, and conflict-resolution fora. Finally, the issues to be addressed during arms control negotiations as frequently involve economic concerns as military ones. Without economic incentives for North Korea, Ukraine or Russia, certain aspects of recent arms control agreements and treaties might not have been so successfully accomplished. Developing policies in this very uncertain and varied international context adds another layer to the already 'thick' fog created by the United States governmental context.

The response to these changes in the threat to world security is being played out against a domestic context that suffers not only from a bewildering organizational mosaic, but also from a lack of public interest and understanding as well as a lack of a consensus on foreign policy priorities and strategies. There continues to be a wide divergence of opinion about the value of arms control to national security. Consequently, discussions can become bogged down in ideological debates between entrenched proponents of conflicting viewpoints.

Furthermore, arms control, as a sub-set of foreign policy, does not have a large, active public that closely monitors every activity and commands the requisite attention and commitment from Congress and the Executive Branch. While numerous non-governmental organizations are active players, they do not have extensive public support. It remains true that while foreign policy will rarely win an election, a foreign policy disaster can lose one. Thus, arms control is often seen as only having a down side for domestic political purposes. In addition, arms control often involves technical and arcane military issues and political concerns that make it difficult to engage the public, except infrequently or during a crisis. Trying to interest the public in what to pursue, how to pursue it, and whether or not to care if it is pursued is a challenge that needs to be better addressed. Public concern and outrage may be the most effective way of gaining the attention and commitment needed from Congress and the Executive Branch.

Finally, it is unlikely that Congress, the President, and specific departments of the Executive Branch could agree today on what is in the 'national security interest'. The ongoing bitter and controversial debate about ballistic missile defences and the value of the Anti-Ballistic Missile Treaty reveal just one such deep divide. Another example is provided by the CTBT, which several presidents (Eisenhower, Kennedy, Carter, and Clinton) perceived as being in America's national interest, although some members of Congress, the Republican party, and individuals in the Pentagon and at the national weapons labs are not convinced.[17] The interpretation of this term 'national security' results from individual beliefs, attitudes, and experiences, and thus will vary widely. If the CTBT is ever to be ratified by the Senate, these parties will have to reach enough of an agreed concept of national interests to allow two-thirds of them to give their 'advice and consent'. While such an accomplishment may currently appear insurmountable, with proper planning, consistent high-level leadership, and time to work issues of concern, it is within reach.

Pursuing Today's Arms Control Agenda with Today's Governmental Context

Trying to plan, fashion, and negotiate multilateral and increasingly multifaceted arms control agreements would be difficult if there were only one organization with centralized leadership. But, as is clear from the discussion above, the United States has an ever more difficult task because of its complicated, and often cumbersome decision-making process. Given the number of potential stakeholders and actors in any one arms control negotiation, this process will not easily be made flexible, creative, innovative, or open to newcomers – all characteristics increasingly important to successful arms controls activities. When the already dense and complex United States governmental context is added to the increasingly intricate international context, questions arise as to how well prepared the United States is to deal with such challenges.

Several aspects of the governmental context described above create barriers that prevent today's arms control agenda from being adequately addressed. First, the Executive Branch and Congress traditionally do not have a similar set of organizational and personal needs; their basic assumptions differ, making it hard to find common ground. The recent increasingly partisan nature of discussions revolving around arms control issues and the diverse new set of threats have caused additional problems. While members of Congress had become comfortable with many of the bilateral strategic issues involved in United States and Soviet arms control discussions, today's agenda includes not only these, but also new issues. These include the worldwide spread and possible use of chemical, biological, or nuclear weapons about which most members of Congress are neither knowledgeable nor focused.

Second, most decision-makers face an uphill battle in defining and then obtaining agreement on concerns. For various reasons, seniors leaders may not provide clear goals or ones that can be easily put into effect; nor can they take the time to explore adequately all of the options, or read all of the materials and information available. Finally, they probably will not be available to provide consistent and credible leadership. The result may be an on-again/off-again effort, with insufficient analysis and planning, and inadequate substantive depth. As arms control agreements become more complex and multifaceted, a participant with a strong staff, good management skills, steady commitment and involvement will significantly dominate the substance, direction, and timing of discussions. Such leadership, though, will be hard to sustain given limited resources and other pressing events; moreover, it may not be constructive if it moves the decision-making process in a direction contrary to the President's goals.

Third, because of the speed and ease of communications and travel, arms control negotiations appear to have no end, moving from formal discussions to *ad hoc* meetings to meetings with allies and other subgroups, and on and on. The fast pace often means that a small group of 'fellow travellers' and their agencies dominate the decision-making process that may be taking place on airplanes and in hotel rooms late at night. While the modern age with its electronic communications and overnight travel to Asia and Europe may facilitate direct discussions with foreign participants, it severely hampers the ability to maintain tight control and a broad bureaucratic consensus since the 'fellow travellers' represent only a few of the concerned agencies and quickly get beyond their original 'talking points' during their sojourn.

Fourth, the massive burden of available information forces senior officials to rely increasingly on their staff, who themselves have to be selective about what they choose to read and consider. One effect of this is that a senior official cannot easily become an on-the-spot expert. Thus decisions, if made without sufficient time for a solid briefing, may be done without adequate information and thought. A second effect is that an official becomes overly dependent on staff for both information and advice. An official can only be as prepared as his staff makes him, so that there is the possibility that he may not be aware of relevant information. In addition, it is easy for bureaucrats to lose sight of the substantive issues. Their focus on the bureaucratic process may make it difficult for the decision-maker to refocus on the substantive issues. Finally, information that might lead to innovative approaches to an arms control negotiation may not be actively sought without significant pressure from senior leaders. Creative thinking does not normally emerge from standard operating procedures or bureaucracies.

Fifth, the proliferation of actors (such as Treasury, Commerce, and Justice) and inter-agency groups required to address new types of arms control needs (such as those dealing with counter-proliferation, counter-terrorism, and the former Soviet Union) have added to an already crowded 'stage'. At a time when the international context may demand more innovation and concerted leadership, the United States may be moving towards an organizational arms control structure that is more diffuse and diverse. Without strong central leadership, discipline will be hard to maintain among the bureaucracies. Controversial decisions may be reopened, the largest agencies will tend to dominate arms control discussions and implementation activities, and endless squabbles will arise over 'turf' issues.

Finally, implementation is coming to the forefront in arms control activities without the United States government, both within the Executive Branch and the Congress, being adequately organized to deal with it. Implementation usually entails re-negotiating aspects of a treaty as the reality of inspections, data exchanges, and data analysis emerges. Although these issues may appear technical, they rest on significant political agreements and deals which require careful discussion and analysis before being modified. Yet, technical experts not only provide the options, but also may drive the decisions. Senior political input may come late, after much time has been wasted discussing technical options that are politically unacceptable or unrealistic. In addition, several agencies may now perceive themselves as having direct responsibility for implementation of the same agreement. For example, despite ACDA's place as the 'national authority' in the CWC's implementing legislation, Commerce Department and the On-Site Inspection Agency claim significant roles for themselves in terms of industry and military facilities. Without clear and consistent support from the White House in implementation discussions, the early phases of implementation of this treaty could become chaotic inside the United States government. A similar problem may emerge once the CTBT enters into force.

Future arms control initiatives may be in trouble if the world is looking to the United States primarily for creativity, flexibility, and leadership. The current decision-making structure, with its increasing number of players, time pressures, and information overload, is not conducive to developing the new approaches required to plan and pursue new arms control initiatives, as well as to implement them.

While many of the features of today's arms control decision-making process are not well suited to the demands of today's arms control agenda, there exist positive aspects that may provide the basis for constructive change. The current process provides a mechanism, albeit imperfect, for the development of policy options, which can then be actively debated and explored. While information may be inadequate and objectives ambiguous, participants have an opportunity to present their positions. The effect of such an approach is twofold: first, it slows down the process and allows additional time for information-gathering and analysis; and second, it forces participants to negotiate with each other and try to find common ground. Even if that is never quite accomplished, it leads to a broader consensus, a hearing for opponents, and an understanding of pitfalls to watch for during actual negotiations and the implementation phase. As George Bunn, a recognized arms control expert, noted in his book about negotiating with the Russians, 'the interagency committee, more than the others helped presidents decide what sort of measures to support by providing a forum for debate and by supplying information on popular, congressional, or allied reactions'.[18] With leadership that centralizes efforts and recognizes the holistic nature of the process, there is still hope that the United States arms control agenda can be responsive to the new demands caused by a multinational, multifaceted arms control agenda.

Conclusion: A Look to the Future

Several conclusions and recommendations emerge from this analysis. First, the argument presented in the introduction was that standard rational actor, organizational, and bureaucratic politics models provide an insufficient explanation for how the United States government functions, especially in the area of arms control. None captures the entire set of factors involved, and thus none provides the practitioner a useful conceptual framework. This study has attempted to begin the process of identifying factors that need to be included in a broader conceptual framework as it relates to arms control. Many of the issues, characteristics, features, and factors discussed need additional analysis, but the general point that all these 'phenomena' make up the governmental context central to the decision-making process remains valid. For a practitioner, what is useful is having an understanding of all factors that might affect his success, that is, a holistic rather than fragmentary analysis. Such an approach will not lead to a simplified model; but, by providing a more comprehensive one, it will provide a more useful one.

Second, much could be gained by a comparative analysis of 'governmental contexts'. With more information becoming available about Soviet/Russian internal discussions, and leaders, as well as other countries' bureaucracies and decision-makers, it may be an opportune time to explore questions about the roles of leaders, bureaucrats, outsiders, and others. A broad study of several countries which analyses the presence, as well as significance, of certain actors and features would provide insights into the decision-making process in general and the unique features of arms control decision-making. Such studies might also lead to creative ideas about how to overcome some of the constraints and barriers common to all participants and thus help develop more effective arms control mechanisms.

Third, if the United States is to continue to be a leader in arms control initiatives, it will have to change the way it does business. Senior political leaders will need to renew their interest in arms control initiatives. Arms control must be acknowledged as an ongoing and extensive process that requires the attention of senior leaders in both the Executive Branch and Congress. Decisions cannot be made *ad hoc*, because without strategic leadership ongoing arms control efforts are too easily deflected, undercut, or stymied. If the agencies recognize that a high value is being placed on the pursuit of arms control decisions (perhaps because the President takes personal charge of top-level meetings or selects key personnel), then there is less opportunity for organizational issues and bureaucratic conflicts to impede progress on the President's arms control agenda. It is also important to reverse the decline in Congressional arms control expertise and interest. If arms control agreements are to be approved and funded adequately, then more Congressional leaders and their staffs must become better informed about the complex set of concerns and policies that arms control agreements involve.

Another issue that needs to be addressed is the quality of arms control staffing. Senior political leaders with responsibility for the arms control agenda need to have sufficient standing within the government, the arms control community, and/or the President's inner circle to be able to demand and receive rapid access to the highest levels of the government. In addition, staffing needs to be adequate and provided to those organizations taking the lead on activities. Staff should also be experienced in the technical and political aspects of negotiations. In order to attract the ongoing involvement of the best staff, agencies such as State and Defense will need to attach more importance to arms control negotiations and implementation activities; agencies that are newer to the arms control arena such as Treasury and Justice will also have to be encouraged – again by senior political leaders – to see the value of assigning high-quality personnel to arms control discussions. Given the increasing demands of today's arms control agenda and context, a lack of technical, managerial, and substantive expertise may limit United States preparations and capabilities to pursue initiatives to a successful conclusion. Since other states are unlikely to provide such resources or leadership, faltering by the United States could severely limit future arms control efforts.

A final area for change involves the bureaucracy and has two aspects. First, the way the bureaucracy is organized to support arms control needs to be re-examined with as fresh and as neutral an eye as possible. The decision to merge ACDA into the State Department should not preclude more comprehensive efforts to re-design the entire United States arms control paradigm. Starting with a blank sheet, how should the United States be organized to ensure that the appropriate agencies are involved, that the necessary short- and long-term planning gets done, and that creativity and innovation are rewarded? Second, the mind-set of those currently involved with arms control activities may need a rude shock. Staffs, probably with extensive oversight from senior management, will have to recognize the interdependence and symbiosis of their efforts and try to problem-solve rather than protect their 'turf'.

As this essay has argued, the arms control decision-making process is dependent upon the effective functioning of bureaucracies, organizations, and people. In order to improve the quality of arms control agreements and their implementation, all three will have to promote better leadership and interagency communication, cooperation, and even collaboration. Behind this effort must reside a strong commitment to the value of arms control, as a means of both reducing threats to United States national security and building a strong, stable international community.

NOTES

Although the views presented here are solely those of the author, I would like to thank the following people for giving me feedback on my ideas and helping in the production of this article: Nancy W. Gallagher, Coit D. Blacker, R. Stephen Day, Debra Miller, O.J. Sheaks, Cheryl Bengston, and Peter Saracino.

1. The term 'arms control' will be used to refer to both arms control and non-proliferation efforts, initiatives, agreements and treaties.
2. Examples of articles and books on governmental decision-making include: John Steinbruner, *The Cybernetic Theory of Decision* (Princeton: Princeton University Press, 1974); Graham

T. Allison, *Essence of Decision: Explaining the Cuban Missile Crisis* (Boston: Little, Brown & Co., 1971); Richard Neustadt, *Presidential Power: The Politics of Leadership* (London: John Wiley & Sons, 1960); Morton H. Halperin, *Bureaucratic Politics & Foreign Policy* (Washington, DC: The Brookings Institution, 1974); Louis C. Gawthrop, *Bureaucratic Behavior in the Executive Branch: An Analysis of Organizational Change* (New York: The Free Press, 1969); and Francis E. Rourke, *Bureaucratic Power in National Policy Making* (Boston, Toronto: Little, Brown, 1986).

3. Two examples of analyses critical of Graham Allison's work are: David A. Welch, 'The Organizational Process and Bureaucratic Politics Paradigms: Retrospect and Prospect', *International Security*, Vol.17, No.2 (1992), pp.112–45; and Jonathan Bevdor and Thomas H. Hammond, 'Rethinking Allison's Models', *American Political Science Review*, Vol.86, No.2 (1992), pp.301–22.

4. Henry Kissinger, *White House Years* (Boston: Little, Brown, 1971), pp.27–9, 30.

5. Terry Deibel, 'Of Presidents and Bureaucrats: A Look at Bureaucratic Politics through the Eyes of National Security Decision-makers', in David C. Kozak and James M. Keagle, *Bureaucratic Politics and National Security: Theory & Practice* (Boulder, CO and London: Lynne, Reinner Publishers, 1988), p.98.

6. Strobe Talbott, *The Master of the Game: Paul Nitze and the Nuclear Peace* (New York: Alfred A. Knopf, 1988), pp.4–19.

7. James W. Fesler, 'Policymaking at the Top of Bureaucracy', in Rourke, *Bureaucratic Power*, pp.322–3.

8. Halperin, *Bureaucratic Politics*, pp.117–24.

9. Comments based on numerous personal conversations by author with individuals inside and outside the United States government, Sept. 1996.

10. George Bunn, *Arms Control by Committee: Managing Negotiations with the Russians* (Stanford, CA: Stanford University Press, 1992), p.215.

11. Gawthrop, *Bureaucratic Behavior*, pp.109–10.

12. Halperin, pp.236–46.

13. Halperin, pp.238–60.

14. Gawthrop, p.89.

15. Bunn, *Arms Control by Committee*, pp.180–2; Deibel in Kozak, pp.95–105. Alexander L. George, *Presidential Decision Making in Foreign Policy: The Effective Use of Information and Advice* (Boulder, CO: Westview Press, 1980), pp.145–87.

16. Bert A. Rockman, 'America's Two Departments of State', in Rourke, pp.355–60.

17. Bunn, pp.233–4.

18. Bunn, p.168.

The Politics of Verification: Why 'How Much?' is Not Enough

NANCY W. GALLAGHER

The Reagan refrain, 'trust but verify', may be the only arms control slogan widely shared by policy-makers, academics, and average citizens across the political spectrum and around the globe. Rivals are unlikely to accept constraints on their own military activities unless they have confidence in procedures for assessing compliance by other states.[1] Yet, consensus in principle on the need for verification quickly disintegrates into controversy about the practical implications. From fights in early negotiations about whether verification decisions should precede or follow arms control, to quarrels in recent years over on-site inspection details, verification disputes have received more sustained attention than any other aspect of arms control. Decades of frustration have convinced many participants that agreement on verification is most likely when it is least necessary – that is, for treaties which only foreclose actions that no one is likely to pursue.

This 'verification paradox' seems less daunting when one knows more about the causes and consequences of verification arguments. Therefore, this article examines the politics of verification, namely the processes through which suspicious states and contentious domestic groups reach agreement on arrangements to judge compliance with cooperative accords. It argues that recurrent difficulties obtaining agreement on verification principles and procedures reflect the specific ideas and strategies which have dominated the politics of verification, not an immutable feature of arms control. In particular, the view of verification as a technical fix and a 'self-help' solution to the political problems of cooperation in an anarchic world has been one of arms control opponents' most potent weapons. This way of thinking about verification remains firmly entrenched in arms control theory and public policy debates, even though most practitioners recognize that verification is inherently political and increasingly multilateral. Thus, the prospects for arms control depend on educating decision-makers about verification dilemmas and finding strategies to promote agreement despite conflicting interests and ideas about international politics.

This essay starts by showing how the verification paradox can become a self-fulfilling prophecy for researchers and policy-makers who work with an overly narrow conception of verification politics. It then uses examples from recent arms control endeavours to develop a broader approach that emphasizes the interactions between two questions ('how much?' and 'what type?'), two types of motives (substantive and strategic), and two political arenas (national and international). It suggests that provisional agreement on verification comes not through 'depoliticization' but through coalitions among groups with different interests and ideas. It concludes with practical implications for improving the politics of verification throughout the arms control process.

The Verification Paradox

States are trapped in a 'security dilemma' when their defensive preparations cause other states to respond in ways that leave both countries feeling less secure. If no one actually has aggressive intentions, states can break the vicious cycle by agreeing to limit their own military activities on the condition that others do likewise. The significance of an arms control accord depends on both the benefits it brings and the likelihood that participants would have chosen that course of action (for example, to destroy all biological munitions or to renounce nuclear weapons) without a cooperative agreement. Reciprocal self-restraint is a normal part of national politics, as when policy-makers conclude that everyone will be safer if no one owns a handgun or joins a vigilante group. Yet, arms control opponents contend that comparable bargains will not work in international politics, because there is no world government to judge compliance, punish violations, and protect law-abiding states from aggression.

Cooperation theorists often view verification as a way for states to obviate this problem and have confidence in compliance without sacrificing their sovereignty.[2] In other words, verification is viewed as a 'self-help' substitute for the functions that a world government would perform. Knowing the 'truth' about compliance lets national leaders deter cheating, detect dangerous violations, and reassure citizens about the benefits of arms control. For example, rational choice theorists have argued that arms control is possible among states with mixed motives if they have the information and the ability to reciprocate cooperative or competitive behaviour.[3] As evidence that verification is the 'critical element' of arms control,[4] many observers note that during the Cold War superpower arms control was limited to agreements that could be verified by satellite surveillance and other national technical means (NTM). Once Soviet resistance to intrusive verification decreased, a series of increasingly important arms control accords could be signed and ratified.[5]

In this view, verification is mainly a technical problem of increasing transparency, that is, knowing what other countries are actually doing when they claim to be in compliance. Since total transparency is rarely possible, the primary policy question asked is, how much certainty do we need for the benefits of cooperation to outweigh the costs and risks?[6] Cost/benefit calculations differ depending on the issue and the context. For example, verification requirements are expected to be much greater when core security capabilities are at stake and the level of distrust is high than they will be for peripheral measures negotiated in a more relaxed political atmosphere.[7]

Depicting verification as a technical solution to security dilemmas overlooks a critical difference between verification in the laboratory and in international relations. Quantum physicists or biochemists can verify research hypotheses because they share a 'paradigm' that tells them how to collect information, analyse data, and interpret results. Since no such paradigm or shared world view exists for international politics, there are no pre-determined principles and procedures to confirm compliance or prove that a promise has been broken. Two decision-makers will reach divergent conclusions from the same data when their assessments are influenced by different assumptions, experiences, contextual information, or conflicting policy concerns.[8] The compliance information that they have, and their confidence in that information, will also depend on design questions, such as who operates monitoring stations and how on-site inspections (OSIs) are conducted. Potential cooperators care intensely that the design and implementation of verification protects their interests and reflects their way of looking at the world. How can states that distrust each other agree on principles and procedures that will not give the other side an unfair advantage? How can domestic groups who disagree about the benefits and risks of arms control agree on national verification requirements?

The sceptics' answer is that they cannot until it does not matter any more. Sceptics note that domestic and international agreement on verification has been easiest when an accord outlawed actions that nobody planned to do (the 1959 Antarctic Treaty); when a huge residual capability minimized the consequences of minor violations (SALT I and II); or after an adversarial relationship improved (superpower arms control after the Cold War). A partial exception that confirms the rule is when strong states dictate verification for weaker players, such as the 1968 Nuclear Non-Proliferation Treaty's (NPT) safeguards that are obligatory only for non-nuclear weapon states (NNWS).

The most common explanation for this dismal track record is that verification decisions become 'politicized' when participants use them as surrogates for deeper disagreements or as devious ways to sabotage arms control.[9] Sometimes states or domestic groups are sincerely interested in cooperation but have divergent ways of calculating verification requirements. For example, the Cold War gulf between the American 'maximalist' verification preferences and the Soviets' 'minimalist' position can be explained in terms of the Soviets' weaker strategic position and American political leaders' greater need for 'open' sources of compliance information to sell their arms control and security policies.[10] Likewise, Reagan-era arguments over settling for 'adequate' verification that could detect militarily significant violations or demanding 'effective' systems that could provide unambiguous evidence of any infraction can be explained in terms of conflicting assumptions about the value of arms control, the Soviets' intentions, and the consequences of low-level cheating.[11] International and domestic disagreements about verification, however, can also be convenient ways to express interest in arms control while avoiding arms limitations. For example, Alva Myrdal, a Swedish delegate to UN talks, saw superpower arguments about verification as a cynical strategy in the 'game of disarmament' that both countries played to pacify world opinion while expanding their arsenals.[12] Likewise, critics of the Reagan administration's arms control policies often accused it of using unobtainable and unnecessary verification demands to blame the Soviet Union for negotiating failures.[13]

If controversies occur when technical questions become 'politicized', the argument goes, the way to promote arms control is to 'depoliticize' verification decisions. One suggestion is to entrust them to an 'epistemic community' of technical experts whose shared commitment to a set of values, causal beliefs, and research methods provides an 'objective' basis for verification design.[14] Yet, verification debates have typically included competing epistemic communities and consensus among scientists has frequently come only through ignoring or finessing key political questions. More often than not, calls to 'depoliticize' verification by turning decisions over to technical experts have been political strategies to obtain a desired outcome by empowering people who share one's starting assumptions.

Another suggestion is to postpone verification decisions until national leaders have answers to more fundamental policy questions. For example, Congressional analysts Mark Lowenthal and Joel Witt suggest that verification should be depoliticized by first establishing a new national consensus about 'what we can expect from arms control, how much risk we are willing to accept, and how much uncertainty we can tolerate'.[15] Allan Krass, a scientist with a long-standing interest in arms control, argued that convergence on a particular set of assumptions about nuclear deterrence would provide the necessary flexibility in verification requirements:

> Despite all the agonizing over verification, it is not the primary reason why so little progress has been made on arms control. In fact, verification is not 'the critical element of arms control.' The critical element is an acknowledgment of the uselessness of marginal military advantages

between nuclear armed states. Once this fact of life is recognized and accepted, verification will begin to look like a solvable problem.[16]

The problem with this solution is that obtaining domestic and international agreement on each issue that influences verification preferences would require a sudden consensus on multiple questions which have divided policy-makers and theorists for decades, if not centuries. Since the end of the Cold War has not diminished arguments over state motivations or security requirements, provisional agreement on verification must not be held hostage to the improbable resolution of enduring debates.

A third type of depoliticization proposal is to find win/win solutions that can satisfy seemingly contradictory verification concerns. The development of satellites and other forms of remote monitoring technology is the classic example, because verifiers could obtain extensive compliance information without intrusive OSIs. Likewise, proposals for 'managed access' inspections seek to reassure participants that procedures can be designed which will provide reliable information about compliance yet protect other sensitive military or economic secrets. When national leaders have been eager for agreement, negotiators have shown remarkable creativity; yet, most win/win solutions still require some willingness to compromise: for example, tolerating low risks of cheating and spying in order to have 'cost effective' inspection procedures. Moreover, win/win solutions simply do not exist for many types of verification dilemma. One response has been to restrict arms control to provisions, such as limits on strategic launch vehicles, that could be easily monitored with existing NTM. Another has been to avoid verification arguments by asserting that 'national honour' is a good enough guarantee of compliance, as occurred with the naval accords signed between the world wars and, less explicitly, with the 1972 Biological Weapons Convention. Each of these proposals for 'depoliticizing' verification, though, will only work under circumstances which severely restrict the opportunities for arms control.

In short, viewing the politics of verification as a derivative problem leads to pessimistic conclusions about the prospects for significant arms control. If verification preferences derive from prior beliefs about national security, then domestic groups and international negotiators will only be able to avoid controversies if everyone already thinks that arms control is highly beneficial, temptations to cheat or spy are low, and the consequences of minor violations are unimportant. This suggests that verification can institutionalize cooperation if, for example, the main players have decided that chemical weapons are a net negative for national security or that over twenty thousand nuclear warheads per superpower is excessive in the post-Cold War world. But it cannot increase support for cooperation when suspicions and incentives for unilateral action remain because participants will always disagree, sincerely or cynically, about 'how much is enough'. If so, arms control can never be more than a minor adjunct to national security policy.

There are good reasons to question the inevitability of the verification paradox. As the next section will show, past research has been based on an incomplete understanding of the politics of verification. It identified important features, such as the domestic and international levels or the sincere and cynical uses of verification arguments, but failed to show how they are interrelated. Concentrating on 'how much is enough' also underestimates the importance of arguments about 'what type is best?' Finally, most writing on the politics of verification occurred in the mid-1980s when arguments among Americans and between the superpowers were especially intense. Earlier authors had plenty of data on the key points of contention, but little evidence about effective ways to build consensus or reach agreement on verification despite conflicting interests and ideas. The unprecedented verification agreements since the mid-1980s, as well as the persistence of many verification arguments, create both the opportunity and the necessity to rethink the politics of verification.

Without a fuller understanding of the politics of verification, the verification paradox risks become a self-fulfilling prophecy. Activists cannot build popular support for significant arms control without a persuasive answer to the chicken-and-egg puzzle posed by the verification paradox. Yet, few scholars continued to study the politics of verification after the first analysts concluded that it was a derivative problem whose solution lay elsewhere. A misplaced belief in the verification paradox also leads to lowest-common-denominator arms control by telling pragmatists that major accords must wait for domestic consensus on security policy and further win/win solutions to conflicting verification concerns. Most importantly, though, the assumption that verification is a technical problem and a self-help process makes domestic support for arms control depend on adversarial types of verification that are fundamentally at odds with significant arms control. As long as these ideas dominate American policy debates and ratification decisions, the United States will be reluctant to make the kinds of verification compromises needed for major multilateral agreements. When such compromises are made, moreover, they will become booby traps that treaty opponents can trigger to sabotage the ratification process.

Rethinking the Politics of Verification

The vast amount of attention paid to arms control verification reflects both the importance of confidence in compliance and the disastrous consequences that could result from verification failures. Opinions differ widely about the amount and type of verification required for a particular arms control accord, as well as the relative dangers posed by imperfect verification or unconstrained competition. Yet, deciding how to judge compliance is a basic problem for any type of cooperation. Without a dictator or an agreed set of principles from which one, and only one, answer can be derived, questions about verification must be answered through political processes. For example, arguments about the legitimacy of wire-tapping or the rules for jury selection show that Americans continue to disagree about the best way to evaluate compliance with domestic laws. Such issues are intensely controversial because alternative approaches reflect divergent principles (for instance, individual liberties versus community needs) and may produce different outcomes (the contradictory verdicts in O.J. Simpson's criminal and civil trials, for example). Thus, it is unrealistic and counter-productive to assume that significant arms control cooperation is only possible after verification preferences converge or are bridged through win/win technologies.

Questions for the Politics of Verification

The politics of verification involve numerous questions that must be addressed explicitly by negotiators or left for individual states to decide. Many are 'how much' types of question. For example, scientists and diplomats spent decades trying to decide how many stations with what technical capabilities should be in an international monitoring system (IMS) for a comprehensive test ban treaty (CTBT). The agreed network is considered capable of detecting and identifying most tests with an explosive yield above 1 kiloton (kt), but a sophisticated tester might be able to evade it by 'decoupling' a 5 kt test – that is, detonating it in an oversized cavity so that the size of its seismic signals is reduced below the IMS threshold.[17] Whether this presents a serious problem depends on assumptions about whether a country that was sophisticated enough to conduct such a test could learn enough to risk detection and whether one or more undetected violations would have significant consequences.

The fine line between verification and espionage (which sometimes exists only in the eye of the beholder) has caused intense debates about how, if at all, national intelligence can be legitimately used in addition to, or in place of, IMS data. Since the United States wanted to keep track of the Soviet testing programme regardless of what, if any, treaty limitations existed, current United States monitoring capabilities are reportedly capable of detecting and identifying a 2–3 kt decoupled explosion at a Russian test site or other areas of particular concern. Americans argue that it would be irrational to agree in advance *not* to raise questions if the national seismic network picked up something that the IMS missed or if a United States satellite detected a suspicious flash that might have been a high altitude test. But China and other NTM opponents respond that the IMS is an agreed system shared by all and that basing a verification decision on anything else would give some states the ability to subject other states to special scrutiny and raise or suppress compliance concerns according to their own national interests. Each side in this debate accuses the other of selfish motives. Even states whose interests are not directly affected still care about the larger implications of choosing between a power politics approach to verification (states with different resources use any information they can find to protect their security) or one based on principles of non-discrimination and equality among states.

The quantity and quality of compliance information also depends on the rights and responsibilities of countries under scrutiny. During the Cold War, the Soviets tried to prevent 'collateral information collection' by proposing that 'host' country nationals should do most verification tasks under international supervision.[18] Americans denounced this as unreliable 'self-verification' and insisted that nationals from the opposing side or non-aligned countries run the monitoring stations and conduct OSIs while the host state facilitated their work by providing easy access and logistical support. The Reagan administration's attempt to make Soviet support for this vision of verification the 'litmus test' of its arms control sincerity[19] was a strategy to blame them for the United States military build-up unless the Soviet Union granted Americans rapid, unimpeded, unconstrained access to sensitive sites throughout the USSR. Victors have forced losers to facilitate 'anytime, anywhere, anything' verification, such as those implemented by the United Nations Special Commission (UNSCOM) in Iraq after the Persian Gulf War. Whenever states have expected to be on both sides of the verification lens, though, negotiators have looked at questions from the perspective of both verifier and verified. Multilateral agreement on managed access inspections for the 1993 Chemical Weapons Convention (CWC) has popularized this approach. Yet, difficulties deciding how the concept could be used to improve the International Atomic Energy Agency (IAEA) safeguards system show that one country's 'legitimate measures to prevent espionage' are another's 'unacceptable attempts to obstruct verification'.[20]

Newspaper articles often fixate on 'the numbers game' because disputes over OSI quotas or acceptable detection probabilities are easily understood by those who think that the most important question is 'how much is enough?' Insider accounts of negotiations, however, consistently reveal that arguments about type of verification matter as much as those about amount. For example, after the Cuban Missile Crisis, American and Soviet negotiators seemed close to agreement on an annual number of CTB inspections (the Soviets offered two or three, the United States wanted eight or ten). The United States was willing to go lower, but only if it knew that inspections could be conducted in an effective manner (easy to initiate quickly, widespread access, reliable personnel, appropriate assistance from the host, and such). Since the Soviets refused to talk about OSI procedures until they knew how frequently the inspections would occur, and the US would only lower their numbers if the Soviets made concessions about type of OSI, negotiations broke down.[21]

Arguments about type of verification are not just round-about efforts to determine who controls access to information. They can also reflect fundamentally different conceptions of verification itself. During the early years of the Cold War, for example, Americans called for verification by an 'objective' international agency while the Soviets questioned whether any organization that was filled with American allies and funded primarily by the United States could be neutral. As United States influence waned and its disillusionment grew with 'politicization' in the United Nations, Americans shifted toward 'reciprocal' measures (that is, adversaries verifying each other's behaviour) to avoid sharing compliance information and verification decisions with third parties. However, since purely reciprocal verification becomes increasingly complicated, expensive, and redundant as more states participate in a treaty regime, most recent multilateral arms control accords have included provisions for some type of central verification agency. The question is whether that agency simply reduces transaction costs by facilitating information flows (maintaining an international arms transfer registry, for example); collects raw data but does no analysis (the United States preference for the CTB's International Data Center); or makes authoritative decisions about when an OSI is needed and whether a violation has occurred (the role played by UNSCOM and the Security Council in Iraq).

United States debates about verification and compliance also reflect different ideas about the type of verification that will have the optimal effects for cooperation. For example, the Reagan administration used a law enforcement analogy to justify its requirements for 'effective' verification. They argued that the 'good guys' must be able to catch and punish every violation or else the 'criminals' would be emboldened to try more serious violations. In this view, the United States needed to control all aspects of the verification process because allowing the Soviets to help collect, analyse, and evaluate compliance information would have been like inviting drug lords to join undercover cops in making sure that stings were done correctly. Most past and present proponents of 'adequate' verification use a different analogy: while foolproof verification, like perfect missile defence, is impossible, it also is unnecessary so long as the United States can deter unwanted actions (nuclear attacks or militarily significant treaty violations). This perspective welcomes cooperative measures to enhance the availability of compliance information, but still assumes that the United States should do its own data analysis and compliance assessments. Its vision of verification-as-deterrence also remained adversarial because it assumes that the countries of greatest concern to the United States will cheat or obstruct the verification process if the opportunity arises.

Some advocates of arms control and cooperative security have proposed an alternative approach in which verification is seen as a type of regulatory management.[22] They assume that parties to an arms control accord have fundamentally compatible security objectives and only sign treaties that they intend to uphold. In this perspective, most compliance concerns are due to ambiguous provisions, misperceptions, confusing rules, changing circumstances, and normal tendencies to test the outer limits of an agreement. Therefore, proponents of a managerial approach argue that members of an arms control regime should work closely at each stage of the verification process so that they understand each other's perspective, avoid misperceptions, and find mutually acceptable methods to strengthen confidence in arms control compliance. Treaty provisions for 'consultations' and 'clarifications' represent a weak form of this approach, while the Acheson-Lilienthal Committee's plan in 1946 for an international Atomic Development Authority with full responsibility for all dangerous nuclear activities is the most comprehensive example.

In short, decisions about arms control verification cannot be reduced to 'technical' questions any more than arguments about wiretapping or jury selection can. Even pieces of the problem that might seem purely technical, such as the strengths and weaknesses of current monitoring options, are shaped by political choices about research and development programmes, plus assumptions about the conditions under which the technologies would be used. Although Americans often depict their verification demands as scientifically determined and thus non-negotiable, decisions about verification design can never be completely 'depoliticized'. Instead, they will always be contested because alternative approaches reflect divergent principles and distribute the benefits, costs, and risks of cooperation in different ways.

Substantive and Strategic Arguments

The preceding discussion surveyed several substantive reasons for verification arguments. When decision-makers face a major arms control dilemma (i.e. strong pressures both for and against cooperation), their choice will often depend on confidence that verification can fulfil its functions without unacceptable costs (financial burdens, infringements on sovereignty) or risks (espionage, contact with foreigners by citizens of a closed society). For example, the original NPT negotiators had to weigh the value of additional assurances that materials from civilian nuclear facilities were not being diverted to military projects against the possibility that more verification requirements would become a disincentive for membership. Even after discoveries about Iraq's progress toward a clandestine nuclear weapons capability spurred widespread agreement on measures to strengthen the IAEA safeguard system, moreover, IAEA members still had great difficulty deciding who should pay for the improvements.

Arguments about verification can also be used for strategic purposes. In national politics, laws are passed and implemented despite ongoing arguments about compliance evaluation. In international politics, though, arms control treaties cannot be signed and ratified unless new verification arrangements are accepted by each state signatory and approved by the necessary number of national policy-makers. Therefore, states and domestic groups which strongly favour cooperation may downplay verification concerns, while those which oppose a treaty may try to exacerbate verification disagreements. In the recent CTB negotiations, for example, many non-nuclear weapon states who believe that the benefits from stopping tests strongly outweigh any costs or risks would have signed a treaty regardless of how arguments about OSIs or NTM were resolved. By contrast, China and France were accused of using extreme verification positions to stall negotiations while they finished their last test series.

Differentiating between substantive and strategic motivations is similar to saying that arguments about verification can be sincere or cynical. Unfortunately, neither participants nor observers can distinguish reliably between the two types of motivations. Instead, there is a tendency to assume that players who share one's own beliefs about verification have legitimate concerns while those who approach the problem differently must be using the politics of verification to promote some other policy goal. Substantive and strategic motivations are also linked in complicated ways. Even when arguments about verification are strategically motivated, their impact on domestic debates and international negotiations depends on their plausibility, namely the extent to which they tap into substantive concerns.

The Politics of Verification as a Two-Level Game

One way to see the connections between different kinds of verification question, motivation, and political arena is to conceptualize arms control debates and negotiations as a two-level game where moves in the national arena affect the chances of international agreement on verification, and vice versa.[23] The players at the national level vary, depending on who has the most influence on security policy in a given country. In the United States, the key players are usually Executive Branch officials, while Congress, attentive elites, and public opinion are a semi-malleable source of pressures and constraints. The same type of analysis can be applied to other countries, but the circle of players might be larger or smaller, more or less heterogeneous, and more or less impenetrable.[24] Arms control opponents can block cooperation by preventing agreement on verification at either level, while supporters must reach agreement in both arenas to 'win'. Success at the international level has traditionally been seen as a consensus among all the relevant states at the negotiating table, although research on international norms suggests that the NPT and other treaties with widespread support can affect behaviour even of non-signatories.[25] Success at the national level depends on the rules for 'ratification' in a given country, that is, the degree of domestic support needed for political leaders to implement arms control promises.[26]

National verification preferences and negotiating strategies result from bargaining among domestic players with different attitudes toward arms control. These attitudes reflect divergent ways of thinking about international relations that have as much to do with participants' education and life experiences as they do with their position in the foreign policy-making process. In the United States, the main distinctions between worldviews can be described by using three 'ideal types' to characterize the middle and ends of a security spectrum, as long as one remembers that real individuals may hold a mix of beliefs or think differently about different arms control issues.

'Arms Control Advocates' believe that cooperation is mutually beneficial, that negotiating partners recognize the need for mutual restraint, and that the risks of arms control pale in comparison with the dangers of unrestrained competition. Peace activists and proponents of cooperative security are in this category, as are more mainstream policy-makers when they argue that the benefits of banning particular weapons (chemical munitions or landmines) dwarf the dangers posed by a few states that might secretly violate or openly reject an accord.[27]

'Cautious Cooperators' agree that arms control would be wonderful if it worked, but they question other states' intentions, and worry about the consequences if potential adversaries cheat, break out of a treaty, or refuse to join a multilateral agreement. This is the group whose preferences underlie the 'Prisoner's Dilemma' model of the arms race upon which much verification research has been based. Public opinion surveys throughout the Cold War showed that large majorities were Cautious Cooperators whose fear of nuclear weapons and support for arms control negotiations was combined with distrust of the Soviets and reluctant support for deterrence as the only realistic route to security for the foreseeable future.[28] The need to win this middle group's support for arms control or weapons development often encouraged policy-makers to depict themselves as Cautious Cooperators even if their own views were actually closer to one end of the security spectrum.[29]

'Unilateralists' do not believe that their country should accept any negotiated constraints on its military capabilities because they have little faith in 'paper treaties' without a supranational power to judge and enforce compliance. They assume that other states are aggressive and will take advantage of arms control partners whenever they can. Unilateralists also fear that disastrous consequences will result even from small violations or relative gains that others obtain from mutual compliance. Unilateralists' antipathy toward arms control only weakens when domestic factors have already ruled out a particular option (for example, atmospheric testing, chemical weapons use, or an expensive strategic modernization programme) and they want other countries to be similarly constrained.[30]

Contrary to the notion of a Cold War consensus, United States policy-makers and citizens have always been divided over these fundamental questions about arms control. The distribution among elites has varied in different administrations: for example, Truman and his top advisers tended toward Unilateralism; Eisenhower was a Cautious Cooperator with a divided group of advisers; and the Kennedy administration tried to mix Arms Control Advocacy and Unilateralism. Players outside the inner circle have different amounts of influence depending on their level of mobilization and their degree of access to top decision-makers. For example, the belligerence of the first Reagan administration energized Arms Control Advocates outside the Executive Branch and prompted many Cautious Cooperators to plead for more moderation. By contrast, the current public passivity on arms control turned CTB negotiation and CWC ratification into a low priority for the Clinton administration even though there has been relatively little strong domestic opposition to either accord.

These domestic divisions mean that some participants argue about verification for its own sake, while others focus on verification as a way to build a coalition for or against arms control. As Table 1 summarizes, Cautious Cooperators are the only players whose attitude toward a treaty depends on the substantive details of verification. Since Arms Control Advocates think that the benefits of cooperation are high and the risks of cheating are low, their own preferences about the amount and the type of verification are flexible. The more firmly they believe in the wisdom of cooperation, the more likely it is that their main goal in the politics of verification will be to persuade Cautious Cooperators that arms control is safe. By contrast, Unilateralists' pessimistic assumptions about other countries' motivations and the serious consequences of small violations make it extremely difficult to satisfy their verification concerns. The further toward the Unilateralist end of the security spectrum players are on a particular issue, the less likely they would be to favour arms control regardless of the verification arrangements. Their main motivation will be strategic as they raise rigid and extreme verification requirements to convince Cautious Cooperators that effective verification is impossible.

TABLE 1
DIVISIONS IN DOMESTIC DEBATES

	Arms Control Advocates	Cautious Cooperators	Unilateralists
Is mutual cooperation desirable?	Yes	Yes	No
Does the other side want cooperation?	Yes	Maybe	No
Would cheating or relative gains matter?	No	Yes	Yes
Resulting Verification Predisposition	Flexible	Crucial	Rigid

In American verification debates, the primary point of convergence has been on the 'myth' that verification is primarily a technical process whose purpose is purely benign (increasing cooperation through detection, deterrence, rewards, and reassurance) and which should ultimately be each country's own responsibility. Lack of experience with major arms control accords means that policy-makers have little empirical evidence about the best approach to verification.[31] Therefore, 'myths' develop that are socially constructed and perpetuated by players who see them as useful or simply accept them without critical reflection. This view of verification plays into American beliefs that scientific objectivity can transcend political differences, that 'openness' and transparency promote peaceful relations, and that superpowers should never defer to others when national security is at stake. Even when Arms Control Advocates understand other countries' concerns about espionage, for example, or personally favour a managerial approach to verification, they often use the dominant language because it appeals to Cautious Cooperators and is simple enough for non-experts to understand. Unilateralists do not believe that anything connected with security can be apolitical or purely benign, yet they espouse this conception of verification as a way to keep raising verification demands and maximizing national control over verification if an accord is inevitable.

A speech by John Holum, the Director of the Arms Control and Disarmament Agency (ACDA), illustrates how arms control supporters can inadvertently create an impossible task for themselves by trying to say what everyone wants to hear about verification.[32] His speech used the

Reaganesque terms 'rigorous' and 'effective' verification, but defined this as 'the ability to detect militarily significant violations, with high confidence, in sufficient time to respond effectively', that is, the notion of 'adequate' verification that Reagan's critics used. As the speech progressed, Holum added other, more difficult, verification requirements. For example, he stated that verification bears a 'political burden' of preserving legislative and popular support for arms control by detecting 'any breach of faith'. Although he may have chosen such language to reassure listeners about ACDA's vigilance, non-experts who did not share his arms control assumptions could easily have understood his speech as conceding the Unilateralists' claim that militarily insignificant violations are politically significant and embracing their demand for 'strict enforcement' of every arms control provision. Holum concluded by saying that ACDA must meet all these verification requirements for an unprecedented number of treaties in an era of shrinking budgets if arms control is to make a lasting contribution to United States security. The net effect of such a speech might not be to increase resources for verification but to raise doubts about the continued relevance of arms control in the post-Cold War world.

The more Americans insist that verification is purely benign, technical, and national in nature, the harder it is to reach agreement with countries where different ideas about verification prevail. During the Cold War, for example, Soviet negotiators routinely depicted verification as a political process that could be used for malign purposes such as espionage, interference with economic development, or false accusations.[33] Both superpowers held a fundamentally adversarial view of verification in that they assumed that the other side would try to gain a competitive edge by hindering, distorting, or otherwise abusing the verification process; thus, both tried to maximize their own control over data collection and analysis. The superpowers' preference for self-help forms of verification conflicts with that of many smaller states for multilateral organizations able to act against the interests of powerful member states. Some Western countries hold a basically benign and technical view of verification, but want to give international verification organizations more responsibility for analysing data, judging compliance, and sometimes even imposing sanctions. In contrast, countries such as China and India assume that verification is political and that the best way to prevent abuses is to keep tight international control over the verification process so that no state can initiate an inspection or declare a violation without overwhelming concurrence from other member states.

As Table 2 illustrates, conflicting conceptions of verification let Unilateralists in different countries use diametrically opposed verification demands to block cooperation. For example, United States and Soviet

Unilateralists both opposed arms control, distrusted each other, and feared that a minor advantage for the other side could have disastrous consequences for their own country. In their early proposals for General and Complete Disarmament (which leaders on both sides saw primarily as a propaganda exercise), Americans demanded foolproof verification arrangements before beginning arms control, while the Soviets insisted that radical disarmament must reduce tensions before they could safely lift the veil of secrecy around their military programmes. Unilateralists on both sides could use this strategy to absolve themselves of blame for the arms race because their position sounded plausible to anyone who accepted their assumptions about verification. But even after the mid-1950s, when some political leaders in the United States and the Soviet Union became more sincerely interested in minor, low-risk measures to restrain the arms race, conflicting conceptions of verification meant that the types of proposal that appealed to Cautious Cooperators in one country usually exacerbated the anxieties of Cautious Cooperators on the other side.

TABLE 2
PREFERENCES IN INTERNATIONAL VERIFICATION POLITICS

Conception of Verification	Divisions in Domestic Debates		
	Arms Control Advocates	Cautious Cooperators	Unilateralists
Purely Benign	7	8	9
Involves Trade-offs	6	5	4
Primarily Malign	3	2	1

Expressed Interest in Verification: 1 = Least 9 = Most

(Note: For simplicity's sake, Table 2 only incorporates the benign-malign division; the technical-political and unilateral-international divisions are two further sources of verification conflicts and misunderstandings.)

Most Americans recognize that both United States domestic politics and international negotiations have important effects on arms control outcomes. But they often assume that these two games are separate and sequential: for example, that electoral politics determine which group of policy-makers will give negotiators their instructions, or that senior officials negotiate on the basis of their conception of the national interest and then bring a finished treaty home for ratification. Moreover, Americans typically underestimate the extent to which domestic factors shape other countries' arms control preferences and their responses to American bargaining strategies. In the politics of verification, however, developments in the domestic politics of any participating state can have important effects on international negotiations, and vice versa, at every stage of the arms control process.

The complex interconnections between national and international politics can be seen in the sequence of events leading up to unprecedented agreements on verification at the end of the Cold War. Gorbachev's 'new thinking' on Soviet security policy reflected a combination of internal and external factors.[34] His attempts to promote cooperative security and *glasnost* in Soviet society decreased Soviet military leaders' power and will to oppose on-site inspections. They also moderated United States verification demands by reassuring American Cautious Cooperators about Soviet intentions and reminding American Unilateralists that they might have to live with the intrusive inspections they were proposing. As the Reagan administration toned down its 'evil empire' rhetoric and moderated its inspection demands, allegations from residual Soviet hard-liners that all United States verification requests were meant to sabotage negotiations or increase espionage opportunities became less plausible, and hence less politically potent. There were still domestic divisions among United States and Soviet policy-makers about how far and how fast to go, just there were still disagreements between superpowers about how much and what type of verification would be best for different arms accords. Nevertheless, each iteration convinced more Cautious Cooperators on both sides that mutually beneficial agreements could be verified in mutually acceptable ways, so support for serious arms control increased. The process was neither automatic nor irreversible, yet it slowly altered policy preferences on both sides until accords that had been unthinkable came within reach.

Blocking and Winning Coalitions

As the previous example illustrates, agreement on verification can be both a cause and a consequence of increased interest in cooperation. When external events decrease Unilateralists' desire to block arms control, agreement on verification helps to institutionalize cooperation that was initiated for other reasons. But as long as Arms Control Advocates, Cautious Cooperators, and Unilateralists have divergent attitudes toward particular arms control proposals, the politics of verification will have an important independent effect on domestic debates and international negotiations.

The end of the Cold War has neither convinced all Americans to become Arms Control Advocates nor created a 'harmony of interests' among all states with potentially threatening military capabilities. Many Americans still believe that this is a 'unipolar moment' when arms control is unnecessary and unwise, that any country which poses a major security risk is an unreliable negotiating partner, and that a single nuclear bomb or a secret cache of chemical weapons in the hands of a 'rogue' state could have devastating consequences unless the United States has retained full freedom of military action. While Washington and Moscow now talk more openly about verification trade-offs, there are still serious disputes about the amount and the type of verification, both between them and among the other countries whose support is essential for stable and significant arms control. Therefore, before suggesting steps to reverse this trend, it is helpful to consider why Unilateralists have historically been able to forge blocking coalitions more easily than Arms Control Advocates could build winning ones.

Since Unilateralists can torpedo arms control by preventing domestic or international agreement on verification, their overarching goal in the politics of verification has been to ensure that the only arrangements which their own Cautious Cooperators would accept were ones that negotiating partners would oppose. The American conception of verification as a benign, technical, self-help process facilitated their efforts in a number of ways. For example, United States Unilateralists maintained that if verification is the key to cooperation, then anyone who is sincere about arms control should start by solving verification problems. This let them put a cooperative face on their own obsession with evasion scenarios, while using Soviet resistance to 'try before you buy' verification invitations as evidence of aggressive intentions that decreased Cautious Cooperators' support for arms control. Likewise, the idea that decisions about verification should be based on scientific criteria allowed Unilateralists to obscure ways in which politically motivated assumptions influenced their technical calculations and let them use uncertainties associated with any inferential activity as a reason why Cautious Cooperators should wait for further research and more precise monitoring methods.

The idea that verification is ultimately a self-help activity has had equally counter-productive effects for cooperation. It gave Unilateralists a trump card to play whenever significant restrictions were in sight because they could always ratchet up United States verification requirements, 'just to be on the safe side'. They could ridicule Soviet requests for direct involvement in data collection and analysis as an example of foxes wanting to guard the chicken coop instead of acknowledging that the Soviets had any legitimate reasons to worry about collateral information collection and want some say in how their own compliance was assessed. Whenever agreement on an arms control treaty seemed inevitable, Unilateralists could insist on 'safeguards' as a self-help solution to residual uncertainties about cooperation. In the test ban case, for example, these have included commitments to increase intelligence capabilities; to intensify underground tests after the 1963 Limited Test Ban Treaty, and to engage in simulations, sub-critical experiments, and other substitutes for testing if a CTB enters into force; and to remain ready to resume prohibited tests on short notice should others cheat or abrogate an agreement. Such safeguards make the best of a bad situation for United States Unilateralists, seem like a prudent plan to Cautious Cooperators, and are the price that Arms Control Advocates reluctantly pay for ratification. Yet, they can have a chilling effect on cooperation by raising doubts about United States intentions, complicating verification, and institutionalizing barriers to more comprehensive arms control.[35]

Arms Control Advocates have had trouble countering Unilateralists' blocking strategies effectively because of their own ideas about verification. Their belief in the value of transparency can make it hard to understand why another country could be legitimately concerned about verification abuse. Thus, they have frequently endorsed the misleading practice of judging other countries' arms control intentions from their response to United States verification proposals.[36] Moreover, Arms Control Advocates long to see international relations rest on something other than power politics. Therefore, they have often pushed for a technical approach to verification in hopes that scientific reasoning will transcend political divisions, and they have been less willing than Unilateralists to manipulate technical arguments for political objectives. Of course, Arms Control Advocates' conviction that the 'facts' associated with nuclear weapons overwhelmingly favour some degree of cooperation has often led them to downplay verification dilemmas and trade-offs in order to reassure Cautious Cooperators. After the CWC was signed, for example, some supporters initially implied that its unprecedented verification provisions had removed all risks from a chemical weapons ban. This created a straw man that treaty opponents could easily destroy by suggesting that verification provisions cost too much money, could not defeat every conceivable evasion scenario, would not apply to non-signatories, and might provide a false sense of security that would erode political support for defences against chemical attacks.

The conception of verification as a self-help way to detect cheating, deter violations, and reassure citizens has been a mixed blessing for arms control. The idea that arms control could enhance United States security if detection probabilities were high enough to deter violations was developed during the Eisenhower years as an alternative to Unilateralists' insistence on 'foolproof' verification. Arms Control Advocates embraced the concept as a way to reduce the number of monitoring stations and inspections needed for Americans to support a CTB. But the new approach did not produce domestic and international agreement because it was highly elastic and extremely adversarial. Unilateralists accepted the new formulation, but assumed that the Soviet Union was so highly motivated to cheat that it would only be deterred by near certain detection. Even that might not be enough if the United States lacked the political will to retaliate against a suspected violation by abrogating the treaty and resuming the competition at a higher level. Unilateralists argued that verification-as-deterrence would not be credible unless the United States could obtain incontrovertible evidence of any violation, had a public confrontation over every compliance concern, and made the United States response to non-compliance as automatic as possible. Thus, the United States continued to negotiate on the basis of verification preferences that perpetuated other countries' concerns about why the United States wanted such intrusive measures and how it would act if it had suspicions that other countries did not share. In short, thinking about verification-as-deterrence has perpetuated the verification paradox because it only reduces monitoring requirements when everybody already agrees that the probability and consequences of non-compliance are low. It also fails to address the inherent contradiction between adversarial verification, which assumes the worst about others' intentions, and significant arms control, which depends on a mixture of common and conflicting interests.

More Promising Approaches to the Politics of Verification

There is no magic formula which can resolve arguments about verification among countries and domestic groups with conflicting interests and ideas about international relations. Instead, the most promising approach is to recognize that decisions involve difficult trade-offs about both amount and type of verification, to understand that players engage in verification arguments for both substantive and strategic reasons, and to think carefully about how different moves affect the chances for agreement at both the national and the international levels. In particular, Arms Control Advocates must find ways to convince Cautious Cooperators that significant agreements can enhance United States security even when they involve some uncertainty about compliance and some delegation of decision-making authority to international organizations. Negotiators know this and each of the recent arms control accords includes a number of compromises on amount and type of verification. But to the extent that public debates keep depicting verification as a self-help solution to the dilemmas of cooperation in an anarchic world, Unilateralists can invoke outdated assumptions to sabotage negotiations or delay ratification of any treaty they dislike.

This analysis has several practical implications for each stage of the arms control process. Attempts to strengthen the verification regime for the 1972 Biological and Toxin Weapons Convention (BWC) are still at a preliminary stage. The original treaty contained no formal verification provisions, and the confidence-building measures added at the 1986 and 1991 review conferences are voluntary. Negotiations on mandatory measures have been slow because key states are conflicted over the value of a legally binding verification regime.[37] Some Western countries have long favoured an intrusive verification regime modelled along the lines of the CWC, while a few non-aligned movement (NAM) countries want more access to biotechnological equipment without obligatory measures to confirm its purely peaceful use. The official United States position has moved from opposition to ambivalence about OSIs; it now seeks more transparency to facilitate its own judgements about compliance, but does not support the level of intrusion and expense that would be needed for high confidence in detection capabilities. The American biotechnology industry's lobbying association publicly says that managed access can be arranged, yet privately resists any inspections that would bring increased costs and risks, but few direct benefits, for them.[38]

Reaching domestic and international agreement on a full-fledged BWC verification regime is a challenging problem because small quantities of BW agents can be produced quickly; delivered with inexpensive dual-use equipment; and used to cause massive fatalities among unprotected troops, civilians, or livestock. Nevertheless, there are ways to promote near-term progress on intermediate measures. One recommendation is to recognize that some participants study verification questions to find mutually acceptable answers while others identify verification problems to complicate prospects for agreement. Ultimately, anyone whose support is required to negotiate, ratify, or implement stronger verification provisions must be drawn into verification discussions. Careful timing, however, can be critical since groups that see arms control and verification as a net negative will participate more constructively if they think that an agreement might be reached without them. The more ambivalent the United States government is, the more incentives Unilateralists have to emphasize the costs and risks of BW verification rather than to weigh which managed access procedures would be more workable and tolerable than others. Cautious Cooperators must be convinced that the net benefits of more formal verification measures will outweigh the costs and risks, but they should rely on analyses done jointly by technical and political experts who understand the perspectives of all the major players but have no stake in obstructing cooperation.[39]

Arms Control Advocates should also think carefully about the amount and type of verification they support. The most open opposition to a legally binding BW verification protocol is currently based on claims that it will restrict access to dual-use equipment. However, the course of CTB negotiations points to other objections that may be raised later for substantive or strategic reasons. Those countries that are most interested in strengthening BWC verification should weigh the benefits for deterrence of preserving uncertainty about OSI details against the danger that key countries or domestic groups will withhold support unless they know precisely what an OSI would entail. More ambivalent players should recognize the contradictions in requesting more transparency yet resisting efforts to clarify obligations, emphasizing the uncertainties associated with verification, and insisting that each country reach its own conclusions. This position might seem prudent to an American Cautious Cooperator, but it could easily be used by NAM critics as evidence that the United States will use biased verification decisions to serve other policy objectives.

The CTB negotiations show that even when all of the major players are officially in favour of cooperation, arguments about verification are still intense and important. Nuclear test ban talks in the United Nations Conference on Disarmament (CD) started in January 1994 and progressed slowly, with a thousand points of disagreement remaining in the working document after two years of negotiations.[40] In hopes of reaching agreement by the 1996 UN General Assembly (the target deadline set by United States legislation and the 1995 NPT Extension Conference), the Chair of the negotiations finally presented a draft text with proposed compromises that became the focus of attention during the final months. Since the CD operates by consensus and several states opposed the revised version of the Chair's text, Australia and other 'friends of the treaty' took the draft CTB to the General Assembly. The treaty was adopted in September 1996 by a vote of 158 to 3, but its future remains unclear because entry into force depends on participation by forty-four states with potential nuclear testing capabilities and India insists that it will 'never sign this unequal treaty, not now, nor later'.[41]

During CTB negotiations, the three most difficult questions about verification involved the place of national intelligence in the verification system, the amount of analysis that the International Data Center (IDC) should do, and the procedures for on-site inspections. The Chair's text used ambiguous language to bridge conflicting positions on the first point. It permits 'the use of national technical means of verification in a manner consistent with generally recognized principles of international law'.[42] This compromise between power and principle tacitly accepts a discriminatory regime where member states have unequal access to compliance information, yet stops short of legitimizing espionage. It does not prevent states from using human sources to assess ambiguous situations, but it precludes them from making accusations which cannot be supported by any other type of compliance information. Some Americans insinuate that countries which want to restrict the use of national intelligence must have something to hide. China, India, and Pakistan have been recent targets of highly publicized United States accusations about treaty non-compliance, secret nuclear testing preparations, and even a close brush with nuclear war. These claims have never been fully substantiated, yet have strained diplomatic relations and affected domestic decisions about nuclear policy in complicated ways. Therefore, nationalist groups in these countries can plausibly depict United States intelligence agencies as loose cannons that must be brought under control − a politically potent, if questionable, allegation.

For two years the United States was the only country that opposed preliminary analysis of IMS data by the technical secretariat on the grounds that such analysis might bias the verification process and that any country who really cared about verification would gladly spend the money required to make sense of the data on its own. Countries with fewer resources and less technical expertise found this position baffling, if not insulting. The United States eventually agreed that the IDC could use standard screening criteria on raw IMS data to prepare a bulletin scoring each seismic event according to how closely its characteristics match those of earthquakes or chemical explosions − as long as the IDC's efforts did not prejudice the right of member states to analyse raw IMS data and reach their own conclusions. Some Americans have suggested, however, that soon after the system is running, the United States should pointedly apply different screening criteria, just to demonstrate that the IDC's set of characteristics is not necessarily the best way to identify suspicious events. This could reduce slightly the already low probability that many of the CTB's Executive Council (the main decision-making body of the Comprehensive Test Ban Treaty Organization) would ignore United States concerns just because an unidentified event received a mixed score on IDC criteria. But it would surely send a strong signal that the United States considered the IDC bulletins unreliable, thus weakening international confidence in the verification regime.

Arguments about OSIs were the most intractable verification issue, and the one where the United States had the greatest difficulty accepting the compromise proposed by the Chair's text. Countries such as the United States, the United Kingdom, and France wanted OSIs to be easily initiated, fast, and comprehensive. They favoured 'red light' procedures whereby inspections would occur upon request by a member state, unless opposed by a majority of Executive Council members. Other states, such as China, Russia, and Israel, wanted more time for consultation and clarification and more leeway for host states to prevent collateral information collection. They also preferred 'green light' procedures whereby an inspection would only occur if approved by a two-thirds majority of the Executive Council. This issue was such a priority for the United States that American negotiators had less energy or inclination to fight for their preferences on other issues, such as more flexible entry into force conditions. While the other nuclear weapon states (NWS) indicated that they would be willing to compromise on a three-fifths majority approval rule, the United States continued to insist that it would go no further than the simple majority approval rule proposed in the Chair's text. This remained unacceptable to China, though, so the United States finally broke its own admonition against reopening negotiations and held private talks in which the two countries converged on the three-fifths formula.

The irony of lengthy arguments over OSIs was that few policy-makers expect OSIs to happen often, if ever, because they are an expensive and confrontational approach that might not yield conclusive evidence even if a violation had occurred. This could expose the initiator to criticism and financial liability for making a 'frivolous' or 'abusive' request. It might even inspire others to initiate retaliatory OSIs on the basis of ambiguous information. The Western states argue that potential violators will not be deterred unless they know that an OSI request would be fulfilled quickly, easily, and thoroughly. Yet, it is not clear why this should make verification more credible if no individual state is likely to request an OSI unless the evidence is clear enough that thirty Executive Council Members would give their approval. The illogic of the deterrence rationale is used by the opposing side as evidence that the Western states must have ulterior motives. United States policy-makers defended their uncompromising stance as essential for Senate ratification, not because such provisions will be invoked often but because they symbolize effective verification. Until the treaty enters into force, though, the United States and other signatories will be legally obligated not to test but will probably be unable to invoke an inspection even if they wanted to.[43]

As this example illustrates, American negotiating positions have often been shaped at home and justified abroad by assertions that a particular type or amount of verification is essential for ratification. Other countries are using this type of two-level strategy increasingly frequently, as in Russia's sudden insistence that it could not ratify a CTB unless the IMS were changed to provide 'equal transparency' at each operational test site. Claiming that one's hands are tied may seem like a clever way to induce other countries to make concessions that cannot be justified in any other way. But empirical research shows that such strategies only work on minor disagreements among friendly states and that leaders who are sincerely interested in cooperation usually prefer to preserve negotiating flexibility even when coming to the table with 'tied hands' might give them a bargaining advantage.[44] Therefore, Arms Control Advocates should think about strategies to broaden the range of verification arrangements that could receive widespread domestic support.

The CWC holds valuable lessons about the politics of verification during ratification because it is the first major multilateral post-Cold War arms control accord and the treaty with the most extensive international verification to date. Signed by 130 countries in early 1993, the CWC was not initially scheduled for a ratification vote by the United States Senate until Fall 1996. The long delay had less to do with the politics of verification than competing priorities for the Clinton administration and other conflicts between the White House and the Republican-controlled Senate. However, a small group of critics used arguments about unverifiability as one of their main lines of attack. While the treaty offers 'unprecedented information-generating opportunities', including extensive declaration requirements, routine monitoring, and challenge inspections, that will enable members to 'piece together' a picture of compliance behaviour, it cannot not guarantee that every violation will be detected.[45] Therefore, Senator Jesse Helms, a long-standing arms control critic and chair of the Senate Committee on Foreign Relations (SCFR), tried one of the Unilateralists' favourite blocking strategies by claiming to support 'a *verifiable* treaty, accomplishing *real* reductions in these abhorrent weapons', but insisting that the CWC did not meet these criteria.[46] When former Senator Robert Dole, then the Republican Party's presidential nominee, came out against the CWC, the Clinton administration postponed the ratification vote until after the 1996 elections. This left little time to secure the Senate's advice and consent before the treaty entered into force on 29 April 1997.[47] Despite very strong public support (one poll found that 84 per cent of respondents favoured ratification) and vigorous attempts to address such issues as chemical weapons defences and the constitutionality of inspection procedures, the fate of the treaty remained uncertain until the final votes were cast on 24 April.[48] To secure a significant victory, CWC supporters had to remove several 'killer conditions' attached to the resolution of ratification, including provisions that set an unrealistically high standard for verification and that prohibited nationals from so-called rogue states from serving on CWC inspection teams in the United States.[49] Although the amended resolution of ratification passed by a comfortable margin, the narrow victory came at a high cost (including the loss of ACDA as an independent agency) and caused deep concern about the prospects for CTB ratification, not to mention progress on other arms control issues.

The difficulties of CWC ratification and the disproportionate influence exercised by a small number of treaty opponents show the need to reframe national debates about verification. Even though the United States arms control policy acknowledged in the late 1950s that perfect verification is neither possible nor necessary, people still routinely ask, 'is the treaty verifiable?' This question invites a yes/no answer and puts treaty supporters in the defensive position of explaining why imperfect verification is still 'good enough'. Opponents can give one vivid example of a cheating scenario far more easily than supporters can explain why each scenario is insignificant or implausible.

Whenever possible, arms control supporters should pose the question in a more positive way: 'how will the treaty be verified?' This reformulation reminds listeners that the United States is constantly trying to assess other states' nuclear, chemical, biological, and conventional military activities regardless of whether or not they are covered by arms control and verification agreements. Since the United States decided unilaterally in 1991 to destroy its entire stock of chemical weapons, the real issue is whether the United States will be safer if most other countries have agreed to do likewise and accepted far-ranging verification provisions than if it refuses to ratify the CWC until all potential enemies have signed and the CIA certifies that it could detect any violation.[50] Moreover, reformulating the question focuses attention on a range of verification capabilities that can be used synergistically rather than a single measure of confidence in detection assigned to each separate treaty prohibition. It also opens the door to a much fuller discussion of the trade-offs involved with different amounts and types of verification.

In a country where soundbites dominate political debates, Arms Control Advocates must have quick ways to reassure Cautious Cooperators that arms control can be beneficial despite verification trade-offs and occasional compliance concerns. The standard formula for 'adequate' verification fits the way that Arms Control Advocates think about security, but it makes many Cautious Cooperators uncomfortable because of their uncertainty about other country's intentions and the significance of low-level violations. Public opinion research in the mid-1980s found that most people used the word 'verification' as a shorthand for 'a low-risk, working relationship that improves only if and when the good faith of the other side has been clearly demonstrated' – a conception that leaves little room for ambiguity, uncertainty, or 'unimportant' violations. One way to challenge such thinking might be to turn the Unilateralists' use of law enforcement analogies on its head by noting that nobody expects perfect compliance with domestic laws or thinks that murder should be decriminalized until the police can catch every perpetrator. Domestic analogies can also be used to educate Cautious Cooperators about the dilemmas involved in any type of compliance evaluation. However, Arms Control Advocates must be careful that their choice of analogies does not reinforce the assumption that verification should ultimately be a self-help, adversarial procedure. Instead, they should explore further the extent to which more managerial models of compliance assessment and enhancement can be used even among states with conflicting interests and perceptions.[51]

Growing experience with arms control implementation offers contradictory evidence that supports conflicting positions in the politics of verification. Attempts to implement the complex requirements of the 1991 Strategic Arms Reduction Treaty, for example, or to adapt the 1990 Conventional Forces in Europe agreement to a world where neither the Warsaw Pact nor the Soviet Union still exists, have involved an ongoing process of consultation, clarification, and dispute resolution that are increasingly multilateral and managerial despite conflicts of interest and lingering doubts about motivations. The Cooperative Threat Reduction Program initiated in 1991 goes even further toward a managerial approach by tacitly acknowledging that concerns about Russian compliance with START I and II, the CWC, the NPT, and a host of other accords may be due to lack of funds, technology, and expertise for safe weapons storage and disposal rather than attempts to gain a strategic advantage through purposive violations.[52] Unfortunately, it also illustrates how difficult it can be to secure and sustain domestic support for programmes that reflect more cooperative, managerial assumptions about arms control. UNSCOM's experience in Iraq, by contrast, has made many observers question whether even the most intrusive, adversarial forms of verification – let alone more cooperative, managerial approaches – can prevent a determined cheater from violating its arms control obligations.[53] It is, however, no more sensible to use Iraq's response to imposed disarmament and verification measures as evidence of other countries' likely behaviour in voluntary arms control regimes than it is to use high rates of compliance with agreements requiring few behavioural changes as evidence that purely managerial forms of verification will ensure compliance with more significant arms control accords.[54]

These examples demonstrate that questions about amount and type of verification are no less controversial today than during the Cold War. Rather, the politics of verification continue to affect the speed, significance, and stability of cooperation at each stage of the arms control process. Although the arenas have changed over the last decade – with more countries at the negotiating table and fewer domestic actors outside the Executive branch vigorously engaged in verification debates – the structure of arguments remains basically the same. Moreover, CWC opponents' use of verification imperfections as an excuse to delay, and nearly derail, ratification shows that absolutist demands continue to be politically potent because few Americans are comfortable thinking about verification trade-offs.

Conclusion

The end of the Cold War brought a tremendous burst of optimism about the prospects for domestic and international agreement on verification. That optimism has been dampened significantly by poor progress on BWC verification, difficulties obtaining a weak CTB treaty, lengthy delays in CWC ratification, and recurrent concerns about the implementation and adaptation of existing verification arrangements. Many people have concluded that the verification paradox is as strong as ever because the same factors that have reduced American verification demands (for example, decreased distrust and lower consequences of minor arms control violations) have also lessened the perceived need for formal arms accords and the willingness to pay for verification. This essay has offered an alternative explanation by suggesting that the ideas and strategies used by Unilateralists to block agreement on verification during the Cold War are still having counterproductive effects on the politics of verification. In particular, the dominant view of verification as a benign and technical, yet fundamentally self-help process has helped Unilateralists condition domestic support for significant arms control on amounts and types of verification that other countries are likely to resist.

Both scholars and policy-makers have a role to play in remedying this situation. The first step is to move away from research and policy statements that reinforce overly narrow conceptions of verification. Thus, theorists should stop equating verification with transparency, maintaining that more 'openness' is necessarily better, and assuming that self-help forms of verification are preferable to more multilateral and/or managerial approaches. Even under conditions of perfect transparency, judgements about compliance will include a subjective component. Thus, there are good reasons for disagreement about the amount of compliance information that states should exchange as well as disputes about how that information should be gathered and assessed. Empirical research can identify some of the benefits and drawbacks associated with different verification arrangements, but attitudes toward verification are so heavily influenced by competing conceptions of international relations that it is unrealistic to expect a scholarly consensus about what methods work best under different conditions.

Pro-arms control policy-makers who understand verification dilemmas must pay more attention to the ways in which efforts to reach agreement at one level affect the chances for agreement at the other. The complex nature of the American arms control decision-making process often produces contradictory or inflexible stances that can raise concerns about American intentions during verification negotiations. Viewing the politics of verification as a two-level game increases sensitivity to the confusions this can cause at the negotiating table. It suggests the need to start thinking about ratification strategies at the beginning of negotiations so that influential senators and other key domestic players have the time and expertise to feel confident in a treaty's verification arrangements despite the inevitable compromises and residual uncertainties. A two-level approach also points to the dangers of using other countries' attitudes toward American verification proposals as evidence of their arms control intentions. Even when such steps provide a short-term surge of domestic support for United States arms control policy, they perpetuate the assumption that significant cooperation depends on full American access to sensitive information and control over how that information is used in the verification process – contradictory conditions that will be increasingly difficult to negotiate for complex multilateral accords covering core security capabilities.

A fuller understanding of verification dilemmas will not produce domestic or international consensus on the appropriate answers. Thus, theorists should approach verification as a political problem in its own right, not a technical fix to the dilemmas of cooperation under anarchy. Instead of urging leaders to 'depoliticize' verification, analysts should pay more attention to promoting provisional agreement on verification among states and domestic groups with conflicting interests and ideas about international politics. The key is to break the Unilateralists' blocking strategy by shifting the terms of domestic debate such that the support of American Cautious Cooperators no longer depends on verification arrangements that decrease risks for Americans by increasing them for negotiating partners. One way to challenge this zero-sum approach is to focus more on verification trade-offs within and across the amount/type dimensions. For example, Arms Control Advocates could justify verification compromises in terms that Cautious Cooperators would understand by explaining that steps to increase compliance information, such as negotiating new transparency measures or giving national intelligence a formal place in multilateral verification arrangements, typically depend on Americans relinquishing some control over how the information will be collected and evaluated. Reluctance to talk about verification trade-offs reflects the fear that Unilateralists will try to postpone arms control until win/win solutions can be found to Americans' own contradictory concerns – for example, demanding a CWC inspection regime that can deter or detect all violations without creating any new costs, inconvenience, or industrial espionage risks for United States chemical companies. Such strategies will only lose their political potency when Americans stop evaluating obtainable verification arrangements against a mythical ideal of perfect transparency, purely benign effects, and total United States control over the verification process.

NOTES

The author would like to thank Anthony Daley, Steven Miller, Amy Sands, and Amy Woolf for helpful comments and suggestions. Many of the arguments presented here are developed and supported more fully in Nancy W. Gallagher, *The Politics of Verification* (Baltimore: Johns Hopkins University Press, forthcoming).

1. 'Monitoring' refers to the collection of information about others' military activities, regardless of whether they are covered by an arms control agreement. 'Verification', by contrast, refers to judgements about the extent to which parties to an arms control accord are upholding their obligations. The verification process includes monitoring, analysis, assessment, consultation, clarification, and any other steps deemed necessary to evaluate compliance.
2. This argument is made most explicitly in Oran Young, *Compliance and Public Authority* (Washington, DC: Resources for the Future, 1979).
3. The classics in this literature are Robert Axelrod, *The Evolution of Cooperation* (New York: Basic Books, 1984) and Kenneth Oye (ed.), *Cooperation under Anarchy* (Princeton: Princeton University Press, 1986). The extreme importance of verification is illustrated by research showing that a one per cent rate of misperception would cause a game of Tit-for-Tat to stabilize in defection 75 per cent of the time. See George Downs, David Rocke, and Randolph Siverson, 'Arms Races and Cooperation', in Oye (ed.), *Cooperation under Anarchy*, pp.140–1.
4. U.S. Arms Control and Disarmament Agency, 'Verification: The Critical Element of Arms Control', Vol.85 (March 1976).
5. For example, William Kincaide maintains that 'progress at the negotiating table is clearly and firmly linked to progress in the methodology of verification', while Ivan Oerlich argues that Americans must think more carefully about the types of arms control agreements they really want now that verification is no longer the limiting factor. See William Kincaide, 'Challenges to Verification: Old and New', in Ian Bellany and Coit Blacker (eds.), *The Verification of Arms Control Agreements* (London: Frank Cass, 1983), p.16, and Ivan Oerlich, 'The Changing Rules of Arms Control Verification', *International Security*, Vol.14, No.4 (Spring 1990), pp.176–84.
6. Allan Krass, *Verification – How Much is Enough?* (London: Taylor and Francis, 1985).
7. J.C. Garnett, 'The Risks Associated with Unverifiable Arms Control Treaties', *Arms Control*, Vol.7, No.3 (Dec. 1986), pp.241–70.
8. Stephen Meyer, 'Verification and Risk in Arms Control', *International Security*, Vol.8, No.4 (Spring 1984), p.113.
9. Krass, *How Much is Enough?*; Michael Krepon, 'The Political Dynamics of Verification and Compliance Debates', in William Potter (ed.), *Verification and Arms Control* (Lexington, MA: D.C. Heath, 1985), pp.137–41; and Mark Lowenthal and Joel Witt, 'The Politics of Verification', in Potter (ed.), pp.153–68.
10. Alan B. Sherr, *The Other Side of Arms Control* (Boston: Unwin Hyman, 1988).
11. James Schear, 'Verification, Compliance, and Arms Control: The Dynamics of the Domestic Debate', in Lynn Eden and Steven E. Miller (eds.), *Nuclear Arguments* (Ithaca: Cornell University Press, 1989), pp.264–321.
12. Alva Myrdal, *The Game of Disarmament* (New York: Pantheon Books, 1976).
13. See, for example, Michael Gordon, 'All or Nothing', *National Journal*, 14 April 1984, p.730.
14. On epistemic communities in arms control, see Emanuel Adler, 'The Emergence of Cooperation: National Epistemic Communities and the International Evolution of the Idea of Nuclear Arms Control', *International Organization*, Vol.46, No.1 (Winter 1992), pp.101–45.
15. Lowenthal and Witt, 'The Politics of Verification', p.168.
16. Allan Krass, 'The Politics of Verification', *World Policy Journal*, Vol.4 (Fall 1985), p.751.
17. Numerous constraints on decoupling exist, but a decoupled 7–10 kt test might not be caught by countries that relied solely on the IMS. For details, see US Congress, Office of Technology Assessment, *Seismic Verification of Nuclear Testing Treaties* OTA-ISC-361 (Washington, DC : USGPO, May 1988), pp.98–106.

18. Collateral information collection refers to the use of agreed verification measures for the purpose of gathering intelligence unrelated to treaty compliance.

19. Eugene Rostow, 'Statement before the Committee of the Armed Services', US Senate, 24 July 1983.

20. Jessica Eve Stern, 'Co-operative Security and the CWC: A Comparison of the Chemical and Nuclear Weapons Non-Proliferation Regimes', *Contemporary Security Policy*, Vol.15, No.3 (Dec. 1994), pp.30–57.

21. Glenn Seaborg, *Kennedy, Khrushchev, and the Test Ban* (Berkeley, CA: University of California Press, 1981), pp.178–89.

22. Policies based on the concept of cooperative security seek to prevent threatening developments through voluntary agreements that prohibit members from amassing the means of aggression. For applications to a range of policy issues, see Janne E. Nolan (ed.), *Global Engagement* (Washington, DC: Brookings, 1994). The contribution that deals most explicitly with verification is Antonia Handler Chayes and Abram Chayes, 'Regime Architecture: Elements and Principles', pp.65–130 in that volume.

23. On two-level games, see Peter B. Evans, Harold K. Jacobson, and Robert D. Putnam (eds.), *Double-Edged Diplomacy* (Berkeley: University of California Press, 1993).

24. For an example applied to Soviet arms control decision-making before and after the Gorbachev revolution, see Matthew Evangelista, 'The Paradox of State Strength: Transnational Relations, Domestic Structures, and Security Policy in Russia and the Soviet Union', *International Organization*, Vol.49, No.1 (Winter 1995), pp.1–38.

25. Thus, the recent CTB negotiations can be defined as a success because all five nuclear weapons states have signed the treaty, a failure because two threshold states (India and Pakistan) have not, or a semi-success because the treaty has strengthened the norm against testing and increased the likelihood of a costly international response should India or Pakistan ever test.

26. In countries without a formal democratic ratification process, this term might refer to military leaders' willingness to abide by the terms of an arms control accord.

27. For an example of an Arms Control Advocate's view of verification in the post-Cold War world, see Antonia Handler Chayes and Abram Chayes, 'From Law Enforcement to Dispute Settlement', *International Security*, Vol.14, No.4 (Spring 1990), pp.147–64.

28. On the consistency in American attitudes toward nuclear weapons, see Everett Carll Ladd, 'The Freeze Framework', *Public Opinion*, Vol.10 (Aug./Sept. 1982), pp.20 and 41.

29. For examples, see Lewis Dunn, 'Arm Control Verification: Living with Uncertainty', *International Security*, Vol.14, No.4 (Spring 1990), pp.165–75; and Oerlich, 'The Changing Rules of Verification'.

30. See Kenneth Adelman, 'Why Verification is More Difficult (and Less Important', *International Security*, Vol.14, No.4 (Spring 1990), pp.141–6.

31. This extends an argument that conflicting 'myths' about the relationship between nuclear weapons and national security persist because the universe of cases is small and the evidence from them is ambiguous enough to support multiple points of view. Peter Lavoy, 'Nuclear Myths and the Causes of Nuclear Proliferation', in Zachary S. Davis and Benjamin Frankel (eds.), *The Proliferation Puzzle*, (London: Frank Cass, 1993), pp.192–212, and Steven Weber, *Cooperation and Discord in U.S.-Soviet Arms Control* (Princeton: Princeton University Press, 1991).

32. John Holum, 'Verification in the Arms Control Implementation Era', Remarks to a Conference on Arms Control and Verification at Southern Methodist University, 18 Nov. 1994.

33. For a concise insider's account of traditional Soviet views on verification, see an article by Roland Timerbayev published under the pseudonym R. Zheleznov, 'Monitoring Arms Limitation Measures', *International Affairs*, Vol.7 (1982), pp.75–84.

34. For explanations focused on internal and external factors, see Jeff Checkel, 'Ideas, Institutions, and the Gorbachev Foreign Policy Revolution', *World Politics*, Vol.45, No.2 (Jan. 1993), pp.271–300 and Jack Snyder, 'International Leverage on Soviet Domestic Change', *World Politics*, Vol.42, No.1 (Oct. 1989), pp.1–30.

35. In a comprehensive study of safeguards, Stephen Flanagan found that they were less likely

to encourage compliance than to 'drive the parties to undertake hedges that ultimately undermine the goals an purposes of an accord'. See 'Safeguarding Arms Control', in Michael Krepon and Mary Umberger (eds.), *Verification and Compliance* (Cambridge, MA: Ballinger, 1988), p.217.

36. For example, Ann Florini writes that increased international support for the norm of transparency 'represents a change of great significance as secretive behavior that was once taken for granted has come to be seen as a signal of nefarious intentions'. Ann Florini, 'The Evolution of International Norms', *International Studies Quarterly*, Vol.40, No.3 (Sept. 1996), p.381.

37. Jonathan B. Tucker, 'Strengthening the Biological Weapons Convention', *Arms Control Today*, Vol.25, No.3 (April 1995), pp.9–12.

38. Milton Leitenberg, 'Biological Weapons Arms Control', *Project on Rethinking Arms Control*, No.16 (College Park: University of Maryland, Center for International and Security Studies at Maryland, May 1996).

39. An *ad hoc* group of international verification experts (VEREX) evaluated different measures from a scientific and technical standpoint and presented BWC members with a list of twenty-one on-site and off-site options. However, their mandate did not include making any value judgments about the various options. See Graham S. Pearson, 'Forging an Effective Biological Weapons Regime', *Arms Control Today*, Vol.24, No.5 (June 1994), pp.14–17.

40. The following account benefited greatly from the ACRONYM analyses of the nuclear test ban negotiations prepared by Rebecca Johnson, director of the Acronym Institute.

41. Ambasador Arundhati Ghose, quoted in Rebecca Johnson, 'The In-Comprehensive Test Ban', Bulletin of the Atomic Scientists, Vol.52, No.6 (Nov./Dec. 1996), p.30. As of March 1997, Pakistan and North Korea were the two other members of the required group that had not signed.

42. The original version of the Chair's text can be found under the document number CD/NTB/WP.330. The revised version presented on 28 June 1996 is CD/NTB/WP.330/Rev.1

43. According to Article 18 of the Vienna Convention on the Law of Treaties (signed in 1969), Parties to a treaty must refrain from acts that would defeat the treaty's object and purpose unless they express the intention not to ratify it.

44. Evans *et al.*, pp.402–3.

45. Michael Moodie, 'Ratify the Chemical Weapons Convention: Past Time for Action', *Arms Control Today*, Vol.26, No.1 (Feb. 1996), p.5.

46. 'Statement by Senator Helms on the Chemical Weapons Convention, April 25, 1996', emphasis in the original.

47. The CWC was scheduled to take effect 180 days after the 65th signatory deposited its instrument of ratification. States that did not ratify the convention before the deadline would not be able to participate in the early stages of implementation and would face sanctions against their chemical industry. Failure to ratify the CWC would have also sent very damaging signals about United States leadership and commitment to arms control.

48. Poll conducted by the Mellman Groups and Wirthlin Worldwide, 20–22 Feb. 1997, results available at http://www.stimson.org/poison/polldata.htm.

49. The argument for this provision was that some states might sign the CWC but secretly develop chemical weapons whose utility would be enhanced if inspectors from that state had learned secrets of chemical weapons defense that could protect soldiers launching a chemical attack. The treaty already gives signatories the right to bar particular inspectors, so the Clinton administration feared that a blanket ban would cause the target states to retaliate by blackballing all American inspectors.

50. In May 1991 President Bush committed the United States unconditionally to destroy its entire stockpile of chemical weapons and to foreswear the use of chemical weapons for any reason against any state upon entry into force of the CWC. For more information, see Amy E. Smithson with the assistance of Maureen Lenihan, *The U.S. Chemical Weapons Destruction Program: Views, Analysis, and Recommendations* (Washington, DC: The Stimson Center, Sept. 1994).

51. See Abram Chayes and Antonia Handler Chayes, *The New Sovereignty* (Cambridge: Harvard University Press, 1995).

52. For details, see the article by Gloria Duffy in this volume.
53. Kathleen Bailey, *The UN Inspections in Iraq* (Boulder: Westview, 1995).
54. George W. Downs, David Rocke, and Peter Barsoom, 'Is the Good News About Compliance Good News About Cooperation', *International Organization*, Vol.50, No.3 (Summer 1996), pp.379–406.

Notes on Contributors

Nancy Gallagher is Assistant Professor of Government at Wesleyan University and the author of *The Politics of Verification* (Johns Hopkins University Press, forthcoming). The 'Bridging the Gaps' project was originated during 1995–96, while she was the first Women in International Security research fellow at the University of Maryland.

Emily Goldman is Director of the International Relations Program at the University of California, Davis, and Associate Professor of Political Science. She is the author of *Sunken Treaties: Naval Arms Control between the Wars* (1994) and co-editor of *U.S. Strategic Adjustment, 1890–1995: Competing Theoretical Explanations* (Colombia University Press, forthcoming). She has also written numerous articles on United States post-Cold War grand strategy and military innovation.

Ann Florini is currently Resident Associate at the Carnegie Endowment for International Peace with support from the Rockefeller Brothers Fund. Her dissertation was on 'Transparency: A New Norm of International Relations' (University of California, Los Angeles, 1995). She has also written numerous articles about the effects of the information revolution on governance and on the evolution of international norms.

Gloria Duffy is CEO of the Commonwealth Club of California. From 1993 to 1995 she served as Deputy Assistant Secretary of Defense, where she headed the Nunn-Lugar progamme. She co-edited *International Arms Control: Issues and Agreements* (1984) and directed a project on Compliance and the Future of Arm Control (1988) for the Center for International Security and Arms Control at Stanford University.

Rebecca Johnson is Director of the London-based Acronym Institute. She has reported, analysed, and published extensively on the Nuclear Non-Proliferation Treaty Review and Extension Conference, the Comprehensive Test Ban Treaty negotiations in the Conference on Disarmament, and other aspects of multilateral arms control.

Amy Sands is Associate Director of the Center for Non-Proliferation Studies at the Monterey Institute of International Affairs, and Director of the Center's Monitoring Proliferation Threats Project. From August 1994 to

June 1996 she was Assistant Director of the Intelligence, Verification, and Information Management Bureau at the US Arms Control and Disarmament Agency. Before joining ACDA, she led the Proliferation Assessments Section of Z Division (intelligence) at Lawrence Livermore National Laboratory.

Index

Printed in the USA/Agawam, MA
November 2, 2015

625491.189

A decade has passed since the superpowers began a series of arms control initiatives which now symbolize the beginning of the end of the Cold War, but the passage of time has not resolved disputes about the role of arms control in preserving peace. Both international relations theorists and foreign policy practitioners must decide which security strategy is most appropriate for a post-Cold War world characterized by the decline in superpower hostility and the rise of regional rivalries; the rapid diffusion of knowledge-intensive technologies; and the increasingly complex relationships between political, military, and economic issues.

How should arms control theory and policy be altered to improve the prospects for cooperation? The essays in this volume address this question by exploring the complexity of national arms control decision-making and multilateral negotiations, and the challenges of reaching domestic and international agreement on verification. Conscious that the gulf between theory and policy is growing at a time when the need for policy-friendly theory is greater than ever, the authors offer a range of jargon-free views from the academic and policy-making worlds. Some argue that growing interdependence creates both the need and the opportunity for a radical reorientation of arms control efforts, while others contend that increasing complexity in arms control problems still constrains what can be negotiated and ratified.

Nancy Gallagher is Assistant Professor of Government at Wesleyan University and the author of *The Politics of Verification* (Johns Hopkins University Press, forthcoming). The project was originated during 1995–96, while she was the first Women in International Security research fellow at the University of Maryland.

FRANK CASS PUBLISHERS
Crown House, 47 Chase Side
Southgate, London N14 5BP

ISBS, 5824 NE Hassalo Street
Portland, OR 97213-3644, USA

CASS

Website: www.frankcass.com

Printed in Great Britain